Effective Education *for* All

Educational PSYCHOLOGY

Critical Pedagogical Perspectives

Greg S. Goodman, *General Editor*

Vol. 25

The Educational Psychology series is part of the Peter Lang Education list.
Every volume is peer reviewed and meets
the highest quality standards for content and production.

PETER LANG
New York • Bern • Frankfurt • Berlin
Brussels • Vienna • Oxford • Warsaw

Effective Education *for* All

Implementing Positive Behavior Support in Early Childhood Through High School

CHUN ZHANG, CARLOS R. MCCRAY, SU-JE CHO, *Editors*

PETER LANG
New York • Bern • Frankfurt • Berlin
Brussels • Vienna • Oxford • Warsaw

Library of Congress Cataloging-in-Publication Data

Effective education for all: implementing positive behavior
support in early childhood through high school /
edited by Chun Zhang, Carlos R. McCray, Su-Je Cho.
pages cm. — (Educational psychology: critical pedagogical perspectives; v. 25)
Includes bibliographical references and index.
1. Behavior modification—United States.
2. Problem children—Behavior modification—United States.
3. Educational psychology. 4. School psychology—United States.
5. Classroom management—United States. I. Zhang, Chun, editor of compilation.
LB1060.2.E44 370.15'28—dc23 2013042468
ISBN 978-1-4331-2125-8 (hardcover)
ISBN 978-1-4331-2124-1 (paperback)
ISBN 978-1-4539-1275-1 (e-book)
ISSN 1943-8109

Bibliographic information published by **Die Deutsche Nationalbibliothek**.
Die Deutsche Nationalbibliothek lists this publication in the "Deutsche
Nationalbibliografie"; detailed bibliographic data are available
on the Internet at http://dnb.d-nb.de/.

The paper in this book meets the guidelines for permanence and durability
of the Committee on Production Guidelines for Book Longevity
of the Council of Library Resources.

29 Broadway, 18th floor, New York, NY 10006
www.peterlang.com

Printed in the United States of America

Table of Contents

Acknowledgments

We all have gone through many barriers and challenges in our lives in order to achieve the American dream we each have in our mind. Having a strong support system will enable and empower us to accomplish our dreams. My accomplishments have been the result of the inspiration and support from those who have shown confidence and love for me. Here, I want to acknowledge the support from my mom, a strong role model and my hero; and my dad who always shares his pride about me; my husband, Yan Liu, who encourages me to do greater things for myself and profession; and my daughter, Tina Liu, who continues to inspire me with her perspectives of work, life, and Christianity.

Chun Zhang
New York, New York

First, I would like to acknowledge my mother and father, Willie and Joyce McCray, whose unyielding support continue to make such endeavors like this possible. I will always cherish their love.

Second, I would like to thank Floyd, D. Beachum, Bruce S. Cooper, Dean James Hennessy, Sheldon Marcus, Gerald Cattaro, Dean Michael E. Dantley, Jeff Brooks, Linda Tillman, Ira Bogotch, and Festus Obiakor for their professional support over the years. You have truly made a difference in a scholar's life.

I would also, like to dedicate this book to Fayth Bryant, Caitlyn Copeland, Alana Melton, Corinne Barnett, Isaiah Wright, and Dailyn Raphael Smith. I hope they look upon this work as they get older and find inspiraion in achieving all their goals in life.

Carlos R. McCray
New York, New York

I wish to express my sincere gratitude to my dear colleague, Dr. Kwang-Sun C. Blair, for guiding me on this book and writing with me. Her guidance and conversations on our chapters and other projects have expanded my knowledge about the area of Positive Behavioral Interventions and Supports to a great extent. I would also like to thank my current and former students at Fordham University. In class, we learn from each other about managing challenging behaviors of children attending urban schools; their questions, their comments and their projects have enabled me to read and research more about Positive Behavioral Interventions and Supports. I am also grateful to Teresa Lopes at Luna Writing and Editing Services who provided her editing services for half of this book. Finally, my deepest gratitude goes to my dear husband, Steven E. Farkas, who always puts my work as priority and offers to read and edit my work.

Su-Je Cho
New York, New York

Most importantly, we, as a team of authors and editors, want to acknowledge the efforts of great teachers, administrators, family members, and policymakers who advocate and provide supportive educational models such as Positive Behavior Support in making school a positive learning environment for students, especially those who were left behind, misunderstood, and given unfair treatment. Providing consistent support for these children at an early age and beyond will help them achieve their American dreams.

Chun Zhang
Carlos R. McCray
Su-Je Cho

Introduction

CYNTHIA HUDLEY

Students who are non-native speakers of English, members of racially and ethnically marginalized groups, and/or economically disadvantaged are far too often represented in the education literature as "at risk" for school failure and behavioral difficulties. The concept of risk at the level of the individual has received a fairly thorough examination, but insufficient attention has been devoted to linking important structural and school characteristics to student learning and behavior. However, structural realities that constrain the success of students deemed "at risk" due to their ethnic and racial heritage or their economic circumstances have been evident in the literature for more than three decades. For example, low-income, ethnic minority students who struggle academically are more often seen as unmotivated or conduct-disordered, while struggling affluent, White children receive services (e.g., counseling, tutoring) to improve learning (Bowles & Gintis, 1976). Such services are less often freely available in urban schools serving racial and ethnic minorities and are economically out of reach for low-income parents to purchase independently. How then can we extend our understanding of school practices and policies as well as students' social circumstances that constrain student opportunities, and how might these understandings promote positive youth development and positive behavior that underpins academic success?

Thinking about the role of school in supporting social and emotional development for any student and reducing disruptive behavior requires an understanding that behavior does not exist solely at the level of the individual but is a product of the transaction between an individual and the environment in which that person must function (Sameroff, 2009). However, the capacity of schools to provide an environment that serves the needs of an increasingly diverse student population has been constrained by declining funding just at the time when student and family needs are increasing exponentially. The nation's economic decline has left many families and schools with dramatically reduced materials, emotional and personnel resources to provide for children's social, emotional, and academic development.

Unfortunately, one of the responses elicited from children by increasingly inattentive and overextended contexts is behavioral disruption, and behavioral disruption in schools is often met with disproportionately punitive responses for children of color (Hudley & Daoud, 2008; King, 1991). For schools, several climate factors that are relevant to social, emotional, and behavioral development can be influenced by the culture of both the perceiver and the student, including inconsistent and punitive discipline, unfamiliar social skills valued by the school culture, and unspoken expectations governing the school culture (Hudley & Gottfried, 2008). Even efforts to induct students into a school's cultural milieu may misfire, as education research consistently finds that practices developed for one group are not equally successful with all groups in a diverse society, often resulting in a significant, culturally defined "achievement gap" (McAllister & Irvine, 2000) and discipline gap (Vincent & Tobin, 2011).

However, there is another substantial body of evidence that school culture can successfully adapt to meet the needs of students from a wide range of cultural, racial, and economic backgrounds and support optimal social and emotional development for all students. The chapters in this volume collect and synthesize important literatures relevant to both student development and school culture, resulting in comprehensive representation of students' needs and the capacity of schools to meet those needs. A comprehensive understanding of the issues is the most reasonable route toward clarifying the relationships between school practices and student outcomes.

Organization of the Book

This edited volume effectively brings together a range of literatures to discuss the impact of school culture on the development and behavior of students from a range of cultural, racial, and linguistic backgrounds. All of the chapters expressly examine culturally and linguistically diverse learners in the schools, and each of the contributors specifically attends to the culture of the school. The organizing principle for the investigation of school culture is the Positive Behavioral Interventions and Supports (PBIS) Model. Taken together, this edited volume will advance research and theory on student development in school context by clarifying the ways in which Positive Behavioral Interventions and Supports can impact behavior and achievement for culturally and linguistically diverse learners.

The first section examines factors that contribute to both social and academic competencies for school success and to school failure. The chapters in this section provide an overview of developmental, cultural, and political perspectives on school success and school failure for these learners. In the first chapter, Diane Rodriguez examines the role of stereotypes and labels in explaining the overrepresentation in special services (e.g., special education) and disciplinary actions (e.g., suspensions) of culturally and linguistically diverse learners, as well as their pervasive underachievement. In Chapter 2, Yi Ding and Dake Zhang examine social and emotional development from both developmental and cultural perspectives. Developmental theories and cultural values are used to explain both universal and culturally unique behaviors that are associated with school success in a given cultural milieu. The third chapter, by Su-Je Cho, Ji-Ryun Kim, Kwang-Sun Cho Blair, and Carlos R. McCray, focuses on several specific characteristics of schools that facilitate either academic success or school failure, and effective strategies for planning and implementing school-wide PBIS.

Section II of this volume explores social and emotional development and school success for culturally and linguistically diverse students in the early childhood and childhood (or elementary) grades. The construct of Positive Behavioral Interventions and Supports is used as a lens to conceptualize school readiness gaps, discipline gaps, school underachievement, and school failure. Chapter 4 by Chun Zhang, Angie Chai, and Kwang-Sun Cho Blair describes the Pyramid Model for early intervention to decrease behavior problems of young children while increasing their academic engagement and success. Chapter 5 by Kwang-Sun Cho Blair, Chun Zhang, and Angie Chai presents a model of culturally relevant Positive Behavioral Interventions and Supports for culturally and linguistically diverse learners. That model is contrasted with extant, highly problematic strategies such as harsher punishment, high suspension and expulsion rates, and disproportionate labeling of emotional disturbance for this population. Chapter 6 by Su-Je Cho, Kwang-Sun Cho Blair and Ji-Ryun Kim presents class-wide Positive Behavioral Interventions and Supports in the elementary school. The chapter details a variety of strategies effective for implementing the three-tier PBIS.

Section III is analogous to the previous section in examining social and emotional development and school success for culturally and linguistically diverse learners in secondary schools, and analyzing strategies and interventions for this population grounded in principles of PBIS. In Chapter 7, Tachelle Banks and Festus Obiakor critically evaluate the assertion that a positive school climate promoting a Positive Behavioral Interventions and Supports system must be adopted by educators and school leadership in order to reduce high levels of school dropout among the most vulnerable student populations. Chapter 8 by Floyd Beachum and Gina Gullo reviews the literature linking culturally relevant Positive Behavioral Interventions and Supports and academic success among African American and Latino students. Culturally relevant PBIS is discussed in the context of culturally relevant leadership and culturally relevant pedagogy in promoting social-cultural justices. Chapter 9 by Christopher Yawn and Lenwood Gibson Jr. presents a school-wide PBIS Model for middle and high school students. The chapter argues that a PBIS system can increase educators' understanding of student behaviors and increase the support needed for middle and high school students to excel.

The final substantive section discusses the implications of social and emotional development and Positive Behavioral Interventions and Supports for educational policy and practice to support the school performance of culturally and linguistically diverse learners. Chapter 10 by Carlos R. McCray, Chun Zhang, Su-Je Cho, and Samual Martin synthesizes research and evidence-based practices that support social and academic development across all ages and grade levels. Chapter 11 by Rosa Milagros Santos and Lillian Durán synthesizes culturally relevant practices, highlighting the roles of educators and school leadership in providing culturally responsive teaching and policymaking to promote positive outcomes for culturally and linguistically diverse learners. Chapter 12 by Carlos R. McCray, Su-Je Cho, Chun Zhang, and Heather Wynne highlights the limitations of existing literature and outlines a vision for future research, practice, and policy to support positive behavioral and academic outcomes for culturally and linguistically diverse learners. The Epilogue by Bruce S. Cooper reiterates various ways to support success for diverse students.

In conclusion, each of the chapters in this volume will make an important contribution to promoting school success for culturally and linguistically diverse learners, from early childhood to high school. This volume offers a unique synthesis of research on social and emotional development, the education of marginalized groups, and the role of positive behavioral support in supporting optimal development and academic achievement for culturally and linguistically diverse learners.

References

Bowles, S., & Gintis, H. (1976). *Schooling in capitalist America: Educational reform and the contradictions of economic life.* New York: Basic Books.

Hudley, C., & Daoud, A. (2008). Cultures in contrast: Understanding the influence of school culture on student engagement. In C. Hudley & A. Gottfried (Eds.), *Academic motivation and the culture of schooling in childhood and adolescence* (pp. 187–217). New York: Oxford University Press.

Hudley, C., & Gottfried A. (2008). *Academic motivation and the culture of schooling in childhood and adolescence*. New York: Oxford University Press.

King, J. (1991). Dysconscious racism: Ideology, identity, and the miseducation of teachers. *Journal of Negro Education, 60*, 133–146.

McAllister, G., & Irvine, J. (2000). Cultural competency and multicultural teacher education. *Review of Educational Research, 70*, 3–24.

Sameroff, A. (2009). *The transactional model of development: How children and contexts shape each other*. Washington, DC: APA.

Vincent, C. G., & Tobin, T. J. (2011). The relationship between implementation of School-Wide Positive Behavior Support (SWPBS) and disciplinary exclusion of students from various ethnic backgrounds with and without disabilities. *Journal of Emotional and Behavioral Disorders, 19*(4), 217–232.

Section I

1. *Factors Influencing Overrepresentation, Underachievement, and School Failure*

Diane Rodriguez

Multiple factors influence academic achievement in school, including motivation and prior knowledge of the learner and his or her classmates, parental support, quality of the teaching, and socioeconomic status. Some factors exert direct influence, while others are more indirect. Poverty, for instance, may diminish the extent to which a learner is able to engage in instruction. Further, poverty can influence the perceptions of school personnel, an indirect consequence that has resulted in overrepresentation of special education services (SES) children in special education. Similarly, culturally and linguistically diverse (CLD) students who are learning English may not recognize words in a textbook—a direct influence on academic achievement—and this may lead to the indirect effect of school personnel concluding that such students are in need of SES. Indeed, CLD students *are* overrepresented in special education. In an effort to reduce such overrepresentation, this chapter seeks to dispel myths, stereotypes, and erroneous labels (e.g., learning disabled, speech impaired, emotionally disturbed), which have been used to explain, excuse, or ignore the poor school performance of this student population. Further, this chapter provides research-based evidence to explain phenomena such as how some students manage to overcome adversarial circumstances. They succeed with strong support systems, such as effective interventions in academics and behavior support.

Before we begin to dispel the myths, we will consider the magnitude of the problem. Its extent is evident in key findings announced by U.S. Secretary of Education Arne Duncan in a statement published on March 6, 2012:

- African-American students, particularly males, are far more likely to be suspended or expelled from school than their peers. Black students make

up 18% of the students in the Civil Rights Data Collection (CRDC) sample, but 35% of the students suspended once, and 39% of the students expelled.
- Students learning English (English Language Learners) comprised 6% of the CRDC high school enrollment, but made up 12% of students retained.
- Only 29% of high-minority high schools offered calculus, compared to 55% of schools with the lowest black and Hispanic enrollment. (U.S. Department of Education, 2012)

Further, the number of CLD students continues to increase in public schools, yet schools in the U.S. are structured to serve English-speaking and acculturated students (Chu, 2011). The Individuals with Disabilities Education Act (IDEA) has always included specific guidelines for determining eligibility for students with disabilities. Alarmingly, misconceptions regarding what constitutes a disability have been so pronounced that IDEA was modified in 2004 to make explicit that limited English proficiency is not a determinant of disability (34 CFR 300.306(b)) (Individuals with Disabilities Education Act, 2004):

In making a determination of eligibility under paragraph (4)(A), a child shall not be determined to be a child with a disability if the determinant factor for such determination is—

(A) lack of appropriate instruction in reading, including in the essential components of reading instruction (as defined in section 6368(3) of this title);
(B) lack of instruction in math; or
(C) limited English proficiency. (20 U.S.C. 1414(b)(5))

The rationale was to avoid misidentifying CLD students as having a learning disability, which has been a serious problem historically. A U.S. Department of Education Office for Civil Rights survey reveals that since the 1970s, there has been persistent overrepresentation of minorities in certain special education eligibility categories (Losen & Orfield, 2002; Sullivan & Bal, 2013; Zhang & Katsiyannis, 2002). This provision was included to assist states in developing guidelines to prevent such inequitable misrepresentation and overrepresentation.

While legislation is helpful, it is insufficient in practice. Training is necessary for both identification and instructional support of CLD students. Orza and Medina (2012) noted: "cultural influences on behavior have largely been ignored in the field of behavior management and must be specifically addressed" (p. 55). Realistically, educators must pay attention to diversity issues because there is still a cultural and ethnic gap between teachers and students (Margolis, 2006; Sullivan & Artiles, 2011). Adding to the problem is the relative lack of research on how key players—that is, teachers—work daily and directly with students experiencing the multiple challenges of such life changes and upheavals. The predominant area of study in this field is the phenomenon of overrepresentation. However, the reasons for the growing disparity in the identification of CLD students in special education are complex. Togut (2011) pinpointed three primary variables that contribute to overrepresentation: social demographics, general education and resource inequity, and the special education process. The reauthorization of IDEA (2004) mandates that states (a) report identification, placement, and discipline data by race and ethnicity; (b) identify problematic policies, procedures, or practices that may contribute to disparities; (c) carry out targeted improvement activities; and (d) require local education agencies (LEAs) with significant disproportionality (based on state criteria) to commit 15% of IDEA funds to early intervention.

Teachers must learn to recognize and understand cultural influences on behavior. For example, educators must be aware that some cultures place more value and emphasis on collective participation and contribution than on individualism and competitiveness. Another example can be found in the verbal and nonverbal communication mode of children and families from diverse backgrounds. Language switching and mixing may be common for many families (Hernandez, Dapretto, Mazziotta, & Bookheimer, 2001; Meuter & Allport, 1999; Orza & Medina, 2012). Many CLD groups value respectful behavior; however, the perceptions and definitions of such behavior may vary, and can conflict with school expectations.

Misconceptions Debunked

Unfortunately, it is a fact that CLD students are overrepresented in special education programs, which perpetuates the pernicious misconception that CLD students are slow learners. Of course Einstein was also considered a slow learner. While this appears absurd in retrospect, lack of familiarity with a language is often perceived as an intelligence deficit. Fortunately, there is a four-fold approach to correcting the problem of overrepresentation. Garcia and Ortiz (2006) identified four key elements to prevent disproportionate representation. The first key element is preventing CLD learners from underachievement and failure in school. In order for educators to do this, they must be able to recognize the differences between school culture and home culture. Teachers need to create a positive classroom environment that fosters and nurtures CLD students. The second key element is to provide early intervention for struggling

CLD learners. Educators must intervene at the earliest possible stage to prevent future academic failures. The third key element is the use of informal assessment to diagnose and prescribe teaching and delivery of instruction. Such data provide teachers with a wealth of information that will allow them to design and differentiate instruction for CLD students. The fourth key element is the availability of a general education problem-solving support system. Collaboration and team efforts are essential to preventing disproportionate representation.

Artiles (2003) ascertained that examining the historical interlocking of race and ability *differences* is important to an analysis of equity and *difference* in education, because the combination of race and ability has been a persistently elusive topic in the history of U.S. education. Many other researchers have addressed the issue of overrepresentation of CLD students. For example, MacMillan and Reschly (1998) stated, "social class, and not ethnicity, would explain more variance in the rates of detection for these high-incidence disabilities, particularly MMR [mild mental retardation]" (p. 20). They further explained that after accounting for variance owing to social class, it is likely that the relative variance in enrollment rates would be explained by ethnicity. Skiba, Poloni-Staudinger, Simmons, Feggins, and Chung (2005) argued that "poverty makes a weak and inconsistent contribution to the prediction of disproportionality across a number of disability categories" (p. 130). Even though research results dispel myths, negative stereotypes persist: "because African American and Hispanic students have been demonstrated to perform more poorly than their Caucasian peers on academic measures ... and often come from more economically disadvantaged backgrounds ... some critics have argued that their rates of referral and eligibility for special education should be higher than the same rates for Caucasian students" (Hosp & Reschly, 2003, p. 76). Meanwhile, Drakeford (2004) contended, "Overrepresentation among African American students in school suspensions and expulsions has been found to escalate as these punishments are used more frequently" (p. 4). He continued his argument, pointing out that several studies have found evidence suggesting race bias. The problem of overrepresentation of minorities in special education due to disciplinary differences needs further investigation. School failure may lead to community problems in general; for this reason, there is an urgent need to address the issue of discipline in the school system.

The goal of Klingner et al. (2005) in addressing the disproportionality of minority children in special education was to assist practitioners, researchers, and policymakers in merging culturally responsive, evidence-based interventions and strategic improvements in practice and policy in order to reduce the inappropriate referral to and placement in special education of CLD learners. A collaborative effort is necessary to ensure that all children and youth are academically and socially successful in the community. First, we must debunk the myths surrounding minority students in special education (see Table 1). Second, we must provide teachers and education staff with professional development workshops, seminars, and college/university courses that prepare them to intervene in community- and school-based prevention programs.

Table 1. Myths vs. Facts About CLD Students

Myth	Fact
CLD students with disabilities are underachievers.	CLD students are overrepresented in special education, and lack of appropriate instruction is not a disability.
It is impossible to change the behavior of CLD students.	It is important to respect and affirm the values and behaviors of CLD students.
The use of reinforcement to change behavior is not appropriate.	All students should be treated equally with respect to encouraging appropriate behavior.

Mapping It Out

In a class discussion for a behavior management project, an education professor asked students to identify a target behavior of CLD students. A novice teacher volunteered that her target behavior was that the student was "calling out." The professor asked: Do you know the dynamics of the culture and values of the student? The novice teacher said no, but reasserted that calling out was an unacceptable behavior. That is when the class started the conversation about target behaviors. Is calling out a major behavior problem for CLD students? The answer is no. Educators need to understand from a biography-driven instructional perspective who their students are. This means that educators teaching CLD students with disabilities need to understand their students linguistically, cognitively, academically, and affectively. Beyond knowing their names and addresses, teachers must become familiar with the customs and values of their diverse students. Knowing these students' strengths and weaknesses will help educators shape the educational environment and help ensure the academic success of CLD students with and without disabilities.

As educators, we need to map out (or plan) the classroom environment for CLD students in order to differentiate instruction for them, and to ensure that they feel welcome. Educators must be aware that for many cultures, open participation is the norm in a group discussion, which makes participation acceptable. A positive and supportive classroom environment creates opportunities for CLD students to experience academic success. As an experienced educator, I would consider calling out a mildly disruptive behavior; notably, this behavior can be modified with techniques to avoid the disruption. Teachers could choose from a variety of strategies including ignoring, signal interferences, humor, proximity control, logical consequences, shaping and modeling to diminish the behavior (Scott, Anderson, & Alter, 2012). Thus, although I understand that calling out can be a distraction for teachers and other students in the classroom, it is a behavior that can be brought under control. Many articles and books have been published about managing behavior (Campbell-Whatley & Lyons, 2013; Kauffman, Pullen, Mostert, & Trent, 2011; Umbreit, Ferro, Liaupsin, & Lane, 2007). In mapping it out for CLD students, a comprehensive program for managing behavior problems in the education setting should include social skills instruction, problem solving, anger management, and appropriate social skills. I recommend that teachers develop and implement educational route planning, which uses complex data to get your students where they need to be in the educational environment.

The teacher enters the classroom with a specific plan to deliver certain instructional content at a specific time, but suddenly s/he encounters a challenging situation with a CLD student. What can the teacher do to manage the difficult classroom behavior of the CLD student and the disruption of the learning environment? Researchers and practitioners have considered that question and their recommendations are helpful. Particularly useful is the *Culturally Responsive Classroom Management Strategies* (CRCM), developed by the Metropolitan Center for Urban Education and New York University's Steinhard School of Culture, Education and Human Development. CRCM is a pedagogical approach designed to guide teachers' management decisions (Metropolitan Center for Urban Education, 2008). CRCM recommends:

1. Recognition of one's own cultural lens and biases
2. Knowledge of the cultural backgrounds of students
3. Awareness of the broader social, economic, and political context
4. Ability and willingness to use culturally appropriate management strategies
5. Commitment to building caring classroom communities

In addition, Shippen, Patterson, Green, and Smitherman (2012) identified preventive practices for reducing misbehavior. They recommend:

1. Reducing the disproportionality of youth of color in special education and alternative settings
2. Transcending high-stakes testing
3. Enhancing alternative education

4. Increasing family involvement in schools
5. Providing quality professional development for educators and staff (p. 299)

Social Cultural Factors to Consider in Service to CLD Students with Special Needs

School personnel—in particular, the multidisciplinary team evaluating CLD students referred to special education due to behavioral issues—must consider a wide variety of factors before deciding on a course of action. Generally speaking, they should consider all of the cultural and linguistic factors that affect the student's functioning at school, home, and in the community. Specific factors to consider include the student's culture, developmental history, health and nutrition history, language use, social and emotional development, social adaptive skills, family orientation, discipline practices, religious practices, educational history, and the parents' and student's perceptions of special education and even of school itself. Collecting information on all of these factors will inform the assessment process and ultimately benefit all primary stakeholders, namely, the student, his or her family, and school personnel. In light of the extensive data collected, the stakeholders should be able to develop and implement an appropriate behavior intervention plan.

Meeting the Needs of CLD Students with Special Needs

One of the most important considerations in meeting the needs of CLD students with special needs is route planning (i.e., planning a development path unique to each learner). The plan must enable the CLD student to attain new learning goals given the learner's current capacity. Teachers should deliver instruction and manage classroom behavior in light of the student's learning style and behaviors, as well as within the necessary linguistic and cultural contexts. This is not to say that CLD students should not be expected to follow the norms for traditional American classroom behavior. By looking at data and behavioral history, the teacher can determine when and where classroom challenges might occur. Educators must then plan and implement effective instructional sets in order to maximize students' success at mastering academic content and appropriate social skills. Providing feedback to these students is a key element of instruction, for both academic learning and social behavior. Scott, Anderson, and Alter (2012) discussed the vast array of rules that govern student movement throughout the classroom, rules derived from peer interaction, teacher routines, and instructional expectations. They contend that successful classroom teachers inculcate three key values in students:

"(1) Respect Self—keep yourself safe and learning; (2) Respect Others—treat other people as you would have them treat you; and (3) Respect Property—treat other people's property as you would have them treat yours." (p. 132).

Significant Events

At first glance, planning classroom instruction and managing behavior appears relatively straightforward. One might assume that if you simply match classroom instructional practices with learner needs, you will have eager and engaged students motivated to learn and behave. However, when considering CLD students with behavioral challenges, lesson planning involves a unique set of complications. One of the challenges is getting to know all of the students. Knowing their names or addresses is not sufficient; teachers must get to know their students well enough that the teacher's words and deeds convey to each student that the teacher sincerely cares about that student's development. Another challenge, which is partly due to differing cultural values and can vary day to day (or hour to hour), is how best to understand the immediate needs of CLD students. Yet another challenge is acquiring sufficient capacity (knowledge, skill, and disposition) to offer an array of services for CLD students when and where they are needed.

How do we go about addressing significant events, which students may come to regard as defining acceptable classroom behavior? Beginner teachers should start by building effective relationships with CLD students. Recognize that CLD students with behavioral challenges bring to the class a unique set of strengths, qualities, talents, and special gifts. Identify those qualities to engage the students in a positive learning environment. Teachers need to be genuine with CLD students, who will surely know if their teachers have empathy, advocate for them, and care about supporting their academic success. Educators must have valuable skills, such as attending, listening, focusing, and observing, in order to help students during the process of academic learning and attainment of appropriate social skills. Teachers should also possess the knowledge, skills, and disposition necessary for reflecting on feelings, responding to content, probing, questioning, and showing empathy. It is important to understand the motivations of student behaviors in order to interpret, confront, challenge, and provide appropriate information to students. Further, for success in the classroom, teachers need to take particular actions, including reinforcing appropriate behaviors, making decisions, and monitoring behavior. Basically, the behavior intervention plan helps teachers monitor student behavior and make decisions according to student need.

Keeping track or monitoring student behavioral data is imperative in the classroom environment. Baca and Cervantes (2004) identified three principles for keeping track of CLD students: (a) acknowledging differences among students; (b) recognizing that differences among students influence how they learn; and (c) providing an array of educational approaches. Well-grounded instruction and a positive learning environment are essential to the educational success of CLD students. More than a decade ago, Ruiz, Rueda, Figueroa, and Boothroyd (1998) advised teachers to transform the historical mind frame of the school environment. Supportive and encouraging staff development increases teachers' capacity to implement strategies and innovative ideas in their instructional practices. Furthermore, through professional development, teachers learn to document student learning outcomes and, importantly, to share with other teachers the experience of changing one's beliefs and attitudes toward teaching. Klingner (2004) concurred that professional development improves practices for students in special education programs. Educators need to see actual examples of successful teaching in order to believe in innovative approaches that will engage CLD students in the curriculum. CLD students must have a clear set of high expectations that are feasible and reachable in order to achieve academic success and positive self-image. Referral, assessment, and placement of CLD students in special education programs must be examined through a careful lens. Ignoring the existence of cultural and linguistic diversity—and the strengths CLD students bring to a school—misses the child as a whole, jeopardizing both learner and teacher and exacerbating disproportionality in special education programs.

Community of Practice

Instructional practices should include goal-oriented behavioral lessons that are conducive to a positive learning environment. CLD students need to know that teacher efforts are focused on their learning. In addition, teachers should relate new content to prior knowledge. Much of teaching is about connecting new content to students' prior experiences, knowledge, culture, language, and community. Many teachers are able to ask questions that prompt students to perceive the relationship between new information and their prior knowledge. CLD students need to see, experience, and feel that the information is relevant and purposeful in their lives. Just as teachers monitor and collect data on student behaviors, they need to monitor students' understanding of new materials. Another key to effective instructional practice is for teachers to be enthusiastic about the content they are teaching.

Teachers should not make the assumption that all CLD students hold similar cultural values, language, and beliefs (Anderman & Anderman, 2010). Many CLD students use a form of discourse different from that of typical classroom communication. Teachers need to acknowledge and affirm cultural and linguistic diversity in order to motivate CLD students to become engaged in classroom discourse. Educators can affirm diversity in the classroom by learning about students and talking to them about their cultures. From discussions with parents about culture, teachers can modify their pedagogy to be more culturally responsive. Kea, Campbell-Whatley, and Richards (2006) affirmed that culturally responsive teaching includes: (a) sociocultural consciousness; (b) an affirming attitude toward students from CLD backgrounds; (c) commitment and skills to act as an agent of change; (d) constructivist views of learning; (e) learning about students; and (f) culturally responsive teaching strategies. Townsend-Walker (2012) concluded that CLD students' perceptions of emotional detachment were apparent across their home, school, and community settings. This is alarming, because students need to feel care, love, and acceptance in all aspects of their lives. Townsend-Walker also found that a few CLD students spoke highly of teachers who cared, respected, and taught them well. This is another example of the importance of connecting with students in the classroom, school, and community.

Designing a personal education plan for CLD students with disabilities that embraces flexibility, consistency, and respect, and that fosters a caring environment conducive to learning is critical. Researchers have recommended crafting functional behavior assessments, behavior intervention plans, and Positive Behavioral Interventions and Supports systems designed specifically for the student with behavioral problems. Teachers must take a few extra steps to create a positive classroom social environment conducive to learning, practice, and academic success. The key component is how the teacher promotes mutual respect between *all* students, including CLD students, and promotes a sense of community among all learners. Rodriguez, Ringler, and O'Neal (2009) investigated the classroom climate of CLD students in a school environment. They concluded that classroom climate affects learning experiences of all learners and is a predictor of the overall perception of the school.

Sharing a Classroom Story

Recently, in a behavior management course, an in-service teacher presented an intervention for CLD students, which could work for many other educators.

Accountability Partners as an Intervention

Edlynne Victoria Safi

As we observe our students in class and all the behaviors they express, we often face negative behaviors that can become disruptive during teaching. As teachers, it is our duty to manage classroom behavior. However, this can become difficult when managing many students at once—but must it be solely the teacher's work to correct behavior? A case study was conducted on a student, referred to as Sean, who has a problematic behavior of being inattentive during the class meeting times that take place in the carpeted area.

Sean is a six-year old Latino student who is enrolled in a special education first-grade class in a public school located in New York City. He does not have an Individualized Education Plan (IEP) but is undergoing evaluations. He has been expressing inattentive behaviors when lesson instruction is taking place. This is a crucial part of the day, and when Sean does not pay attention, he becomes lost during individual work. Sean demonstrates his inattentiveness by crawling under tables, becoming fixated and playing with an object such as a piece of crumpled paper or an eraser, and by looking in the opposite direction of the teacher giving instruction. As I planned for an intervention to correct Sean's behavior, I decided to give Sean an *accountability partner*; this partner will be a fellow classmate. The purpose of the accountability partner is to bring Sean back to paying attention when he is off task. Whenever Sean is displaying inattentiveness, such as crawling under the table, displaying wandering eyes, or fidgeting with an object, the accountability partner will simply tap Sean on the shoulder and remind him of what he should be doing. This will then remind Sean that he needs to be paying attention to the teacher during instruction.

This process of the accountability partner has advantages and disadvantages. As a teacher, one of the advantages is that it alleviates pressure for the teacher, since s/he doesn't have to stop during instruction to get the student to reengage in the lesson. Using accountability partners as a behavior intervention for a particular student also benefits other students, as the partner grows by gaining experience on how to behave as a mature student. Allowing a child to have the responsibility of holding someone accountable builds leadership skills, and this is crucial during the young and impressionable years. Another benefit of putting an accountability partner in place is that the child who is under the intervention no longer gets embarrassed when reprimanded for being off task. Prior to the intervention, when Sean was off task, his teacher would pause during instruction and call out his name to remind him of what he should be doing. This kind of strategy can cause stress to a student, as s/he is now put on the spot to the class in a negative light; when a student is embarrassed or under stress, the student often remains unfocused and off task. When an accountability partner is in place, the transition of being off-task to being on-task is done discreetly, which can lead to better student success.

Although implementing accountability partners as an intervention can be successful for the student at risk, it does also have some disadvantages. As the student who is the accountability partner becomes partially responsible for the student at risk, for example, Sean, this close partnership between the two students can lead to both students becoming distracted during instruction. This was the case for Sean and Lindsey on certain days of the intervention. The students would sometimes end up chitchatting during the meeting-area times rather than listening to the teacher. This kind of behavior is understandable since children are very social. It is important that when you are implementing the accountability partner intervention that you choose the partner wisely. Pairing a stronger and more disciplined student to the student at risk is key, but you also must make sure that the partner is friendly, as you do not want any bullying to occur.

In sum, accountability partners as an intervention for behavior management does lead to success and has many positive aspects, but as with all interventions, it may not work for every student. To promote positive classroom behaviors, you as the teacher need to use discernment in making choices in what the student needs and if this intervention is a good fit.

Conclusion

The education system continues to face the challenges of misidentification of CLD students in special education. More professional development and courses are needed for educators to understand the differences between language diversity and language disorders, between problematic behavior and different cultural values and beliefs, and the impact of the lack of instruction that CLD students receive, which contributes to low academic achievement. Educators must create a classroom environment where students feel confident and own their academic success. Building positive relationships with CLD students through the use of Positive Behavioral Interventions and Supports is the key element to positive classroom management, and will minimize referrals to special education due to behavioral differences. Effective teaching requires an educational environment that is conducive to student learning, that fosters academic and social growth. At the building level, team players in effective schools put in place a proactive school-wide discipline program or School-Wide Positive Behavioral Interventions and Supports (SWPBIS) program that facilitates and maintains a positive school environment for all students. It is imperative that we be vigilant to the danger of stereotyping when discussing different cultures (Zirpoli, 2012). Valuing and addressing diversity are important components of a successful classroom and school environment. Researchers have recommended that educators implement and enforce fair, equitable, culturally sensitive and appropriate classroom rules, models of knowledge, and respect for diverse cultures (Klingner et al., 2005; Orza & Medina, 2012; Schwartz, 2001).

By collaborating with family members, teachers demonstrate that they value the extended partnership in educating the CLD student, including siblings, grandparents, friends, church members, and community leaders. Such a practice exemplifies an understanding of the dynamics of CLD communities. Many CLD families face challenges such as low self-esteem, lack of trust, inability to have fun, shame, anger, sadness, rejection and discrimination, lack of support, and adjustment to a new lifestyle, cultural shock, language difference, and immigration status. In light of such life challenges, educators must maintain a sense of respect and seek to facilitate and build a positive parent-school relationship. Educators can create a comprehensive collaboration system, together with CLD students, families, and the community. They must help CLD students follow established school and classroom rules. Teach them classroom rules with high expectations to avoid miscommunications and misunderstandings. Most importantly, they must be consistent with all students.

What is the impact of the overrepresentation of CLD students in special education programs? According to researchers such as Gay (2010), Drakeford (2004), and Townsend-Walker (2012), the importance of considering culture when implementing educational discipline models cannot be overemphasized. Educators, parents, community members, children, and other stakeholders need to work together and collaborate in order to ensure that CLD students are not overrepresented in special education. We must ensure that educators understand different cultural practices within their own disciplines to prevent unnecessary student referrals to special education programs. Teacher education programs have to put more emphasis on bringing practical and realistic diverse living experiences into the program. For CLD students, there is no one-size-fits-all instructional method. CLD students need a variety of opportunities to be successful in school and in society. We must believe in their intelligence and guide them to a better outcome. We must say *basta* (enough!) to the misunderstanding and misjudging of CLD children and youth, each of whom brings rich cultural and linguistic diversity into our schools and communities every day. It is time to embrace that richness, and to transform the lives of our population of CLD children and youth so that they may realize their potential to excel and make outstanding contributions to society. Fostering growth takes continuous effort and reflection on how we can make enriching school environments safe educational places for learners, which surely includes making them feel like a member of the community. There is much to do.

References

Anderman, E. M., & Anderman, L. H. (2010). *Classroom motivation.* Upper Saddle River, NJ: Pearson.

Artiles (2003). Special education's changing identity: Paradoxes and dilemmas in views of culture and space. *Harvard Education Review, 73*(2), 164–202.

Baca, L., & Cervantes, H. (2004). *The bilingual special education interface.* Upper Saddle River, NJ: Pearson.

Campbell-Whatley, G. C., & Lyons, J. E. (2013). *Leadership practices for special and general educators.* Upper Saddle River, NJ: Pearson.

Chu, S. Y. (2011). Perspectives in understanding the schooling and achievement from culturally and linguistically diverse backgrounds. *Journal of Instructional Psychology, 38*(3), 201–209.

Drakeford, W. (2004). *Racial disproportionality in school discipline practice.* Denver, CO: Practitioner Brief Series National Center for Culturally Responsive Educational System.

Garcia, S., & Ortiz, A. (2006). *Preventing disproportionate representation: Culturally and linguistically responsive prereferral interventions.* Denver, CO: Practitioner Brief Series National Center for Culturally Responsive Educational System.

Gay, G. (2010). *Culturally responsive teaching* (2nd ed.). New York: Teachers College Press.

Hernandez, A. E., Dapretto, M., Mazziotta, J., & Bookheimer, S. (2001). Language switching and language representation in Spanish-English bilinguals: An fMRI study. *NeuroImage, 14*, 510–520.

Hosp, J. L., & Reschly, D. J. (2003). Referral rates for intervention or assessment: A meta-analysis of racial differences. *Journal of Special Education, 37*, 67–80.

Individuals with Disabilities Education Act, Pub. L., No. 108–446, 118 Stat. 2647 (2004).

Kauffman, J. M., Pullen, P. L., Mostert, M. P., & Trent, S. (2011). *Managing classroom behavior: A reflective case-based approach.* Upper Saddle River, NJ: Pearson.

Kea, C., Campbell-Whatley, G., & Richards, H. V. (2006). *Becoming culturally responsive educators: Rethinking teacher education pedagogy.* Denver, CO: Practitioner Brief Series National Center for Culturally Responsive Educational Systems.

Klingner, J. (2004). The science of professional development. *Journal of Learning Disabilities, 37*(3), 248–255.

Klingner, J., Artiles, A., Kozleski, E., Harry, B., Zion, S., & Tate, W. (2005). Addressing the disproportionate representation of culturally and linguistically diverse students in special education through culturally responsive educational systems. *Education Policy Analysis, 13*(38). Retrieved from http://epaa.asu.edu/ojs/article/view/143

Losen, D. J., & Orfield, G. (2002). *Racial inequity in special education.* Cambridge, MA: Harvard Education Press.

MacMillan, D. L., & Reschly, D. J. (1998). Overrepresentation of minority students: The case for greater specificity or reconsideration of the variables examined. *Journal of Special Education, 32*(1), 15–24.

Margolis, J. (2006). New teachers, high-stakes diversity, and the performance-based conundrum. *Urban Review*, *38*(1), 27–44.

Metropolitan Center for Urban Education. (2008). *Culturally responsive classroom management strategies.* New York: NYU Steinhardt.

Meuter, R. F., & Allport, A. (1999). Bilingual learners switching in naming: Asymmetrical costs of language selection. *Journal of Memory and Language*, *40*, 25–40.

Orza, J. L., & Medina, J. (2012). Diversity in the classroom. In T. J. Zirpoli, *Behavior management: Positive application for teachers* (6th ed.) (pp. 55–85). Upper Saddle River, NJ: Pearson.

Rodriguez, D., Ringler, M., & O'Neal, D. (2009). English language learners' perceptions of school environment. *Journal of Research in Childhood Education*, *23*(4), 513–527.

Ruiz, N. T., Rueda, R., Figueroa, R., & Boothroyd, M. (1998). Bilingual special education teachers' shifting paradigms: Complex responses to educational reform. *Journal of Learning Disabilities*, *28*(10), 622–635.

Schwartz, W. (2001). *School practices for equitable discipline of African American students.* New York: ERIC Clearinghouse on Urban Education (ED455343).

Scott, T. M., Anderson, C. M., & Alter, P. (2012). *Managing classroom behavior using Positive Behavior Support.* Upper Saddle River, NJ: Pearson.

Shippen, M. E., Patterson, D., Green, K., & Smitherman, T. (2012). Community and school practices to reduce delinquent behavior: Intervening on the school-to-prison pipeline. *Journal of the Teacher Education Division of the Council for Exceptional Children*, *35*(4), 296–308.

Skiba, R. J., Poloni-Staudinger, L., Simmons, A. B., Feggins, L. R., & Chung, C. G. (2005). Unproven links: Can poverty explain ethnic disproportionality in special education? *Journal of Special Education*, *39*, 130–144.

Sullivan, A. L., & Artiles, A. (2011). Theorizing racial inequality in special education: Applying structural theory to disproportionality. *Urban Education*, *46*, 1526–1552.

Sullivan, A. L., & Bal, A. (2013). Disproportionality in special education: Effects of individuals and school variables on disability risk. *Exceptional Children*, *79*(4), 475–494.

Togut, T. D. (2011). The Gestalt of the school-to-prison pipeline: The duality of overrepresentation of minorities in special education and racial disparity in school discipline on minorities. *Journal of Gender, Social Policy, and the Law*, *20*(1), 164–179.

Townsend-Walker, B. (2012). Teacher education and African American males: Deconstructing pathways from the school house to the "big house." *Teacher Education and Special Education*, *35*(4), 320–332.

Umbreit, J., Ferro, J., Liaupsin, C. J., & Lane, K. L. (2007). *Functional behavior assessment and function-based intervention: An effective approach.* Upper Saddle River, NJ: Pearson.

U.S. Department of Education. (2012, March 6). *New data from U.S. Department of Education highlights educational inequities around teacher experience, discipline, and high school rigor.* Retrieved from http://www.ed.gov/news/press-releases/new-data-us-department-education-highlights-educational-inequities-around-teache

Zhang, D., & Katsiyannis, A. (2002). Minority representation in special education: A persistent challenge. *Remedial and Special Education*, *23*(3), 180–187.

Zirpoli, T. J. (2012). *Behavior management: Positive application for teachers* (6th ed.). Upper Saddle River, NJ: Pearson.

2. *Developmental and Cultural Perspectives of Social and Emotional Development and Its Relation to School Success*

YI DING AND DAKE ZHANG

Educators and researchers have recognized the influence of children's social and emotional development on their later academic achievement and school success. Children with age-appropriate social skills and emotional competence are likely to have more opportunities to socialize with peers, develop positive relationships with teachers and caregivers, and enjoy positive school experiences (Landry & Smith, 2010). Conversely, children who do not develop social and emotional competence are at greater risk for negative school experiences such as being rejected, feeling isolated, and encountering punitive discipline. Childhood behavioral problems are often associated with poor social skills, emotional dysregulation, low tolerance of frustration, and poor problem solving in social contexts such as the classroom (Denham, 2006). Developmentally, young children with poor social and emotional competence are prone to difficulty with the transition to kindergarten, poor academic readiness, social and behavioral problems in later school years, and long-term academic and social challenges (Barbarin et al., 2006; Bornstein, Hahn, & Haynes, 2010; Fantuzzo, Bulotsky, McDermott, Mosca, & Lutz, 2003). Thus, the social and emotional competence of students has been of great concern to educators.

Another critical issue in the U.S. education system is the disproportionate representation of culturally and linguistically diverse (CLD) students placed in special education and targeted for disciplinary actions such as suspensions (e.g., Dunn, 1968; Waitoller, Artiles, & Cheney, 2010). Most of the attention in the literature has focused on the overrepresentation of African American and Hispanic students (e.g., Artiles & Trent, 1994; Harry & Klingner, 2006), whereas less attention has been paid to the under-identification of Asian American students in special education (Hui-Michael & Garcia, 2009). The disproportionate representation of CLD students in special education suggests that the procedures for educational placement and disciplinary actions are not applied equally across ethnic groups and indicates a need to examine (a) both developmental and cultural factors associated with the social and emotional development of CLD students and (b) the relation of social-emotional competence to school success. Successful school experiences are based on both adaptive school adjustment and adequate academic outcomes (Dickinson, McCabe, & Essex, 2006). This chapter begins with a review of typical social and emotional development in children and its link to school success. Then, the chapter addresses the developmental and cultural aspects of social and emotional development of CLD children.

Development of Social and Emotional Competence and Link to School Success

Social and emotional development begins in infancy. Through social exchanges with caregivers, infants are exposed to social reciprocity. As infants grow physically and cognitively, simple social exchanges evolve into complex social interactions. Children's interactional histories lay the foundation for their later social-emotional competence (Thompson, 2006). In turn, the emergence of social and emotional competence leads to children's successful experiences at home, in the community, at school, and in their adult lives (e.g., Guralnick, 2010).

Two Sides of the Same Coin

Empirical studies have supported the importance of social-emotional competence to school success (Carlton & Winsler, 1999). Kindergarteners with positive social-emotional competence demonstrate not only more positive attitudes toward school and smoother adjustment to school routines, but also better academic performance (Ladd, Birch, & Buhs, 1999; Ladd, Kochenderfer, & Coleman, 1996). It is much like the old saying, "The rich get richer." Children with adequate social and emotional competence are likely to have friends at school, to be liked by others, to establish and maintain new friendships, and to initiate positive relationships with teachers (e.g., Buysse, Goldman, West, & Hollingsworth, 2008). In turn, they possess more positive attitudes toward school, participate more actively in school activities, are more open to suggestions for improvement, and achieve more in school in comparison to those who lack social and emotional competence. Children with appropriate and effective social-emotional competence are able to negotiate complex social contexts and to achieve personal goals (Brown & Conroy, 2011). Subdomains of social and emotional competence, such as positive relationships with teachers, positive self-image, emotional knowledge, social abilities, and emotional regulation, are often predictors of academic success (e.g., Carlton, 1999; Jacobsen & Hofmann, 1997; O'Neil, Welsh, Parke, Wang, & Strand, 1997; Shields et al., 2001).

Conversely, deficient social-emotional development has been associated with a variety of challenges. For example, aggressive children or those who are victimized by peers often have difficulty adjusting to school routines and are at risk for academic difficulties, delinquency, and substance abuse (Gagnon, Craig, Tremblay, Zhou, & Vitaro, 1995; Haapasalo & Tremblay, 1994; Kochenderfer & Ladd, 1996). Children with social-emotional deficits often experience negative interactions with peers (Campbell, 2002; Webster-Stratton & Reid, 2003), display oppositional defiant behaviors with adults, and have difficulties interacting with teachers (Walker, Ramsey, & Gresham, 2004). Children with negative peer and teacher interactions are more prone to peer rejection and expulsion from early childhood settings (Gilliam & Shahar, 2006).

Long-lasting deficits in social and emotional competence are often manifested in children's behavioral adjustment in the form of externalizing behaviors, internalizing behaviors, and maladaptive behaviors (Mash & Barkley, 2002). Externalizing behaviors include inattention, dysregulation, noncompliance, impulsivity, aggression, and other disruptive behaviors. Internalizing behaviors include depression, social withdrawal, anxiety, shyness, hypersensitivity, and somatic complaints. Maladaptive behaviors often refer to deficient mastery of conceptual, social, and practical skills, such as inadequate self-direction, lack of community living skills, and inappropriate communication skills. There has been increasing interest among researchers in exploring relations between children's social and emotional competence and their behavioral adjustment, which is critical for school readiness and later school success.

Lack of Social-Emotional Competence and Effects on School Success

Lack of social-emotional competence in preschool children is often attributed to poor parent-child relationships. Based on the attachment theory, poor parent-child relationships are often characterized by mistrust, inconsistent child care, and lack of support (Brown & Conroy, 2011). When children do not receive adequate social and emotional support from parents, they are more likely to encounter subsequent psychological, social, and emotional difficulties. Thompson (2006) argued that healthy development is hindered by inadequate support and emotional instability. Abusive, punitive, or conflicting family circumstances are risk factors for children's poor social-emotional competence, conduct difficulties, and externalizing and internalizing behavior problems (Cassidy, 1995).

Negative early life experiences tend to foster a negative social and emotional developmental trajectory that limits future social opportunities (McCabe & Altamura, 2011). When children do not possess adequate social-emotional competence, they are less likely to establish and maintain friendships and more likely to develop emotional regulation difficulties due to peer rejection and experiences of being ignored or neglected. With fewer social interaction opportunities, children have fewer chances to practice their social skills. Children learn to socialize and socialize to learn. Troubles in peer relationship, deficits in social skills, and negative emotions have been shown to be factors in internalizing and externalizing behavioral problems in children (Merrell, 2003).

With inadequate social-emotional competence, children suffer not only social rejection, but also academic difficulties because their behavioral problems may interfere with their ability to learn and perform successfully in academic settings (Vaughn, Hogan, Lancelotta, Shapiro, & Walker, 1992). Transition to kindergarten can be challenging for children with poor social-emotional competence (Huffman, Mehlinger, & Kerivan, 2000; Qi & Kaiser, 2003). Children with poor social-emotional competence often demonstrate delays in academic skills (Barbarin et al., 2006), are viewed as more difficult to assist by teachers due to lack of cooperation and self-regulation (Rimm-Kaufman, Pianta, & Cox, 2000), and tend to have additional future behavioral difficulties (Fantuzzo et al., 2003). In short, adequate social and emotional competence is one of the fundamental skills for future academic and school success. However, for CLD children who have the additional challenge of developing social-emotional competence within diverse cultures, a variety of individual and environmental factors warrant further examination.

Individual Factors of Social and Emotional Development in CLD Children

Cognition

Adequate cognitive abilities are related to children's social and emotional development. Despite disagreement regarding the definition of intelligence, experts have greater agreement on three descriptors associated with intelligence: abstract thinking or reasoning, the capacity to acquire knowledge, and problem-solving ability (Sattler, 1990). Contemporary theories of learning focus on how knowledge is represented, organized, and processed, and current theorists are interested in social dimensions of learning. Intelligence or effective problem-solving skills are often characteristics of children who are socially and academically competent (Masten et al., 1999). With effective problem-solving or coping skills, children with average to above-average intelligence are able to protect themselves from aversive situations (Masten & Coatsworth, 1998), obtain positive attention from teachers, and maintain friendships with peers (Farber & Egeland, 1987; Werner & Smith, 1992). A negative correlation was found between intelligence and disruptive behavior and academic failure (Masten, Best, & Garmezy, 1990).

Children from CLD backgrounds might differ from the majority culture in their cognitive processing. Some cultures emphasize a holistic approach to learning new concepts, whereas other cultures focus on an analytic approach to learning new concepts. Some cultures prefer to teach children to process information from broader concepts (e.g., fruit) to narrower concepts (e.g., banana), whereas other cultures prefer to process information from narrower to broader concepts. For example, mailing addresses in Western countries typically start with the name of recipient (first line), the room number of the apartment/suite/etc. or number on the street (second line), the city, state, corresponding zip code (third line), and the country (fourth line). However, the format of mailing addresses in China is reversed, starting with the country, the city and province, the room number of the apartment/suite/etc., the name of the recipient, and ending with the postal code if applicable. Another example is the order of personal names. In many Western countries, the order is given name, middle name or initial, and family name (e.g., David C. Johnson). However, in many Asian countries, the order is family name, middle name (if applicable), and given name. Thus, a native Chinese child will be called Ping (given name) Liu (family name) in the U.S. and Liu Ping in China. These daily living examples indicate that cultures can alter and shape how children perceive concepts, process information, and represent information obtained.

Language

Language is probably the most powerful tool for young children to make connections with peers, caregivers, and teachers. Communication is essential to helping children to express needs, exchange ideas, share toys, and negotiate with peers and adults. Communication plays an important role in the development of children's social, emotional, cognitive, and motor skills. However, for many CLD children, especially those with disabilities, learning to communicate in English as a second language does not come naturally or easily. Without effective communication, young children might resort to naïve behaviors, such as crying or pushing, to escape a task or request a preferred object. Such maladaptive behaviors are often deemed as socially and emotionally inappropriate for a school environment. Most educators or related school personnel are familiar with the typical developmental trajectory of language development in children. However, the developmental trajectory becomes more complicated when the children are English language learners (ELLs). Cummins (1984) made a distinction between two types of language proficiency: Basic Interpersonal Communication Skills (BICS) and Cognitive Academic Language Proficiency (CALP). CALP demands more cognitive involvement, requires broader content-specific concepts and vocabulary (Chamberlain, 2005), and might take five to seven years to acquire, whereas proficiency in BICS might take two to three years. Thus, a child from a CLD background who speaks English as a second language might take several years to master adequate social and communication skills in a school setting. Prior to the successful mastery of BICS, CLD children might display social and emotional difficulties.

Cultural differences are evident in language development, and individuals from different cultures often utilize different approaches to foster language development in their children (Heath, 1983). For example, Western cultures encourage self-disclosure of feelings and emotions that children experience, whereas such self-disclosure is encouraged less by Asian parents. In the context of parent-child play, parents from some cultures prefer verbally engaging their children and expect frequent verbal feedback from their children, whereas parents from other cultures prefer to focus on hands-on skills and behavioral demonstrations. Thus, during social interactions, children from the former group might have better communication/explanation skills and children from the latter group might have better demonstration skills.

Temperament

Children's temperament is a factor in the development of social competence (Dixon & Smith, 2000; Masten & Powell, 2003). Children differ in the ways they respond to new people, environments, challenges, and opportunities (Chess, Thomas, & Birch, 1968; Karr-Morse & Wiley, 1997). In general, three broad temperament factors related to social interactions include (a) reactivity or negative emotionality; (b) self-regulation; and (c) approach-withdrawal, inhibition, or sociability (Oades-Sese, Esquivel, Kaliski, & Maniatis, 2011). A sociable and positive-natured temperament was found to be one of the resiliency factors for children in poverty (Werner & Smith, 1992; Wyman, Cowen, Work, & Parker, 1991). However, temperament is also influenced by environmental factors, such as parenting styles, socioeconomic status (Sanson, Oberklaid, Pedlow, & Prior, 1991), and culturally specific beliefs and norms (Chen, Rubin, & Li, 1995; Smart & Sanson, 2001).

Behaviors

Adaptive behaviors are broadly defined as the ways in which children complete everyday functional tasks that reflect age-appropriate expectations for independence (Horn & Childre, 2004). However, the types of behaviors that are considered age appropriate are based on cultural expectations (Anderson & Webb-Johnson, 1995). Existing data and empirical studies have shown that certain groups of CLD children are overrepresented in a number of disability categories in special education (e.g., Artiles & Trent, 1994; Coutinho & Oswald, 2000; U.S. Department of Education, 2009). Bauermeister (1995) found that one-third of the Puerto Rico students in a representative group would be classified as having attention-deficit hyperactivity disorder (ADHD) using mainland U.S. norms that indicate a lower tolerance for inattention and hyperactivity. Anderson and Webb-Johnson (1995) questioned the overrepresentation of African American male students with diagnosis of emotional and/or behavioral disorders (EBD). They argued that many of the problem behaviors in these students were attributable to low engagement in academic activities and different perceptions of what constitutes emotional and/or behavioral disorders.

Environmental Factors Contributing to Social and Emotional Development in CLD Children

Poverty and Neighborhood Community Characteristics

Children do not grow and develop in a vacuum. The environments in which they live have an impact on their overall development as individuals, such as what and how they learn, when they develop particular skills, and how they interact with others. According to Bailey and Wolery (1992), individuals, families, organizations, and agencies are an organized whole entity and the subcomponents of the entity are interrelated and interdependent. Based on the ecological perspective (Bronfenbrenner, 1992), a change in one part of the system (environment) might influence other parts. In the U.S., race, socioeconomic status (SES), and neighborhood characteristics associated with risk factors are often interrelated (Duncan, Brooks-Gunn, & Klebanov, 1994). Children from low SES families are more likely to live in urban neighborhoods where they are exposed to aversive experiences such as violence and substance abuse. These children have been shown to suffer from higher levels of anxiety, irritability, stress, and hypervigilance (Gorman-Smith & Tolan, 1998). These psychological conditions might contribute to children's social and emotional difficulties that are reflected in externalizing behaviors and that result in discipline referrals (Gregory, Skiba, & Noguera, 2010).

Children's coping mechanisms are shaped by their exposure to and experiences with different environmental threats. Having a "tough front" or physically protecting oneself to avoid potential victimization might be a necessary survival skill in a community characterized by violence (Anderson, 1999; Stewart, Schreck, & Simons, 2006), whereas such behavioral manifestations might be viewed as unfriendly and unsociable characteristics in the safety of a typical school setting. Dance (2002) advocated for the need to examine the "code of the street" when addressing challenging behaviors in students from high-crime neighborhoods, considering that these students might have to adjust to different social norms in their school settings. Race and ethnicity remain a significant predictor of disciplinary referrals, suspensions, and expulsions, after controlling for parental education, family structure, and the urbanicity of neighborhoods (Wallace, Goodkind, Wallace, & Bachman, 2008). Students enrolled in schools with higher rates of low-income students (Raffaele Mendez, Knoff, & Ferron, 2002; Wu, Pink, Crain, & Moles, 1982) or from low-SES families (McCarthy & Hoge, 1987; Skiba, Michael, Nardo, & Peterson, 2002) have a higher likelihood of being targeted for school discipline, and these conditions appear to be mild contributors to disproportionate discipline sanctions of CLD children (Wallace et al., 2008).

Parenting Styles

A famous Chinese proverb states that "Parents are their child's first teachers." By nature, children inherit many physical and psychological features from their parents. Through nurturing, family routines, customs, and parenting styles, parents reinforce their children to behave in specific ways. Baumrind's (1967, 1971) early conceptualization of the dimensions of parenting styles, which include authoritative, authoritarian, and permissive styles, has had a long impact on the literature that explains individual differences in relation to parenting characteristics (Parke & Buriel, 2006; Winsler, Madigan, & Aquilino, 2005). Based on Baumrind's approach, researchers have described two dimensions of parenting styles: parental acceptance/responsiveness and demandingness/control (Grolnick, 2003; Maccoby & Martin, 1983). Joint consideration of these two dimensions has yielded four main parenting styles addressed in the literature: (a) authoritative (warm, responsive/restrictive, demanding), (b) permissive (warm, responsive/permissive, undemanding), (c) authoritarian (rejecting, unresponsive/restrictive, demanding), and (d) uninvolved (rejecting, unresponsive/permissive, undemanding) (Rinaldi & Howe, 2012).

Empirical studies have reported a variety of child outcomes associated with parenting styles. For example, more effective social skills and academic achievement were positively associated with the authoritative parenting style (e.g., Baumrind, 1991; Baumrind, Larzelere, & Owens, 2010), whereas externalizing and attention problems were associated with permissive and authoritarian parenting styles (e.g., Baldry & Farrington, 1998; Kaufmann et al., 2000; Milevsky, Schlechter, Netter, & Keehn, 2007). In a group of Canadian toddlers, Rinaldi and Howe (2012) found that permissive parenting by mothers and authoritarian parenting by fathers uniquely and significantly predicted externalizing behaviors, while authoritative parenting by fathers was predictive of adaptive behaviors. In Chinese elementary children, children's temperament (effortful control and anger/frustration) had bidirectional relations with parenting styles, suggesting higher effortful control and lower anger/frustration were associated with higher authoritarian parenting across time and in both directions (Lee, Zhou, Eisenberg, & Wang, 2013). In Australian adolescents, a six-year longitudinal study found that authoritarian parenting in seventh grade predicted later (low) psychological flexibility, and adolescent psychological flexibility in ninth grade predicted later decreases in authoritarian parenting and increases in authoritative parenting (Williams, Ciarrochi, & Heaven, 2012). Based on Williams et al. (2012), inflexible parents tend to raise inflexible children, whereas flexible adolescents reinforce flexible parenting styles. In sum, parenting styles and children's functioning demonstrate bidirectional relations. With improvement in parental coping skills and reduction in parenting stress, parents might be able to manifest more positive, less punitive, and more consistent parenting styles, which in turn might aid children in their social and emotional development (Healey, Flory, Miller, & Halperin, 2011).

Aside from universal understanding of parenting styles, family is a social-cultural-economic arrangement that influences children's social and emotional development (Alizadeh, Talib, Abdullah, & Mansor, 2011). Traditional Western philosophy supports problem solving through active and direct manipulation or control to change the environment, whereas Confucian philosophy stresses rules to promote loyalty, respect, and harmony among family members (Moodley & West, 2005). Western culture emphasizes defining and attacking problems directly, whereas Asian cultures tend to accommodate or cope with problems indirectly (Sue & Sue, 2008). In parenting, direct confrontation and explicit elaboration might be used less often by Asian parents. For example, if a child is invited to a birthday party on a Sunday morning, a Caucasian parent might respond in a direct way: "I'm sorry, but our family is having lunch at your grandma's house." An Asian parent might respond by saying, "This is a great opportunity to hang out with your friends; however, I am unsure whether we can make it because your grandma has been asking us to have lunch at her house." Both approaches indicate that the parents do not prefer for the child to attend the birthday party; however, the former response is explicit and the latter tries to avoid conflict and to achieve harmony among family members.

Acculturation Level of the Family

One of the developmental challenges encountered by CLD children is their exposure to school experiences, including interactions and interpersonal relationship building with peers and adjustment to teacher expectations (Oades-Sese et al., 2011). Berry's acculturation framework (1997, 2003) has been one of the most widely referenced theories in the multicultural education literature. Based on Berry, two dimensions of acculturation are (a) immigrants' maintenance of their heritage culture and (b) immigrants' adoption of the mainstream culture. Joint consideration of both dimensions yields four levels of acculturation: integration (embrace both heritage culture and mainstream culture), marginalization (embrace neither culture), separation (exclusively embrace heritage culture), and assimilation (exclusively embrace mainstream culture). Depending on the acculturation level of a CLD family, there might be a gap between school expectations and family expectations for the children's social and emotional development.

Integration and separation were positively associated with life satisfaction, and marginalization was negatively associated with self-esteem in youths from four cultural backgrounds (Vietnamese, Pakistani, Turkish, and Chilean) residing in Norway (Sam, 2000). Korean American adolescents with the integration mode of acculturation reported the fewest emotional and behavioral problems, whereas those with marginalization mode reported the most problems (Shrake, 1996). Hispanic American children with assimilated parents were rated higher on social competence in comparison to those with less assimilated parents (Pawliuk et al., 1996).

Language proficiency of children from CLD backgrounds is also associated with the acculturation level of the family. Children from CLD families might exhibit minimal to completely fluent proficiency in both native and mainstream languages (Gutierrez-Clellen, 1999). Based on Brice (2002), bilingualism can be classified into five categories in English-Spanish speaking children: (a) a Spanish-dominant speaker, (b) an English-dominant speaker, (c) a balanced-bilingual speaker, (d) a mixed bilingual (or limited-bilingual) speaker, and (e) a low-bilingual speaker. Children who have limited-bilingual or low-bilingual skills might encounter particular difficulties in social interactions in mainstream cultural settings.

Cultural Values

Culture generally refers to the customs, values, traditions, and history of a particular group. For individuals raised in CLD families in the U.S., the cultural values imposed by White European American society can lead to conflicting feelings and cause potential harm. For example, in terms of family support for child rearing, White educators might emphasize the nuclear family's role in children's development and education; however, traditional Hispanic families might emphasize interdependent support from extended families (Uba, 1994), and African American families have a kinship system (relatives of a variety of blood ties may act as the extended family; Hines & Boyd-Franklin, 2005). Without the awareness of the value differences, educators might misunderstand behaviors (e.g., grandparents picking up children from school instead of parents) and make judgments (e.g., minority parents are not as involved in children's education as White European American parents) that are detrimental to minority families.

Different societies and cultures possess different perceptions on time management. The U.S. White European American culture is characterized as being preoccupied with the future (Katz, 1985; Kluckhohn & Strodtbeck, 1961). Because of the future orientation, the society values (a) youth achievement and (b) controlling one's destiny by future planning. However, Native Americans and African Americans tend to value a present-time orientation, whereas Asian Americans and Hispanic Americans possess a past-present focus (Sue & Sue, 2008). In the U.S. mainstream culture, youth is valued more highly than age; in contrast, respect for elders and ancestors is stressed in Native American and Asian American cultures. Difficulties may occur when educators are not aware of differences rooted in the time perspective and misperceive CLD children (e.g., do not establish time management skills; do not possess a planner; do not take a proactive role in making progress) (Hines & Boyd-Franklin, 2005).

In terms of the relational dimension, the U.S. culture is characterized as an achievement-driven society and the concept of individualism is emphasized. It is believed that the individual is the psychosocial unit of operation; the individual holds accountability for his/her own behaviors; independence and autonomy are highly valued; and one should be internally directed and controlled (Sue & Sue, 2008). Relationship in Asian cultures, such as China and Japan, is lineal in nature, and identification with others is wide and linked to ancestor worship. Collectivism is stressed in many Asian cultures. Obeying the wishes of ancestors or decreased parents and using identity in relation to the historical past are common practice in Asian cultures. However, such behaviors might be misinterpreted as the inability to establish an independent identity and not being accountable for one's own behaviors.

Regarding the activity dimension, White U.S. cultural values stress an action (doing) orientation, which means that human beings have to master and control nature, must do things to solve problems, and take a pragmatic and utilitarian view of life (Sue & Sue, 2008). Educators expect that children should be proactive, self-initiating, and fight against inaction. However, Native Americans and Hispanic Americans endorse a being or being-in-becoming mode of activity (Sue & Sue, 2008). Through self-containment, poise, and harmony with the universe, they cope with many challenging situations. Educators who are unfamiliar with Native American values might conclude that children from this particular cultural group are aloof, passive, noncompetitive, or inactive.

Teachers' Expectations

It is generally believed that teachers' expectations for students are race- and ethnicity-specific. It is a well-known notion that teachers' expectations may influence students' academic achievement and other types of functioning through self-fulfilling prophesies. Generally speaking, European American and Asian American students consistently outperform African American and Hispanic American students in reading and mathematics achievement tests, according to measures in fourth and eighth grades (National Center for Education Statistics, 2003). Low test performance might in turn lower teachers' expectations for African American and Hispanic American students (Ferguson, 2003).

Research findings regarding teachers' expectations have shown mixed results. For example, some studies have supported the notion that teachers hold higher expectations for European American than for African American students (Coates, 1972; Sbarra & Pianta, 2001), whereas other findings have not supported such observations (Kehle, Bramble & Mason, 1974; Pigott & Cowen, 2000). Teachers' expectations for Hispanic American students were similar to those for African American students and were less similar to expectations for Asian American students (Jensen & Rosenfeld, 1974), indicating that teachers did not view children from CLD backgrounds as a homogenous group. Furthermore, researchers found that teachers held more positive attitudes toward Asian American than toward European American students (Chang & Sue, 2003).

In a meta-analysis, Tenenbaum and Ruck (2007) examined 39 articles published from 1971 to 2003 that directly tested for teachers' expectations; special education, disciplinary, or reading group referral; and spoken language or teacher feedback between CLD and European American students. It was found that teachers held the highest expectations for Asian American students and that teachers held more positive expectations for European American students than for Hispanic or African American students. The findings suggested that teachers' expectations and speech patterns varied depending on students' ethnic backgrounds. In other words, teachers' expectations contributed to more positive or neutral speech patterns toward European American students, in comparison to African American and Hispanic American students. Tenenbaum and Ruck (2007) argued that differentiated teachers' expectations and speech contribute to an unfair classroom climate, which might place African American and Hispanic American students in disadvantageous positions for academic, social, and emotional development.

Conclusion

Universal and unique developmental trajectories contribute to children's social and emotional development. Children who experience difficulties in social-emotional development are more likely to encounter challenges when they pursue academic and school success. Cultural values and perspectives play a key role in shaping and reinforcing children's behaviors. With a growing number of young children with CLD backgrounds enrolling in U.S. schools, many of whom are bilingual or have English as a second language (Fry & Gonzales, 2008), there is an urgent need to provide developmentally appropriate and culturally responsive practices to children from CLD families. To meet the needs of an increasingly diverse student composition in the U.S., Hui-Michael and Garcia (2009) recommended that ongoing professional development should be provided to educators and related service providers to (a) foster their cultural self-awareness, (b) increase their understanding of cultural values and how such values influence children's learning, and (c) enhance their skills to provide alternative culturally sensitive assessment and intervention to CLD children.

References

Alizadeh, S., Talib, M. B. A., Abdullah, R., & Mansor, M. (2011). Relationship between parenting style and children's behavior problems. *Asian Social Science*, *12*(7), 195–200.

Anderson, E. (1999). *Code of the street: Decency, violence, and the moral life of the inner city.* New York: W. W. Norton.

Anderson, M., & Webb-Johnson, G. (1995). Cultural contexts, the seriously emotionally disturbed classification, and African American learners. In B. Ford, F. Obiakor, & J. Patton (Eds.), *Effective education of African American exceptional learners* (pp. 151–188). Austin, TX: PRO-ED.

Artiles, A., & Trent, S. (1994). Overrepresentation of minority students in special education: A continuing debate. *Journal of Special Education*, *27*, 410–437.

Bailey, D. B., & Wolery, M. (1992). *Teaching infants and preschoolers with disabilities* (2nd ed.). Columbus, OH: Macmillan.

Baldry, A. C., & Farrington, D. P. (1998). Parenting influences on bullying and victimization. *Legal and Criminological Psychology*, *3*, 237–254.

Barbarin, O., Bryant, D., McCandies, T., Early, D., Pianta, R., & Howes, C. (2006). Children enrolled in public pre-K: The relation of family life, neighborhood quality, and socioeconomic resources to early competence. *American Journal of Orthopsychiatry*, *76*(2), 265–276.

Bauermeister, J. J. (1995, Summer). ADD and Hispanic (Puerto Rican) children: Some thoughts and research findings. *Attention!*, *2*, 16–19.

Baumrind, D. (1967). Child care practices anteceding three patterns of preschool behavior. *Genetic Psychology Monographs*, *75*, 43–88.

Baumrind, D. (1971). Current patterns of parental authority. *Developmental Psychology Monographs*, *4*(1), 1–103.

Baumrind, D. (1991). Parenting styles and adolescent development. In J. Brooks-Gunn, R. Lerner, & A. C. Peterson (Eds.), *The encyclopaedia of adolescence* (pp. 746–758). New York: Garland.

Baumrind, D., Larzelere, R. E., & Owens, E. B. (2010). Effects of preschool parents' power assertive patterns and practices on adolescent development. *Parenting: Science and Practice*, *10*, 157–201. doi:10.1080/15295190903290790

Berry, J. W. (1997). Immigration, acculturation, and adaptation. *Applied Psychology: An International Review*, *46*(1), 5–68.

Berry, J. W. (2003). Conceptual approaches to acculturation. In K. M. Chun, P. B. Organista, & G. Marin (Eds.), *Acculturation: Advances in theory, measurement, and applied research* (pp. 17–37). Washington, DC: American Psychological Association. doi:10.1037/10472-004

Bornstein, M. H., Hahn, C., & Haynes, O. M. (2010). Social competence, externalizing and internalizing behavioral adjustment from early childhood through early adolescence: Developmental cascades. *Development and Psychopathology*, *22*, 717–735.

Brice, A. E. (2002). *The Hispanic child: Speech, language, culture, and education*. Boston, MA: Allyn & Bacon.

Bronfenbrenner, U. (1992). *Ecological systems theory*. London, UK: Jessica Kingsley.

Brown, W. H., & Conroy, M. A. (2011). Social-emotional competence in young children with developmental delays: Our reflection and vision for future. *Journal of Early Intervention, 33*(4), 310–320.

Buysse, V., Goldman, B. D., West, T., & Hollingsworth, H. (2008). Friendships in early childhood: Implications for early education and intervention. In W. H. Brown, S. L. Odom, & S. R. McConnell (Eds.), *Social competence of young children: Risk, disability, and intervention* (pp. 77–97). Baltimore, MD: Paul H. Brookes.

Campbell, S. B. (2002). *Behavior problems in preschool children: Clinical and developmental issues* (2nd ed.). New York: Guilford.

Carlton, M. P. (1999). Motivation and school readiness in kindergarten children. *Dissertation Abstracts International, 60*(11-A), 3899A.

Carlton, M. P., & Winsler, A. (1999). School readiness: The need for a paradigm shift. *School Psychology Review, 28*, 338–352.

Cassidy, J. (1995). Attachment and generalized anxiety disorder. In D. Cicchetti & S. L. Toth (Eds.), *Emotion, cognition, and representation. Rochester Symposium on Developmental Psychopathology* (Vol. 6, pp. 343–370). Rochester, NY: University of Rochester Press.

Chamberlain, S. P. (2005). Recognizing and responding to cultural differences in the education of culturally and linguistically diverse learners. *Intervention in School and Clinic, 40*(4), 195–211.

Chang, D. F., & Sue, S. (2003). The effects of race and problem type on teachers' assessment of student behavior. *Journal of Consulting and Clinical Psychology, 71*, 235–242.

Chen, X., Rubin, K. H., & Li, B. (1995). Social and school adjustment of shy and aggressive children in China. *Development and Psychopathology, 7*, 337–349.

Chess, S., Thomas, A., & Birch, H. G. (1968). *Temperament and behavior disorders in children*. New York: New York University Press.

Coates, B. (1972). White adult behavior toward Black and White children. *Child Development, 43*, 143–154.

Coutinho, M., & Oswald, D. (2000). Disproportionate representation in special education: A synthesis and recommendations. *Journal of Child and Family Studies, 9*(2), 135–156.

Cummins, J. (1984). *Bilingual education and special education: Issues in assessment and pedagogy*. San Diego, CA: College Hill.

Dance, L. (2002). *Tough fronts: The impact of street culture on schooling*. London: Routledge.

Denham, S. (2006). Social-emotional competence as support for school readiness. What is it and how do we assess it? *Early Education and Development, 17*, 57–89.

Dickinson, D., McCabe, A., & Essex, M. (2006). A window of opportunity we must open to all: The case for high-quality support for language and literacy. In D. K. Dickinson & S. B. Neuman (Eds.), *Handbook of early literacy research* (pp. 11–28). New York: Guilford Press.

Dixon, W. E., Jr., & Smith, P. H. (2000). Links between early temperament and language acquisition. *Merrill-Palmer Quarterly, 46,* 417–440.

Duncan, G. J., Brooks-Gunn, J., & Klebanov, P. K. (1994). Economic deprivation and early childhood development. *Child Development, 65,* 296–318.

Dunn, L. (1968). Special education for the mildly retarded: Is much of it justifiable? *Exceptional Children, 7,* 5–24.

Fantuzzo, J., Bulotsky, R., McDermott, P., Mosca, S., & Lutz, M. (2003). A multivariate analysis of emotional and behavioral adjustment and preschool educational outcomes. *School Psychology Review, 32,* 185–203.

Farber, A., & Egeland, B. (1987). Invulnerability among abused and neglected children. In E. J. Anthony & B. J. Cohler (Eds.), *The invulnerable child* (pp. 253–288). New York: Guilford Press.

Ferguson, R. (2003). Teachers' perceptions and expectations and the Black–White test score gap. *Urban Education, 38,* 460–507.

Fry, R., & Gonzales, F. (2008, August). *One-in-five and growing fast: A profile of Hispanic public school students* (Report). Washington DC: Pew Hispanic Center. Retrieved from http://pewhispanic.org/files/reports/92.pdf

Gagnon, C., Craig, W. M., Tremblay, R. E., Zhou, R. M., & Vitaro, F. A. (1995). Kindergarten predictors of boys' stable behavior problems at the end of elementary school. *Journal of Abnormal Child Psychology, 23,* 751–766.

Gilliam, W. S., & Shahar, G. (2006). Preschool and child care expulsion and suspension. *Infants & Young Children, 19,* 228–245.

Gorman-Smith, D., & Tolan, P. H. (1998). The role of exposure to violence and developmental problems among inner-city youth. *Development and Psychopathology, 10,* 101–116.

Gregory, A., Skiba, R. J., & Noguera, P. A. (2010). The achievement gap and the discipline gap: Two sides of the same coin? *Educational Researcher, 39*(1), 59–68.

Grolnick, W. S. (2003). *The psychology of parental control: How well-meant parenting backfires.* Hillsdale, NJ: Erlbaum.

Guralnick, M. J. (2010). Early intervention approaches to enhance the peer-related social competence of young children with developmental delays: A historical perspective. *Infants & Young Children, 23,* 73–83.

Gutierrez-Clellen, V. F. (1999). Language choice in intervention with bilingual children. *American Journal of Speech-Language Pathology, 8,* 291–302.

Haapasalo, J., & Tremblay, R. E. (1994). Physically aggressive boys from ages 6 to 12: Family background, parenting behavior, and prediction of delinquency. *Journal of Consulting and Clinical Psychology, 62,* 1044–1052.

Harry, B., & Klingner, J. (2006). *Why are so many minority students in special education?* New York: Teachers College Press.

Healey, D. M., Flory, J. D., Miller, C. J., & Halperin, J. M. (2011). Maternal positive parenting style is associated with better functioning in hyperactive/inattentive preschool children. *Infant and Child Development, 20,* 148–161.

Heath, S. B. (1983). *Ways with words: Language, life, and work in communities and classrooms.* Cambridge, UK: Cambridge University Press.

Hines, P. M., & Boyd-Franklin, N. (2005). African American families. In M. McGoldrick, J. Giordano, & N. Garcia-Preto (Eds.), *Ethnicity and family therapy* (2nd ed., pp. 87–100). New York: Guilford.

Horn, E., & Childre, A. (2004). Assessing adaptive behavior. In M. McLean, M. Wolery, & D. B. Bailey Jr. (Eds.), *Assessing infants and preschoolers with special needs* (pp. 487–516). Upper Saddle River, NJ: Pearson.

Huffman, L. C., Mehlinger, S. L., & Kerivan, A. S. (2000). Risk factors for academic and behavioral problems at the beginning of school. In L. C. Huffman et al., *Off to a good start: Research on the risk factors for early school problems and selected federal policies affecting children's social and emotional development and their readiness for school.* Chapel Hill, NC: Child Mental Health Foundations and Agencies Network (FAN).

Hui-Michael, Y., & Garcia, S. B. (2009). General educators' perceptions and attributions about Asian American students: Implications for special education referral. *Multiple Voices for Ethnically Diverse Exceptional Learners, 12*(1), 21–37.

Jacobsen, T., & Hofmann, V. (1997). Children's attachment representation: Longitudinal relations to school behavior and academic competency in middle childhood and adolescence. *Developmental Psychology, 33*, 703–710.

Jensen, M., & Rosenfeld, L. (1974). Influence of mode of presentation, ethnicity, and social class on teachers' evaluations of students. *Journal of Educational Psychology, 66*, 540–547.

Karr-Morse, R., & Wiley, M. S. (1997). *Ghosts from the nursery: Tracing the roots of violence.* New York: Atlantic Monthly Press.

Katz, J. H. (1985). The sociopolitical nature of counseling. *The Counseling Psychologist, 13*, 615–624.

Kaufmann, D., Gesten, E., Lucia, R. C. S., Salcedo, O., Rendina-Gobioff, G., & Gadd, R. (2000). The relationship between parenting style and children's adjustment: The parents' perspective. *Journal of Child and Family Studies, 9*, 231–245.

Kehle, T. J., Bramble, W., & Mason, E. (1974). Teacher's expectations: Ratings of student performance as biased by student characteristics. *Journal of Experimental Education, 43*, 54–60.

Kluckhohn, F. R., & Strodtbeck, F. L. (1961). *Variations in value orientations.* Evanston, IL: Row, Patterson, & Co.

Kochenderfer, B. J., & Ladd, G. W. (1996). Peer victimization: Cause or consequence of school maladjustment? *Child Development, 67*, 1305–1317.

Ladd, G. W., Birch, S. H., & Buhs, E. S. (1999). Children's social and scholastic lives in kindergarten: Related spheres of influence? *Child Development, 70*, 1373–1400.

Ladd, G. W., Kochenderfer, B. J., & Coleman, C. C. (1996). Friendship quality as a predictor of young children's early school adjustment. *Child Development, 67*, 1103–1118.

Landry, S. H., & Smith, K. E. (2010). Early social and cognitive precursors and parental support for self-regulation and executive function: Relations from early childhood into adolescence. In B. Sokol, U. Muller, J. Carpendale, A. Young, & G. Iarocci (Eds.), *Self and social regulation: Social interaction and the development of social understanding and executive functions* (pp. 385–418). New York: Oxford University Press.

Lee, E. H., Zhou, Q., Eisenberg, N., & Wang, Y. (2013). Bidirectional relations between temperament and parenting styles in Chinese children. *International Journal of Behavioral Development, 37*(1), 57–67.

Maccoby, E. E., & Martin, J. A. (1983). Socialization in the context of the family: Parent-child interaction. In P. H. Mussen (Series Ed.), *Handbook of child psychology: Socialization, personality, and social development* (4th ed., Vol. 4, pp. 1–101). New York: Wiley.

Mash, E., & Barkley, R. (2002). *Child psychopathology* (2nd ed.). New York: Guilford Press.

Masten, A. S., Best, K., & Garmezy, N. (1990). Resilience and development: Contributions from the study of children who overcome adversity. *Development and Psychopathology, 2*, 425–444.

Masten, A. S., & Coatsworth, J. D. (1998). The development of competence in favorable and unfavorable environments: Lessons from research of successful children. *American Psychologist, 53*, 205–220.

Masten, A. S., Hubbard, J. J., Gest, S. D., Tellegen, A., Garmezy, N., & Ramirez, M. (1999). Competence in the context of adversity: Pathways to resilience and maladaptation from childhood to late adolescence. *Development and Psychopathology, 11*, 143–169.

Masten, A. S., & Powell, J. L. (2003). A resilience framework for research, policy, and practice. In S. S. Luthar (Ed.), *Resilience and vulnerability: Adaptation in the context of childhood adversities* (pp. 1–26). New York: Cambridge University Press.

McCabe, P. C., & Altamura, M. (2011). Empirically valid strategies to improve social and emotional competence of preschool children. *Psychology in the School, 48*(5), 513–540.

McCarthy, J. D., & Hoge, D. R. (1987). Social construction of school punishment. *Social Forces, 65*, 1101–1120.

Merrell, K. W. (2003). *Behavioral, social, and emotional assessment of children and adolescents.* Mahwah, NJ: Lawrence Erlbaum.

Milevsky, A., Schlechter, M., Netter, S., & Keehn, D. (2007). Maternal and paternal parenting styles in adolescents: Associations with self-esteem, depression and life-satisfaction. *Journal of Child and Family Studies, 16*, 39–47.

Moodley, R., & West, E. (Eds.). (2005). *Integrating traditional healing practices into counseling and psychotherapy.* Thousand Oaks, CA: Sage.

National Center for Education Statistics. (2003). *The nation's report card.* Retrieved from http://nces.ed.gov/nationsreportcard/

Oades-Sese, G., Esquivel, G., Kaliski, P., & Maniatis, L. (2011). A longitudinal study of the social and academic competence of economically disadvantageous bilingual preschool children. *Developmental Psychology, 47*(3), 747–764.

O'Neil, R., Welsh, M., Parke, R. D., Wang, S., & Strand, C. (1997). A longitudinal assessment of the academic correlates of early peer acceptance and rejection. *Journal of Clinical Child Psychology, 26*, 290–303.

Parke, R. D., & Buriel, R. (2006). Socialization in the family: Ethnic and ecological perspectives. In W. Damon, R. M. Lerner, & N. Eisenberg (Eds.), *The handbook of child psychology: Social, emotional, and personality development* (6th ed., Vol. 3, pp. 429–504). New York: Wiley.

Pawliuk, N., Grizenko, N., Chan-Yip, A., Gantous, P., Matthew, J., & Nguyen, D. (1996). Acculturation style and psychological functioning in children of immigrants. *American Journal of Orthopsychiatry, 66*, 111–121. doi:10.1037/h0080161

Pigott, R. L., & Cowen, E. L. (2000). Teacher race, child race, racial congruence, and teacher ratings of children's school adjustment. *Journal of School Psychology, 38*, 177–196.

Qi, C. H., & Kaiser, A. P. (2003). Behavior problems of preschool children from low-income families: Review of the literature. *Topics in Early Childhood Special Education, 23*(4), 188–216.

Raffaele Mendez, L. M., Knoff, H. M., & Ferron, J. M. (2002). School demographic variables and out-of-school suspension rates: A quantitative and qualitative analysis of a large ethnically diverse school district. *Psychology in the Schools, 39*, 259–276.

Rimm-Kaufman, S. E., Pianta, R. B., & Cox, M. J. (2000). Teachers' judgments of problems in the transition to kindergarten. *Early Childhood Research Quarterly, 15*, 147–166.

Rinaldi, C. M., & Howe, N. (2012). Mothers' and fathers' parenting styles and associations with toddlers' externalizing, internalizing, and adaptive behaviors. *Early Childhood Research Quarterly, 27*, 266–273.

Sam, D. (2000). Psychological adaptation of adolescents with American backgrounds. *Journal of Social Psychology, 140*(1), 5–25.

Sanson, A., Oberklaid, F., Pedlow, R., & Prior, M. (1991). Risk indicators: Assessment of infancy predictors of preschool behavioral maladjustment. *Journal of Child Psychology and Psychiatry, 32*, 609–626.

Sattler, J. (1990). *Assessment of children* (3rd ed.). San Diego, CA: Jerome M. Sattler.

Sbarra, D. A., & Pianta, R. C. (2001). Teacher ratings of behavior among African American and Caucasian children during the first two years of school. *Psychology in the School, 38*, 229–238.

Shields, A., Dickstein, S., Seifer, R., Giusti, L., Magee, K. D., & Spritz, B. (2001). Emotional competence and early school adjustment: A study of preschoolers at risk. *Early Education & Development, 12*, 73–96.

Shrake, E. (1996). *Perceived parenting style, ethnic identity, and associated problem behaviors among Korean American adolescents* (Unpublished doctoral dissertation). University of California, Los Angeles.

Skiba, R. J., Michael, R. S., Nardo, A. C., & Peterson, R. L. (2002). The color of discipline: Sources of racial and gender disproportionality in school punishment. *Urban Review, 34*, 317–342.

Smart, D., & Sanson, A. (2001, Winter). Children's social competence. *Australian Institute of Family Studies, 59,* 10–15.

Stewart, E. A., Schreck, C. J., & Simons, R. L. (2006). "I ain't gonna let no one disrespect me": Does the code of the street reduce or increase violent victimization among African American adolescents? *Journal of Research in Crime and Delinquency, 43,* 427–458.

Sue, D. W., & Sue, D. (2008). Counseling the culturally diverse: Theory and practice (5th ed.). Hoboken, NJ: John Wiley.

Tenenbaum, H. R., & Ruck, M. D. (2007). Are teachers' expectations different for racial minority than for European American students? A meta-analysis. *Journal of Educational Psychology, 99*(2), 253–273.

Thompson, R. A. (2006). The development of the person: Social understanding, relationships, conscience, self. In W. Damon & R. M. Lerner (Editors-in-Chief) & N. Eisenberg (Vol. Ed.), *Handbook of child psychology: Social, emotional, and personality development* (6th ed., Vol. 3, pp. 24–98). Hoboken, NJ: John Wiley.

Uba, L. (1994). *Asian Americans.* New York: Guilford.

U.S. Department of Education. (2009). Individuals with Disabilities Education Act (IDEA).

Vaughn, S., Hogan, A., Lancelotta, G., Shapiro, S., & Walker, J. (1992). Subgroups of children with severe and mild behavior problems: Social competence and reading achievement. *Journal of Clinical Child Psychology, 21*(2), 98–106.

Waitoller, F. R., Artiles, A. J., & Cheney, D. (2010). The miners' canary: A review of overrepresentation research and explanations. *Journal of Special Education, 44*(1), 29–49.

Walker, H. M., Ramsey, E., & Gresham, F. M. (Eds.). (2004). *Antisocial behavior in school: Evidence-based practices* (2nd ed.). Belmont, CA: Wadsworth.

Wallace, J. M., Jr., Goodkind, S., Wallace, C. M., & Bachman, J. G. (2008). Racial, ethnic, and gender differences in school discipline among U.S. high school students: 1991–2005. *Negro Educational Review, 59,* 47–62.

Webster-Stratton, C., & Reid, M. J. (2003). Treating conduct problems and strengthening social emotional competence in young children (ages 4–8 years): The Dina Dinosaur treatment program. *Journal of Emotional and Behavioral Disorders, 11,* 130–143.

Werner, E. E., & Smith, R. S. (1992). *Overcoming the odds: High-risk children from birth to adulthood.* Ithaca, NY: Cornell University Press.

Williams, K. E., Ciarrochi, J., & Heaven, P. C. (2012). Inflexible parents, inflexible kids: A 6-year longitudinal study of parenting style and the development of psychological flexibility in adolescents. *Journal of Youth and Adolescence, 41*(8), 1053–1066.

Winsler, A., Madigan, A. L., & Aquilino, S. A. (2005). Correspondence between maternal and paternal parenting styles in early childhood. *Early Childhood Research Quarterly, 20,* 1–12.

Wu, S., Pink, W., Crain, R. L., & Moles, O. (1982). Student suspension: A critical reappraisal. *Urban Review, 14,* 245–272.

Wyman, P. A., Cowen, E. L., Work, W. C., & Parker, G. R. (1991). Developmental and family milieu correlates of resilience in urban children who have experienced major life stress. *American Journal of Community Psychology, 19,* 405–426.

3. *Creating a Culturally Responsive School Climate with School-Wide Positive Behavioral Interventions and Supports*

SU-JE CHO, JI-RYUN KIM, KWANG-SUN CHO BLAIR,
AND CARLOS R. MCCRAY

School violence is a national concern for schools and communities across the United States (Kondrasuk, Greene, Waggoner, Edwards, & Nayak-Rhodes, 2005). A report by National Center for Educational Statistics indicated that students ages 12 to 18 were victims of approximately 583,000 violent crimes in 2004 (Dinkes, Cataldi, Kena, & Baum, 2006). School-wide violence can take several forms including bullying, intimidation, gang activity, locker theft, weapon use, assault, and other behaviors that often result in a person being victimized (Espelage & Horne, 2008). These behaviors are usually targeted against peers. However, similar forms of student violence are directed against educators. Such violence ranges from disrespectful behavior to intimidation, verbal threats or gestures, theft, property damage, and in some cases, physical assault (American Psychological Association, n.d.). Among these acts, student verbal aggression against teachers was most frequently reported by teachers in several studies (e.g., Mooij, 2011).

Students exposed to violent behaviors or victims of such behaviors are likely to experience a range of negative social-emotional, academic, and developmental outcomes. Dempsey and Storch (2008) found that students being victimized by aggressive peers in childhood have a tendency to develop social anxiety and depression in adulthood. Similarly, in investigating the relationship between frequent involvement in bullying and aggressive impulsivity and perceptions of school climate using a large-scale data of 24,345 elementary-, middle-, and high-school students. O'Brennan, Bradshaw, and Sawyer (2009) found that bully/victims displayed a higher level of internalizing symptoms, problems in peer relationships, and have poorer perceptions of the school environment and academic performance.

Students exposed to violence and victimization at school are at high risk of dropping out (Peguero, 2011). Of the high-school dropouts, more than half are students of color, and most are from low-income families; low-income students fail to graduate at five times the rate of middle-income peers and six times that of higher-income peers (National Center for Education Statistics, 2012). To ensure that all students, including those from culturally and linguistically diverse (CLD) backgrounds, attain academic proficiency, creating and maintaining safe environments where students can learn appropriate academic and social skills is a prerequisite.

Given the high percentage of students engaging in and being victimized by high-risk behaviors, addressing student problem behaviors has been the most pressing concern for educators (Sprague et al., 2001; Walker & Shinn, 2002). A number of studies (e.g., Gregory, Cornell, & Fan, 2012) reported that high rates of violence directed toward peers and teachers were strongly associated with disorganized school structures, negative school climates, lack of administrative and collegial social supports, and high residential crowding. On the contrary, lower rates were as a result of organized school structures and support systems, clear and consistent school-wide disciplinary policies, and positive relationships between faculty and students and among students.

School-Wide Positive Behavioral Interventions and Supports (SWPBIS) has been widely accepted as an effective way to create positive school cultures (Sugai & Horner, 2009). SWPBIS has been associated with school improvements in classroom behavior, academic performance, and school climate (Sugai, Horner, Lewis-Palmer, & Todd, 2005). However, the implementation of SWPBIS in urban schools, where poverty-stricken neighborhoods are more prevalent, has been challenging due to a number of variables, some of which will be described below (Gottlieb, Alter, Gottlieb, & Wishner, 1994; McCurdy, Kunsch, & Reibstein, 2007). In addition, more students in urban schools have been found to require secondary and tertiary supports compared to other settings (Turnbull, Turnbull, & Wilcox, 2002; Warren et al., 2003).

Researchers reported that student violence is a multi-systematic issue that manifests from community, school, school personnel, and student factors (Espelage et al., 2013). This chapter describes various factors that are associated with student behavior and academic performance in schools. This chapter further describes key elements for successful implementation of

SWPBIS establishing universal primary prevention in the school as the first step as a way to promote positive school climates for *all* students including those with CLD backgrounds and those who exhibit challenging behaviors.

Factors Associated with Student Performance in Schools

A number of factors in school settings have an impact on the implementation of SWPBIS. Significant factors in implementing SWPBIS may include, but not limit to the high rates of problem behavior, divergent cultural and contextual community issues, collaborative processes, competency of the workforce, and district and administrative leadership (Putnam & Colleagues, 2009). Understanding these factors is necessary to ensure successful implementation of SWPBIS. In the next section, we discuss the school, teacher, parent, and community characteristics that are associated with student performance in schools and that have an impact on the implementation of SWPBIS.

School Factors

Various school factors have been found to influence student performance and achievement scores. For example, Aske and Corman (2008) examined the relationship between several school characteristics and student achievement scores in reading, writing, and math using the data from elementary schools in the Denver metropolitan region collected from 2001 to 2007. The findings showed a strong relationship between student achievement scores and student attendance rates, student enrollment stability, and the free-lunch variables. The findings also revealed a statistical difference between student achievement scores and student racial backgrounds. However, the difference was no longer significant when the SES variable was held constant, indicating poverty affects student academic performance more negatively than their racial backgrounds. The longitudinal data further showed that as the percent of students eligible for the free-lunch program increased, the percent of students' test scores fell. The analysis of the 2001–2002 data revealed that when student attendance rates increased by 1%, the percent of students' test scores increased by 1.47%.

Low-performing schools have a higher percentage of special education students, African American students, and students from low socioeconomic status based on data from 626 schools in New York City (Stiefel, Schwartz, & Iatarola, 2001). Similar results were reported in other studies (e.g., Borman, Carter, Aladjem, & LeFloch, 2004; Carr, 2006). CLD students, especially those with disabilities, are likely to receive more and harsher disciplinary actions than their White peers (Krezmien, Leone, & Achilles, 2006; Skiba et al., 2008). Researchers (e.g., Krezmien et al., 2006) argued that harsh punishments are ineffective. A supportive school climate is more likely to enhance social and academic success of students. Cartledge and Kourea (2008) characterized culturally competent classrooms as (1) being disciplined, not punitive, (2) being fair, (3) providing evidence-based proactive systems, (4) including evidence-based social skill instruction, and (5) using individualized behavior plans.

Class size has been found to be significantly related to student achievement in various subjects regardless of student backgrounds (e.g., Merritt et al., 2011; Shin, 2012). For example, Merritt, Rimm-Kaufman, Berry, Walkowiak, and Larsen (2011) examined if class size predicts achievement for low-income third-grade students. The study sample was 205 third graders, with the majority of them from CLD and economically disadvantaged backgrounds. The schools the students attended participated in a three-year longitudinal cluster randomized control trial of the Responsive Classroom Approach. They found that class size was a significant predictor of math achievement for the sample, explaining 28% of the classroom-level variance. The result further showed that students gained 11 points higher on the third-grade math achievement test for every three fewer students in a classroom. Similarly, Shin (2012) found that African American students benefit more than students of other races and ethnicities from reduced class size in first- through third-grade academic achievement in four key academic subjects.

Benefits of class-size reduction have been evident in California's billion-dollar class-size reduction program. In the late 1990s, the state of California implemented the class-size-reduction (CSR) program throughout the state to reduce K–3 class sizes by roughly ten students per class. The CSR program resulted in creating 25,000 new teaching positions, many of which were filled by teachers without certification and experience (Jepsen & Rivkin, 2009). In investigating the effects of CSR on reading and math achievement, they found that the ten-student reduction in class size increased reading and math achievement scores in the early grades for students of all racial and ethnic backgrounds by 0.10 and .06 standard deviations of the school average test score distribution, respectively, while holding other variables constant. The authors concluded that although CSR was found to increase student achievement scores, "the benefits cannot justify the substantial cost."

Exclusionary approaches (e.g., discipline referrals, suspension, and expulsion) for challenging behaviors are still commonly practiced in many schools including those in New York City. Students displaying problem behaviors in these schools are likely to experience social, emotional, and academic failures because they lose valuable opportunities to learn critical academic and social skills (Cartledge & Kourea, 2008). These deprived opportunities have been known to contribute to further exclusions, academic failure, and school disengagement, such as school dropouts (Office of Special Education Programs, 2001; Skiba, 2002). At least the students freed from exposure to problem behavior are better able to focus on the academic tasks at hand. Tobin and Sugai (1999) in their longitudinal research found that the number of discipline referrals in sixth grade was strongly associated with chronic discipline problems in later middle school. They also reported that three or more suspensions in ninth grade predicted school failure.

Instead of excluding students with challenging behaviors from the learning context, Sugai and Horner (2002) proposed a school-wide behavior management system as an alternative approach. In this approach, the researchers suggested that classroom teachers and the school as a whole provide direct instruction on appropriate social skills so students can learn the desired behavior without losing their instructional time. Schools can effectively support students by teaching school-wide behavioral expectations, consistently reinforcing desired behaviors, and providing consequences for undesired behaviors consistently (Lane, Kalberg, & Menzies, 2009; Sugai, & Horner, 2002). Using the data collected from 77 schools, Vincent and Tobin (2012) found that SWPBIS significantly reduced rates of exclusionary policies although disproportionate rates of exclusionary policies for the students from CLD backgrounds still remained high. These findings indicate that schools should be more culturally responsive in supporting CLD students even within a SWPBIS context.

Teacher Factors

Teacher characteristics seem to be strongly associated with student success in school. Effective teachers foster positive teacher-student relationships. Thus, a high-quality teacher-student relationship should be established as a means of reducing challenging behavior in classrooms while also promoting effective student learning (Marzano, Marzano, & Pickering, 2003). This positive relationship can be a foundation for successful behavior management as well as effective teaching and learning. Students who do not have the necessary social-emotional skills cannot learn effectively in school. Students should learn interpersonal skills such as collaborating with others and how to manage their feelings, empathy, problem solving, and self-control via a social skills curriculum designed by their teachers (Whitted, 2011).

Social support provided by teachers has been found to be one of the most significant predicting variables for positive student outcomes (Wentzel, Donlan, & Morrison, 2012). The more support students perceived from their teachers, the better academic performance the students achieved including increased academic initiative, interest in diverse subjects, and school engagement (Danielsen, Wiium, Wilhelmsen, & Wold, 2010; Wentzel et al., 2012). Elias and Haynes (2008) found a positive correlation between perceived teacher support and social-emotional competence and improved academic performance among students from low socio-economic backgrounds. Similarly, McNeely and Falci (2004) reported that a stratified sample of 80 adolescents receiving emotional support (e.g., fairness and caring) from their teachers were less likely to display problematic behaviors (e.g., substance use, violent behavior, inappropriate sexual activity, and suicide) as compared to their peers with little teacher support. In addition, positive teacher-student relationships characterized by a high level of closeness and a low level of conflict seem to enhance positive adaptation of students with severe behavior issues in school. Social support would contribute to decreasing behavior problems in school and increasing student academic achievement (Baker, Grant, & Morlock, 2008; Danielsen, Samdal, Hetland, & Wold, 2009).

In order to provide sufficient and proper social and emotional support, teachers should be culturally responsive and competent (Cartledge & Kourea, 2008). To do so, they should be aware of their own and students' cultures and understand how their own cultural norms could affect their teaching and judgment of others' behaviors (Gay, 2002; Weinstein, Tomlinson-Clarke, & Curran, 2004). If teachers are aware of culturally different behaviors, they can accept or proactively respond to students' behavior and teach desired behaviors without using unnecessary punishment.

Similarly, teachers who support students' different cultures should hold high expectations for students' behaviors and academic performances regardless of their backgrounds and keep intact the students' sense of responsibility for learning. Teachers' beliefs about students' behavior and academic performance are closely associated with students' actual performance. In reality, teachers tend to have different expectations based on students' racial and socioeconomic backgrounds (Diamond, Randolph, & Spillane, 2004; Ferguson, 2003). Teachers should be aware of their own expectations for students and apply the same high expectations for all students in their classrooms.

Family and Community Factors

Students from communities of low socioeconomic status tend to experience risk factors including poverty, limited resources, substandard housing, and high crime rates. Impoverished families may not have sufficient levels of quality interactions with their children to foster the development of appropriate social skills because parents have to focus on securing basic resources including employment, childcare, and safe housing (Evans, Gonnella, Marcynyszyn, Gentile, & Salpekar, 2005; Kozol, 2005). The lack of social skills is likely to cause delays in academic and language development and may lead to engagement in challenging behaviors including aggressions (Burchinal, Peisner-Feinberg, Bryant, & Clifford, 2000).

A high level of family involvement in their children's education has been identified as one of the key elements for improving social-emotional development and school success of children (Christenson & Havsy, 2004; Patrikakou, Weissberg, Redding, & Walberg, 2005). The more parents become involved in the education of their children, the higher the rates of children's attendance, homework completion, school completion, and academic performance (Barnard, 2004; Jeynes, 2005).

In order to create a positive climate in the school and effectively manage challenging behavior, it's necessary to have family and community involvement in school activities. Sheldon and Epstein (2002) reported that regardless of prior rates of discipline in a school, when schools implement activities where family and community can be involved, the rate of disciplinary referrals decreased. Thus, schools should make efforts to invite families and community leaders to school activities that have positive impacts on students' social and academic performance.

To summarize, we have described various factors that contribute to school success or failure. Unfortunately, schools have little control over most of these factors unless they put in substantial resources at a great cost. Fortunately, there are several schools in the United States that have improved student and school outcomes by establishing low-cost, school-wide support programs (Dwyer, 2002; Kern & Manz, 2004; Sugai, Horner, & Gresham, 2002). Research has provided convincing evidence that when all staff members in all school settings actively teach, model, and consistently reinforce appropriate behavior, the climate at school will improve and the number of students with challenging behaviors will decrease.

Key Elements for Successful Implementation of School-Wide PBIS

This section describes the key elements for successful implementation of sustainable SWPBIS. The key elements include but are not limited to school-wide agreements, school-wide teams, professional development, resources, partnership with families and community leaders, and data-based decision making.

School-Wide Agreements

Because SWPBIS involves all school personnel, its implementation should be grounded in agreements among staff regarding the procedures, and obtaining their willingness to implement them (McKevitt & Braaksma, 2008). Sugai et al. (2005) recommended having at least 80% of staff willing to implement PBIS procedures. The authors suggested an anonymous ballot as the best way to obtain the accurate count of staff in favor of PBIS for the school. If it is less than 80%, then the school may experience difficulties with planning, implementation, sustainability, and effectiveness of SWPBIS (Sugai et al., 2005).

For a school to obtain 80% buy-in, McKevitt and Braaksma (2008) summarized common arguments against using PBIS and several strategies for responding to these arguments using the existing research. First, some teachers may believe their responsibility is only to teach academics. These teachers should be taught that social skills are strongly correlated with academic performance, and students must be systematically taught appropriate social skills to achieve positive academic outcomes. Second, time is another issue for some educators. PBIS can save time in the long run because it prevents behavior problems, which diverts time away from teaching academics. Literature reviews (e.g., Scott & Barrett, 2004) may convince these educators of the time-saving aspects of PBIS and can be used to teach these educators. Third, some teachers would argue that their approach is sufficient in meeting the behavioral needs of all students. This claim should be accepted only if the school's discipline data or other convincing data supports it. Last, some educators may believe positive reinforcement and acknowledgment of expected behavior is actually harmful. They need to be taught that rewards have been demonstrated to improve student motivation and thus, academic performance. The literature documents these strategies as being effective, and thus schools should utilize such literature to turn the majority toward SWPBIS.

The researchers compiled feasible elements of school-wide agreements including (1) school-wide expectations and rules (i.e., be respectable, be responsible), (2) rules defined operationally by setting, (3) data-based decision making, (4) recognition of expected behavior (i.e., token economy, award ceremonies), and (5) consistent consequences for violating rules and expectations.

School-Wide Teaming

Teaming for SWPBIS refers to the process of "working as a cohesive, integrated, and representative collection of individuals who lead the systems change and implementation process" (Office of Special Education Programs, 2004, p. 26).

Sugai et al. (2005) recommend that SWPBIS be planned, implemented, monitored, and evaluated with the leadership of a team of four to eight professionals. The team should include at least one administrator, staff from general education and special education, related services professionals such as a school psychologist, a guidance counselor, and a behavior specialist, and one or more family members. McKevitt and Braaksma (2008) recommended creating a family advisory group and a student advisory group (if it is a middle school or high school). Through a family advisory group, family members raise their viewpoints and concerns; while through a student advisory group, students provide their input on the development and implementation of SWPBIS.

For SWPBIS to be successful, research suggests that collaborators are selected based on two criteria: (1) those having interest in working toward a positive climate in school, and (2) those having skills in behavior, resources, management, prevention, communication, and program development (McKevitt & Braaksma, 2008). To have the team function effectively, members should take certain roles according to their expertise and interests, and their roles should be clearly defined and, ideally, written out. McKevitt and Braaksma (2008) suggested several useful tips that PBIS leadership teams consider during planning and implementing SWPBIS. First, a team facilitator is designated to move the agenda forward and ensure the team remains focused on the topic at hand. Second, a time keeper and recorder is designated to identify action items and hold the team accountable to the purpose of each meeting. Third, teams meet on a regular schedule to ensure they have adequate and predictable planning time. Fourth, members with skills in facilitating group communication and participation are identified to ensure that all members express and discuss ideas and concerns.

Each team member is crucial, but the administrator may play a most significant role in the success of SWPBIS. George, White, and Schlaffer (2007), describing the implementation of SWPBIS in two exemplary schools, outlined various roles that the administrators should play. Their roles include initiating initial assessments, conducting preliminary research, articulating rationale for change, creating a vision, rallying support among their respective staffs, and managing every aspect of the intervention implementation. Similarly, Schwahn and Spady (1998) asserted that the administrators should listen, problem solve, and be visible when things do not go well.

Professional Development

Professional development is one of the most crucial elements in the successful implementation of SWPBIS. Because the PBIS framework and its procedures are relatively new to staff in many schools, all school staff—including school secretaries and custodians—should be aware of the PBIS framework and be trained in the basics of its implementation. This way, any adults in school can acknowledge positive behaviors displayed by students. McKevitt and Braaksma (2008) asserted that professional development should first focus on the leadership team. A sequence of professional development workshops given to the leadership team should convey "the core knowledge across the continuum to allow implementation with fidelity and measurable student outcomes" (Lewis, Barrett, Sugai, & Horner, 2010). After the training, the leadership team should be able to identify a coach who has advanced training in behavioral theory and treatments so as to provide support and guidance to school staff in implementing and monitoring PBIS procedures and progress (Sugai et al., 2005).

Sugai et al. (2005) provided a framework for training leadership teams and the rest of school staff. Training for leadership teams should occur over a three-year period. In the first year, four days of training spread across the school year should address the universal prevention component of PBIS. Training in the second and third year should focus on implementation of the secondary and tertiary prevention interventions. After obtaining training, the leadership team should be responsible for training the rest of the school staff in PBIS practices. Although finding adequate time is often difficult, such training for staff may occur during staff meetings, after school, or during teacher days (when students are not in school) (McKevitt & Braaksma, 2008).

The content of professional development is well established and it should be delivered in two phases (Lewis et al., 2010). The content is designed to apply at the district level, but it can be used at the school level with minor modifications if the district to which the school belongs has not implemented PBIS. Content at the initial phase should focus on the essential features of SWPBIS, the purpose and rationale of the district in implementing it, and the commitment on the part of the district and/or school (e.g., forming a team, technical assistance). The second phase is for training and technical assistance and focuses on measurable team outcomes with a specific plan to measure related student outcomes. (See "Core Content Foci Across the SWPBIS Continuum" in Lewis et al., 2010, pp. 16–21, for details on phase of implementation and specific content knowledge per each phase.)

Resources

Although SWPBIS does not require substantial monetary resources, some funding may be required for various purposes. At the school level, funding is needed to pay for (a) faculty release time to attend professional development workshops and obtain materials (e.g., posters and banners), (b) reinforcement items (e.g., tokens), (c) stipends for substitute teachers while team members or staff are meeting or attending training, and (d) a data collection system (e.g., electronic data collection system) (McKevitt & Braaksma, 2008). Designating two coaches, one external at the district level and one internal at the school level, is highly recommended and ought to be budgeted (Lewis et al., 2010). These coaches should be free from teaching duties and have flexibility in setting their time during typical school days. An external coach from the district can provide technical assistance to leadership teams in schools. An internal coach is a staff member within the school who is familiar with school-wide behavioral issues. Some roles of the internal coach are to serve as a resource person for the school team during SWPBIS meetings and assist the team and school staff in problem solving. Administrators and the leadership team at the school may seek to obtain monetary resources to begin implementing PBIS by fundraising or applying for district, state, or federal grants (McKevitt & Braaksma, 2008). However, because no funding is permanent, McKevitt and Braaksma (2008) advised that schools maximize existing resources for SWPBIS implementation.

Partnership with Families and Community Members

As described earlier, collaborative school-family relationships have been found to positively influence school climate changes and student outcomes. Families and community leaders (i.e., school board members) are valuable resources to school leadership teams because they have diverse expertise and experiences. As team members, these individuals will provide different perspectives and opinions, and assistance in the SWPBIS planning and implementation. However, reaching the desired level of family and community involvement may be a challenge to some schools. According to Minke and Anderson (2005), this challenge is in part due to the fact that teachers and administrators alike lack training on collaborating with families, and effective communication and coping skills to deal with emotionality, conflict, and strained relationships.

Leadership teams can utilize several venues to engage families and community members in SWPBIS practices. McKevitt and Braaksma (2008) offered several useful tips. First, newsletters, newspaper articles, and parent meetings can be effectively used to keep people informed. Second, schools can organize assemblies and develop posters as ways to encourage participation in school activities related to the implementation of PBIS. Third, schools can conduct surveys or focus group interviews to obtain feedback useful in improving PBIS practices. When involving families, developing trust and respect between families and schools is the first step (Albright, Weissberg, & Dusenbury, 2011). To advance this relationship, both two-way school-home communication and family involvement at home and school should be established using the following strategies suggested by Albright and colleagues (2011):

- Strategies for two-way home-school communication
  - Assess the different preferences, perceptions, and practices of the children and families you work with
  - Involve or highlight children in information shared with families
  - Be positive and communicate respect, support, and appreciation
  - Share information about classroom policies and practices
- Strategies for family involvement at home and school
  - Create a skill chart to record how social emotional learning skills are being incorporated at home
  - Share strategies, tools, or resources that match children's learning styles and skills
  - Use interactive materials to engage children and families
  - Distribute regular newsletters to keep parents informed and involved
  - Share specific strategies and practical tips to promote children's social emotional learning
  - Invite families into the classroom to observe and actively participate in social emotional learning
  - Hold social emotional learning parenting workshops or group meetings
  - Focus on social emotional learning as part of progress reports, report-card sharing, and parent-teacher conferences

With these strategies, schools may be more likely to establish trusting partnerships with families. Similar strategies can be applied to collaborating with community members. However, prior to and after establishing partnerships, each school should conduct its own need assessment to understand their contexts and figure out the best way to support collaboration between families and the school, and between the school and other community stakeholders (e.g., small-business employers offering students part-time work).

Data-based Decision Making

The hallmark of SWPBIS is an emphasis on data-driven evaluation. School leadership teams are the crucial decision-making body. With their leadership, schools should determine whether SWPBIS has been effective and perform several tasks described below (George & Kincaid, 2008):

- assess the fidelity of SWPBIS processes
- provide data on student performance (i.e., academic performance data, office discipline referrals, and suspension data)
- assist in developing an action plan for problem areas

George and Kincaid suggested that data be collected throughout the academic year and findings be frequently disseminated to provide stakeholders (involved in the PBIS planning and implementation) with information on the progress of activities and student performance. Ongoing evaluation will allow for the leadership team to adjust their efforts throughout the year.

Evaluation instruments will allow the leadership team to assess various areas including training effectiveness and satisfaction, technical assistance, team processes, activities implemented, and student outcomes (George & Kincaid, 2008). Schools can use the "School-Wide Benchmarks of Quality Scoring Form (Revised)" (Kincaid, Childs, & George, 2005) for evaluation processes. This instrument is designed to assess the development and implementation of school-wide PBIS. The form lists 53 benchmarks of quality in SWPBIS programs within ten critical elements and is completed by school teams periodically to identify areas of strengths and weakness. The "Benchmarks of Quality" and its form have been widely used by states and districts to guide technical assistance and training, to identify model schools (if used at the district level), and to evaluate outcomes related to level of SWPBIS implementation (McKevitt & Braaksma, 2008).

Conclusion

School violence has been a major concern for the nation's schools and communities. Students and educators alike have been reported as being victimized by various forms of school-wide violence and as a result, they feel unsafe in schools. A prerequisite to ensuring that all students attain academic proficiency, including students from culturally and linguistically diverse (CLD) backgrounds, is to create and maintain safe environments where students can learn appropriate academic and social skills. Research shows that this is a multi-systematic issue that manifests from community, school, school personnel, and student factors (Espelage et al., 2013). We have described various factors contributing to student behavior and academic performance, including school factors (i.e., student attendance rates, class size), personnel factors (i.e., teacher-student relationship, teacher support), family and community factors (i.e., family involvement), and student factors (SES, race/ethnicity, disability). Unfortunately, schools have little control over most of these factors unless they put in substantial resources at great cost.

Research that investigates the relationship between school climates and student performance shows that student behavior problems are strongly associated with disorganized school structures, negative school climates, and lack of administrative support. The School-Wide Positive Behavioral Interventions and Supports (SWPBIS) framework has proved to be an effective tool in improving school climates and student behaviors. We described the key elements for successful implementation of SWPBIS establishing universal primary prevention in the school as the first step as a way to promote positive school climates for *all* students, including those with CLD backgrounds and those who exhibit challenging behaviors. To successfully implement sustainable SWPBIS, at least 80% of staff has to show their willingness to implement SWPBIS procedures. Furthermore, a leadership team of professionals and family and community members guides the staff and provides them with technical assistance. Effects of the SWPBIS implementation need be determined with ongoing data collection and analyses on the process and outcomes. Literature has provided sufficient data that when schools implement SWPBIS with fidelity, the school climate will improve and the number of student problem behaviors will decrease. Finally, administrators and staff of schools that have yet to establish a school-wide behavior intervention should gather to learn about SWPBIS and seek effective ways to implement it at their schools. Abundant information and practical resources in the literature and national centers await.

References

Albright, M. I., Weissberg, R. P., & Dusenbury, L. A. (2011). *School-family partnership strategies to enhance children's social, emotional, and academic growth.* Newton, MA: National Center for Mental Health Promotion and Youth Violence Prevention, Education Development Center, Inc.

American Psychological Association, Center for Psychology in Schools and Education. (n.d.). *Violence against teachers: A silent national crisis* [Online brochure]. Retrieved from http://www.apa.org/ed/schools/cpse/activities/violence-against-teachers.pdf

Aske, D., & Corman, R. (2008). The relationship between school characteristics and student performance on standardized tests in the Denver metro region. *Proceeding of the Academy of Educational Leadership, 13*(2), 79–84.

Baker, J. A., Grant, S., & Morlock, L. (2008). The teacher-student relationship as a developmental context for children with internalizing or externalizing behavior problems. *School Psychology Quarterly, 23*(1), 3–15.

Barnard, W. M. (2004). Parent involvement in elementary school and educational attainment. *Children and Youth Services Review, 26*(1), 39–62.

Borman, K. M. Carter, K., Aladjem, D. K., & LeFloch, K. C. (2004). *Putting the pieces together: Lessons from comprehensive school reform research* (pp. 109–150). Washington DC: National Clearinghouse for Comprehensive School Reform.

Burchinal, M. R., Peisner-Feinberg, E., Bryant, D. M., & Clifford, R. (2000). Children's social and cognitive development and child-care quality: Testing for differential. *Applied Developmental Science, 4*, 149–165.

Carr, W. (2006). Education without theory. *British Journal of Educational Studies, 54*(2), 136–159.

Cartledge, G., & Kourea, L. (2008). Culturally responsive classrooms for culturally diverse students with and at risk for disabilities. *Exceptional Children, 74*, 351–371.

Christenson, S. L., & Havsy, L. H. (2004). Family-school-peer relationships: Significance for social, emotional, and academic learning. In J. E. Zins, R. P. Weissberg, M. C. Wang, & H. J. Walberg (Eds.), *Building academic success on social and emotional learning: What does the research say?* (pp. 59–75). New York: Teachers College Press.

Danielsen, A. G, Samdal, O., Hetland, J., & Wold, B. (2009). School-related social support and students' perceived life satisfaction. *Journal of Educational Research, 102*(4), 303–320.

Danielsen, A. G, Wiium, N., Wilhelmsen, B. U., & Wold, B. (2010). Perceived support provided by teachers and classmates and students' self-reported academic initiative. *Journal of School Psychology, 48*(3), 247–267.

Dempsey, A. G., & Storch, E. A. (2008). Relational victimization: The association between recalled adolescent social experiences and emotional adjustment in early adulthood. *Psychology in the Schools, 45*(4), 310–322.

Diamond, J. B., Randolph, A., & Spillane, J. P. (2004). Teachers' expectations and sense of responsibility for student learning: The importance of race, class, and organizational habitus. *Anthropology & Education Quality, 35*(1), 75–98.

Dinkes, R., Cataldi, E. F., Kena, G., & Baum, K. (2006). *Indicators of school crime and safety: 2006* (NCES 2007–003/NCJ 214262). U.S. Departments of Education and Justice. Washington, DC: U.S. Government Printing Office.

Dwyer, K. P. (2002). Tools for building safe, effective schools. In M. R. Shinn, H. M. Walker, & G. Stoner (Eds.), *Interventions for academic and behavior problems II: Preventive and remedial approaches* (pp. 167–212). Bethesda, MD: National Association of School Psychologists.

Elias, M. J., & Haynes, N. M. (2008). Social competence, social support, and academic achievement in minority, low-income, urban elementary school children. *School Psychology Quarterly, 23*, 474–495.

Espelage, D., Anderman, E. M., Brown, V. E., Jones, A., Lane, K. L., McMahon, S. D., … Reynolds, C. (2013). Understanding and preventing violence directed against teachers: Recommendations for a national research, practice, and policy agenda. *American Psychologist, 68*(2), 75–87. Retrieved from http://www.apa.org/pubs/journals/releases/amp-68-2-75.pdf

Espelage, D., & Horne, A. (2008). School violence and bullying prevention: From research-based explanations to empirically based solutions. In S. Brown & R. Lent (Eds.), *Handbook of counseling psychology* (4th ed., pp. 588–598). Hoboken, NJ: Wiley.

Evans, G. W., Gonnella, C. A., Marcynyszyn, L. A., Gentile, L. E., & Salpekar, N. A. (2005). The role of chaos in poverty and children's socioemotional adjustment. *Psychological Science*, *16*, 560–565.

Ferguson, R. F. (2003). Teachers' perceptions and expectations and the Black-White test score gap. *Urban Education*, *38*, 460–507.

Gay, G. (2002). Culturally responsive teaching in special education for ethnically diverse students: Setting the stage. *Qualitative Studies in Education*, *15*, 613–629.

George, H. P., & Kincaid, D. K. (2008). Building district-level capacity for Positive Behavior Support. *Journal of Positive Behavior Interventions*, *10*(1), 20–32.

George, M., White, G., & Schlaffer, J. (2007). Implementing School-Wide Behavior change: Lessons from the field. *Psychology in the Schools*, *44*(1), 41–51.

Gottlieb, J., Alter, M., Gottlieb, B. W., & Wishner, J. (1994). Special education in urban American: It's not justifiable for many. *The Journal of Special Education*, *27*, 453–465.

Gregory, A., Cornell, D., & Fan, X. (2012). Teacher safety and authoritative school climate in high schools. *American Journal of Education*, *118*, 1–25.

Horner, R. H., Sugai, G., Todd, A. W., & Lewis-Palmer, T. (2005). School-Wide Positive Behavior Support. In L. Bambara & L. Kern (Eds.), *Individualized supports for students with problem behaviors: Designing positive behavior plans* (pp. 359–390). New York: Guilford Press.

Jepsen, C., & Rivkin, S. (2009). Class size reduction and student achievement: The potential tradeoff between teacher quality and class size. *Journal of Human Resources*, *44*(1), 223–250.

Jeynes, W. H. (2005). A meta-analysis of the relation of parent involvement to urban elementary school student academic achievement. *Urban Education*, *40*(3), 237–269.

Kern, L., & Manz, P. (2004). A look at current validity issues of schoolwide behavior support. *Journal of Behavioral Disorders*, *30*, 47–59.

Kincaid, D., Childs, K., & George, H. (2005). *School-wide benchmarks of quality scoring form* (revised) (Unpublished instrument), University of South Florida. Retrieved from http://flpbs.fmhi.usf.edu/pdfs/Benchmarks%20Scoring%20Form_RevFinal.pdf

Kondrasuk, J. N., Greene, T., Waggoner, J., Edwards, K., & Nayak-Rhodes, A. (2005). Violence affecting school employees. *Education*, *125*, 638–647.

Kozol, J. (2005). Apartheid in America? *Phi Delta Kappan*, *87*, 264–275.

Krezmien, M. P., Leone, P. E., & Achilles, G. M. (2006). Suspension, race, and disability: Analysis of statewide practices and reporting. *Journal of Emotional and Behavioral Disorders*, *14*, 217–226.

Lane, K. L., Kalberg, J. R., & Menzies, H. M. (2009). *Developing schoolwide programs to prevent and manage problem behaviors*. New York: Guilford Press.

Lewis, T., Barrett, S., Sugai, G., & Horner, R. (2010, September). *Blueprint for school-wide positive behavior training and professional development* (Version 3). National Technical

Center on Positive Behavioral Interventions and Supports. Retrieved from http://www.pbis.org/common/pbisresources/publications/PBIS_PD_Blueprint_v3.pdf

Marzano, R. J., Marzano, J. S., & Pickering, D. J. (2003). *Classroom management that works: Research-based strategies for every teacher.* Alexandria, VA: Association for Supervision and Curriculum Development.

McCurdy, B. L., Kunsch, C., & Reibstein, S. (2007). Secondary prevention in the urban school: Implementing the behavior education program. *Preventing School Failure: Alternative Education for Children and Youth, 51*(3), 12–19.

McKevitt, B. C., & Braaksma, A. D. (2008). Best practices in developing a Positive Behavior Support system at the school level. In A. Thomas & J. Grimes (Eds.), *Best Practices in School Psychology* (pp. 735–747). Bethesda, MD: National Association of School Psychologists.

McNeely, C., & Falci, C. (2004). School connectedness and the transition into and out of health-risk behavior among adolescents: A comparison of social belonging and teacher support. *Journal of School Health, 74*(7), 284–292.

Merritt, E. G., Rimm-Kaufman, S. E., Berry, R. Q., Walkowiak, T. A , & Larsen, R. A. (2011, Fall). *The contribution of mathematics instructional quality and class size to student achievement for third grade students from low income families.* Poster session presented at the Society for Research of Educational Effectiveness Conference, Washington DC.

Minke, K. M., & Anderson, K. J. (2005). Family-school collaboration and Positive Behavior Support. *Journal of Behavior Interventions, 7*(3), 181–185.

Mooij, T. (2011). Secondary school teachers' personal and school characteristics, experience of violence and perceived violence motives. *Teachers and Teaching: Theory and Practice, 17*, 227–253.

National Center for Educational Statistics (2012). Trends in high school dropout and completion rates in the United States: 1972–2009. Washington, DC: U.S. Department of Education.

O'Brennan, L. M., Bradshaw, C. P., & Sawyer, A. L. (2009). Examining development differences in the social-emotional problems among frequent bullies, victims, and bully/victims. *Psychology in the Schools, 46*(2), 100–115.

Office of Special Education Programs (2001). *Prevention research and the IDEA discipline provisions: A guide for school administrators.* Washington, DC: U. S. Department of Education.

Office of Special Education Programs Center on Positive Behavioral Interventions and Supports (2004). School-Wide Positive Behavior Support Implementers' blueprint and self-assessment. Eugene, OR: University of Oregon.

Patrikakou, E. N., Weissberg, R. P., Redding, S., & Walberg, H. J. (2005). School-family partnerships: Enhancing the academic, social, and emotional learning of children. In E. N. Patrikakou, R. P. Weissberg, S. Redding, & H. J. Walberg (Eds.), *School-family partnerships for children's success* (pp. 1–17). New York: Teachers College Press.

Peguero, A. A. (2011). Violence, schools, and dropping out: Racial and ethnic disparities in the educational consequence of student victimization. *Journal of Interpersonal Violence, 26*, 3753–3772.

Putnam, R., McCart, A., Griggs, P., & Choi, J. H. (2009). Implementation of School-Wide Positive Behavior Support in urban settings. In W. Sailor, G. Dunlap, G. Sugai, & R. Horner (Eds.), *Handbook of Positive Behavior Support* (pp. 443–463). New York: Springer.

Schwahn, C., & Spady, W. (1998). Why change doesn't happen and how to make sure it does. *Educational Leadership, 55*(7), 45–47.

Scott, T. M., & Barrett, S. B. (2004). Using staff and student time engaged in disciplinary procedures to evaluate the impact of school-wide PBS. *Journal of Positive Behavior Interventions, 6*, 21–27.

Sheldon, S. B., & Epstein, J. (2002). Improving student behavior and school discipline with family and community involvement. *Education and Urban Society, 35*(1), 4–26.

Shin, Y. (2012). Do Black children benefit more from small classes? Multivariate instrumental variables estimators with ignorable missing data. *Journal of Educational and Behavioral Statistics, 37*(4), 543–574.

Skiba, R. J. (2002). Special education and school discipline: A precarious balance. *Behavioral Disorders, 27*(2), 81–97.

Skiba, R. J., Simmons, A. B., Ritter, S., Gibb, A. C., Rausch, M. K., Cuadrado, J., & Chung, C. (2008). Achieving equity in special education: History, status, and current challenges. *Exceptional Children, 74*, 264–288.

Sprague, J., Walker, H., Golly, A., White, K., Myers, D. R., & Shannon, T. (2001). Translating research into effective practice: The effects of a universal staff and student intervention on key indicators of school safety and discipline. *Education and Treatment of Children, 24*(4), 495–511.

Stiefel, L., Schwartz, A. E., & Iatarola, P. (2001). *Determinants of school performance in New York elementary schools: Results and implications for resource use* (Condition Report prepared for the Education Finance Research Consortium, sponsored by the NYS Boards of Regents). Retrieved from http://www.albany.edu/edfin/CR01_SIS_Report.pdf

Sugai, G., & Horner, R. H. (2002). The evolution of discipline practices: School-Wide Positive Behavior Supports. In J. K. Luiselli & C. Diament (Eds.), *Behavior psychology in the school: Innovations in evaluation, support, and consultation* (pp. 23–50). New York: Haworth.

Sugai, G., & Horner, R. H. (2009). Responsiveness-to-intervention and School-Wide Positive Behavior Supports: Integration of multi-tiered approaches. *Exceptionality, 17*, 223–237.

Sugai, G., Horner, R. H., & Gresham, F. M. (2002). Behaviorally effective school environments. In M. R. Shinn, H. M. Walker, & G. Stoner (Eds.), *Interventions for academic and behavior problems II: Preventive and remedial approaches* (pp. 315–350). Bethesda, MD: National Association of School Psychologists.

Sugai, G., Horner, R. H., Lewis-Palmer, T., & Todd, A. (2005). *School-Wide Positive Behavior Support training manual.* Eugene, OR: Educational and Community Supports, University of Oregon.

Tobin, T. J., & Sugai, G. M. (1999). Using sixth-grade school records to predict school violence, chronic discipline problems, and high school outcomes. *Journal of Emotional and Behavioral Disorders, 7*(1), 140–153.

Turnbull, H. R., Turnbull, A. P., & Wilcox, B. L. (2002). Family interests and Positive Behavior Support: Opportunities under Individuals with Disabilities Education Act. In J. Lucyshyn, G. Dunlap, & R. Albin (Eds.), *Families and Positive Behavior Support: Addressing problem behavior in family contexts* (pp. 349–370). Baltimore, MD: Paul H. Brookes.

Vincent, C. G., & Tobin, T. J. (2012). The relationship between implementation of School-Wide Positive Behavior Support (SWPBS) and disciplinary exclusion of students from various ethnic backgrounds with and without disabilities. *Journal of Emotional and Behavioral Disorders, 19*(4), 217–232.

Walker, H. M., & Shinn, M. R. (2002). Structuring school-based interventions to achieve integrated primary, secondary, and tertiary prevention goals for safe and effective schools. In M. R. Shinn, G. Stoner, & H. M. Walker (Eds.), *Interventions for academic and behavior problems: Preventive and remedial approaches.* Silver Spring, MD: National Association of School Psychologists.

Warren, J. S., Edmonson, H. M, Griggs, P., Lassen, S. R., McCart, A., Turnbull, A., & Sailor, W. (2003). Urban applications of School-Wide Positive Behavior Support: Critical issues and lessons learned. *Journal of Positive Behavior Interventions, 5*(2), 80–91.

Weinstein, C. S., Tomlinson-Clarke, S., & Curran, M. (2004). Toward a conception of culturally responsive classroom management. *Journal of Teacher Education, 55*(1), 25–38.

Wentzel, K. R., Donlan, A., & Morrison, D. (2012). Peer relationships and social-motivational processes. In A. M. Ryan & G. W. Ladd (Eds.), *Peer relationships and adjustment at school* (pp. 79–108). Charlotte, NC: Information Age.

Whitted, K. S. (2011). Understanding how social and emotional skill deficits contribute to school failure. *Preventing School Failure, 55*(1), 10–16.

Section II

4. *Effective Positive Behavioral Interventions and Supports for Students in Early Years and Grades: Practices and Policies*

CHUN ZHANG, ANGIE CHAI, AND KWANG-SUN CHO BLAIR

Current Status of Diversity in Schools

A report from the U.S. Department of Education, *The Condition of Education 2011*, uses national statistical data to provide information about the latest trends in education (Aud et al., 2011). The report summarizes recent demographic data of school-aged students and their teachers. Ford (2012) highlights three undeniable realities that are revealed in the report. First, students attending U.S. public schools are more racially, ethnically, and linguistically diverse than ever before. Next, the diversity in schools is expected to continue to grow. Finally, despite the rapid changes in student demographics, the racial and ethnic demographics of educators remain relatively unchanged, with data showing that 85% of teachers are White and 75% are female (Aud et al., 2011).

Achievement Gap and Discipline Gap

According to national tests of academic achievement, students from certain racial groups score significantly lower than those from other groups. More specifically, research indicates that African American, Hispanic, and Native American students are not performing as well as Euro-American or Asian American students (Ogbu, 2003; Planty, Provasnik, & Daniel, 2007). This trend is commonly referred to as "the achievement gap" and the differences in performance correspond closely with differences in socioeconomic and racial status. Although the achievement gap appears to be narrowing, the differences are still substantial and continue to raise concerns. Also, national statistics reveal the continuing trend of disproportionality or overrepresentation of Black, Hispanic, and English language learners (ELLs) in special education programs (Donovan & Cross, 2002; Heller, Holtzman, & Messick, 1982; Skiba et al., 2008).

Another area of concern that has received great attention in recent years involves the impact of cultural and linguistic diversity on behavioral issues in schools. Researchers have examined rates of discipline referrals across school populations and found that African American students have been referred to school administrators at disproportionately higher rates compared to their Euro-American peers (Skiba et al., 2011). Similarly, African American students are overrepresented in rates of exclusionary rates and consequences such as out-of-school suspensions and expulsions (Vincent & Tobin, 2011). In contrast to discipline rates for African American students, Euro-American and Asian American students are underrepresented with both groups having relatively lower rates of exclusionary consequences. This trend of under- and overrepresentation has been referred to as "the discipline gap," however, there has been relatively little attention given to this issue (Gregory, 1997; Gregory & Mosely, 2004; Skiba et al., 2008). The achievement gap and discipline gap appear to co-exist and are likely to directly affect each other. Unfortunately, both trends link African American students and other minority groups to negative outcomes. Thus, there is a great need for further investigation and intervention to increase academic achievement as well as social, emotional, and behavioral supports for these groups.

For over half a century, researchers, educational leaders, and policymakers have been discussing how racial and ethnic dissimilarities between students and teachers can lead to cultural differences and misunderstandings that negatively affect a student's experience in school (Oberg, 1960; Trent, Kea, & Oh, 2008). Educators have reported that one of the most challenging issues in schools involves problematic student behaviors (Squires & Bricker, 2007). Cultural and linguistic factors have been found to complicate the approaches to handling challenging behaviors. It is important to examine how differences between values, beliefs, and child-rearing practices can affect a student's behavior and progress in school. Both achievement gap and discipline gap have been linked to the mismatch of mainstream culture in schools to the cultures of the students in the minority groups. In this chapter, we will discuss some cultural influences on social emotional development, and will present a Positive Behavioral Interventions and Supports model for supporting young children, which has practical applications for working with all students, especially with African American students. We will focus on understanding and supporting young children's social and emotional development, with implications for African American children and their families and professionals working with them.

The Role of Cultural Competence in Working with Minority Students

In response to these increasing issues of cultural clashes between teachers, other professionals, and students, there has been a push for educators to be culturally competent. It is suggested that teachers who are more culturally responsive can better meet the needs of students from cultures that are different from their own (Trent et al., 2008). Becoming culturally competent involves understanding more about the backgrounds of students and families. For example, some researchers have discussed nine learning characteristics of African American students that highlight behaviors that are often misinterpreted or misunderstood by teachers who do not understand the cultures of their students (Boykin, 1983; Boykin, Tyler, & Miller, 2005; Ford & Kea, 2009). These characteristics include spirituality, harmony, affect, communalism, movement, verve, expressive individualism, orality, and social time orientation.

Misunderstanding or insensitivity to cultural differences can lead to mistaking behavior or learning style that's accepted or even valued in another culture as behavior that is miscategorized as an emotional or behavioral disorder (Webb-Johnson, 2002). One research study found that teachers perceived African American students to be more defiant, rule breaking, or disruptive than other groups (Wentzel, 2002). In addition, students may be referred for special education based on a lack of culturally responsive behavior management skills from the professionals. These issues can result in disproportionate discipline outcomes, misdiagnosis, and special education services for students from culturally and linguistically diverse (CLD) backgrounds (Cartledge & Kourea, 2008; Skiba et al., 2008; Webb-Johnson, 2002). The mismatch of cultural values, beliefs, and definitions of appropriate behaviors can contribute to teaching or behavior management styles that cause unintended outcomes for CLD students, including young children. This following section will address the challenging behaviors of young children, especially African American students who experience higher percentages of dropout, expulsion, and school failure. They, in particular, need early intervention and support to prevent school failure, expulsion, and other severe negative consequences.

Understanding Young Children's Challenging Behaviors

An increasingly large number of young children are entering early childhood settings at a very early age. More and more caregivers, including educators, report that addressing challenging behaviors with young children is one of the most difficult parts of interacting with young children (Hemmeter, Fox, Jack, & Broyles, 2007; Squires & Bricker, 2007). Understanding social and emotional development, challenging behaviors, the development of social and emotional skills, and knowing how to nurture a young child's positive self-image or self-esteem rather than reacting to the challenging behaviors through the use of punitive methods will have a lasting impact on the child's healthy social and emotional development and positive child-adult interactions and relationships.

A challenging behavior is defined as any behavior that is harmful to the child or others; interferes with a child's cognitive, social, or emotional development; or puts a child at high risk for later social problems or school failure (Kaiser & Rasminsky, 2011). Behaviors such as hitting, biting, tantrums, yelling, screaming, or withdrawal are barriers to young children's development of social competence and positive social relationships (Campbell, Spieker, Burchinal, Poe, & The NICHD Early Child Care Research Network, 2006). Caregivers, including educators, need to be aware that the demonstration of challenging behaviors is a part of typical child development during the early years. For example, tantrums from a toddler who cries for 10 minutes if another child takes away his or her favorite toy may be considered age-appropriate behaviors. A 3-year-old boy may bite another child when another child knocks down his block building. These behaviors may occur due to the child's limited ability to express his or her feelings or thoughts. However, as the child matures into preschool and kindergarten years, it is expected that the child's increase in social skills, emotion regulation ability, language abilities, and cognitive problem-solving abilities would decrease tantrums and some other challenging behaviors (Campbell et al., 2006). These challenging behaviors should also be reduced and replaced by appropriate behaviors as the child develops language, social and emotional regulation, and cognitive problem-solving skills (Benedict, Horner, & Squires, 2007; Campbell, 1995). If these abilities do not mature and the challenging behaviors persist into preschool or later, the prognosis for the child becomes increasing negative.

Typical child development involves the maturation of specific social and emotional skills throughout the early childhood years. With teaching, scaffolding, and support, most young children will develop self-regulation and coping strategies to build positive social relationships, interact with adults and other children, and engage in social and pre-academic activities. Unfortunately, if challenging behaviors are ignored and not addressed appropriately, these behaviors will have long-term negative consequences on the child's social and emotional, and academic development.

Children who exhibit challenging behaviors will face multiple difficulties in school including peer rejection, negative perception by teachers, negative interactions with teachers and peers, and lack of support for developing social skills and competence (Stormont, 2002). One study found that children are being expelled from state preschool programs at three times the rate of school-age students (Gilliam, 2005). Another study by Hemmeter, Corso, and Cheatham (2006) surveyed more than 500 early childhood educators and found that their highest-rated training need was addressing challenging behavior. Researchers indicated that if challenging behaviors are not addressed by third grade, they will significantly alter or impact the students' social, emotional, and academic development and outcomes (Stormont, Smith, & Lewis, 2007). Thus, it is important to provide early support for young children to gain the appropriate social, emotional, and related skills within their earliest encounters with peers and adults. The following behavior support model provides support and interventions to directly teach social skills and expected school behaviors to students. Professionals and family members play a key role in helping young children develop social competence for the sake of their healthy emotional well-being and academic success.

Positive Behavioral Interventions and Supports: A Promising Model

There should be a strong emphasis in early childhood education and curriculum on building young children's social and emotional competence so that they will develop self-regulation and coping skills to participate and engage in academic development and social relationship building. Teachers need to have the knowledge and skills to help their students develop age- and individually appropriate social skills to support their academic and social and emotional development. A promising behavior support model called Positive Behavioral Interventions and Supports or School-Wide Positive Behavioral Interventions and Supports (SWPBIS) is gaining widespread attention and has been implemented to help teachers and family members address challenging behaviors of young and older students in schools across the United States (see Figure 1 below). However, the implementation of this behavior support model in early childhood settings is sporadic depending on the awareness, knowledge, and

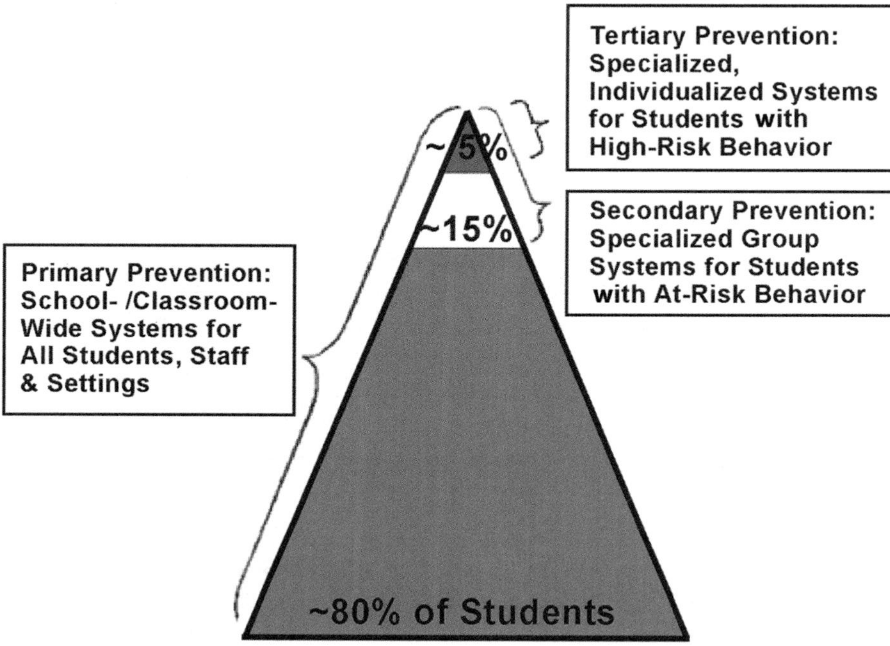

Adapted from OSEP Technical Assistance Center on Positive Behavioral Interventions & Supports (www.pbis.org).

Figure 1. Continuum of School-Wide Instructional and Positive Behavioral Interventions and Supports.

skills of the teachers and principals and their ability to implement such a model at classroom and school levels. Research on Positive Behavioral Interventions and Supports demonstrates that, when implemented appropriately or successfully, classwide supports will be sufficient to manage and address the challenging behaviors of 80–85% of the students; about 5–15% of students will respond to small group behavior supports or interventions; and about 1–7% will require or need intensive, individualized interventions (Crone & Horner, 2003).

The system-wide application of Positive Behavioral Interventions and Supports is structured around a three-tiered model that is preventive and proactive. It includes teaching social skills, providing behavioral supports, monitoring, and evaluating student behaviors in natural routines, schedules, and activities (Krasch & Carter, 2009). Barbetta, Norona and Bicard (2005) summarized that in essence, "prevention is the most effective form of behavior management. That is, the most efficient way to reduce or eliminate misbehaviors is to prevent their occurrence or escalation from the beginning"

(p. 11). In schools where SWPBIS is implemented, SWPBIS needs several key components. At the primary level (or Tier 1), the school identifies and defines behavior expectations for all students; school staff are trained and are involved in teaching students these expectations in a preventive approach in classrooms and other settings in school. In addition, a school builds a rewards/behavior reinforcement system for providing students feedback, encouragement, and support. At the secondary level (or Tier 2), supports/interventions for students who are at risk for problem behaviors are developed and provided. This secondary support system can be extra support in addition to the primary prevention and will use evidence-based interventions such as social-skills training for those students who need additional behavioral support. At the tertiary level (or Tier 3), students with persistent, intensive, and severe challenging behaviors will receive an individualized behavior support plan that is developed by a team through the process of completing a functional behavior assessment.

At the primary level, preventive interventions can include designing environments that are predictable, consistent, positive, and safe for all students; explaining, teaching, and implementing behavior expectations such as being nice, doing best work, and helping others (Carr et al., 2002; Horner, Sugai, Todd, & Lewis-Palmer, 2005). At the secondary level, interventions will focus on providing additional support to some students who do not respond to Tier 1 interventions such as the use of an individualized picture schedule for those who have difficulty with transitions (Crone & Horner, 2003). Finally, at the tertiary level, interventions focus on providing more intensive supports to a small number of children who do not respond to either Tier 1 and/or Tier 2 interventions (Crone, Horner, & Hawken, 2004; Lewis & Sugai, 1999). The SWPBIS model focuses on providing prevention and support (at Tier 1 and Tier 2 levels) in order to decrease the number of students needing intensive behavior support (at Tier 3 level), thus helping most children develop appropriate behaviors in natural environments, and providing those few with more intensive and individualized behavior and instructional support. This in itself reduces the number of children needing special education and other related services.

PBIS and Its Implementation in Early Childhood

The implementation of program-wide Positive Behavioral Interventions and Supports in early childhood settings follows the essential elements of SWPBIS, but has been tailored to address the unique needs of young children and the early childhood programs (Fox & Hemmeter, 2009). However, there has been a relatively small amount of research done about using PBIS in early childhood settings when compared to the existing research on the use of PBIS in elementary, middle, and high school settings. There is an increasing need for effective approaches to address problematic behaviors in young children.

Stormont, Lewis, and Beckner (2005) discuss several specific adaptations of SWPBIS to facilitate its implementation in early childhood programs. These adaptations take into account the differences for the educational environments for preschool children and school-age children, and the developmental appropriateness of behavior intervention strategies for young children. First, the structure of a PBIS program in early childhood would most likely be considered program-wide rather than school-wide since early childhood programs may be spread out across a school district rather than housed within one school. Next, a program-wide team may be larger than typical SWPBIS teams as they may include administrators across various programs in a school district or additional professionals that work within the programs. The team should work together to ensure that everyone involved including family members is prepared to support behavioral expectations and collect data on children's behaviors. It is also essential to provide professional development opportunities to promote knowledge about PBIS for staff, such as paraprofessionals or assistant teachers, who may not have received the information through other sources.

In addition, educators should use developmentally appropriate strategies to help students learn the behavioral expectations emphasized in an early childhood PBIS program (Stormont et al., 2005). These strategies include but are not limited to using praise, using pictures and other visual representations of behavioral expectations, using puppet shows, taking photographs of students who are exhibiting the highlighted behaviors and positing them in the classroom, and describing expectations using words and actions that young children understand. Additionally, student acknowledgment or reinforcement systems, such as a token economy, may need to be modified to be age-appropriate for young children (Crone et al., 2004; Hemmeter et al., 2007).

Benedict et al. (2007) studied the implementation of PBIS in 15 preschool classrooms, including six Head Start classrooms and three integrated special-education classrooms. Various adaptations were made to adjust the PBIS model for preschool classrooms. Modified PBIS strategies included the creation of well-defined learning centers in preschool classrooms and exposure to clearly defined and developmentally appropriate behavioral expectations, such as the use of quiet voices inside, listening ears, and safe hands. For preschool children, explicit teaching of these expectations could occur every day. Also, the preschool teachers were provided with additional consultation to improve the implementation of universal PBIS practices. The authors found that when teachers received support from a PBIS consultant, preschool teachers were more likely to use universal PBIS practices such as implementing classroom rules, schedules, transition supports, and specific verbal praise and positive statements.

The Pyramid Model

In early childhood education and early intervention, the Pyramid Model has been developed as a tiered intervention model (Fox, Dunlap, Hemmeter, Joseph, & Strain, 2003; Fox, Carta, Strain, Dunlap, & Hemmeter, 2010; Hemmeter, Ostrosky, & Fox, 2006). The model is a promotion, prevention, and intervention framework of evidence-based practices, which support social, emotional, and behavioral development of infants, toddlers, and preschoolers. The Pyramid Model has been developed by two national, federally funded research and training centers: the Center on the Social and Emotional Foundations for Early Learning (CSEFEL: www.vanderbilt.edu/csefel/) and the Technical Assistance Center on Social Emotional Intervention for Young Children (TACSEI: www.challengingbehavior.org). As shown in Figure 2, the model describes three tiers of promotion and intervention practices: universal promotion for all children; secondary preventions for children at risk of social-emotional delay; and tertiary interventions for children with persistent challenging behavior.

The first level of Tier 1, Nurturing and Responsive Caregiving Relationships, focuses on promotion of social-emotional development through the provision of nurturing and responsive caregiving relationships to children, partnerships with families, and collaborative relationships among intervention and classroom team members. The second level of Tier 1, High-Quality Supportive Environments, highlights the provision of supportive environments through the provision of predictable and supportive environments and family interactions within home and community settings and the provision of supportive high-quality programs that are culturally and developmentally appropriate. Tier 2, Targeted Social Emotional Supports, addresses social skills and emotional regulation of children who need more focused interventions. Systematic and focused instruction aims to teach children social-emotional skills. Tier 3, Intensive Interventions, uses the approach of individualized PBIS to support children who have persistent social competence skill deficits and challenges (Fox et al., 2010). The Teaching Pyramid Observation Tool for Preschool Classrooms (TPOT: Hemmeter, Fox, & Snyder, 2008) has been used to assess fidelity of the Pyramid Model implementation in early childhood programs. The TPOT is a rating scale that includes 141 indicators related to the Pyramid Model practices. It is

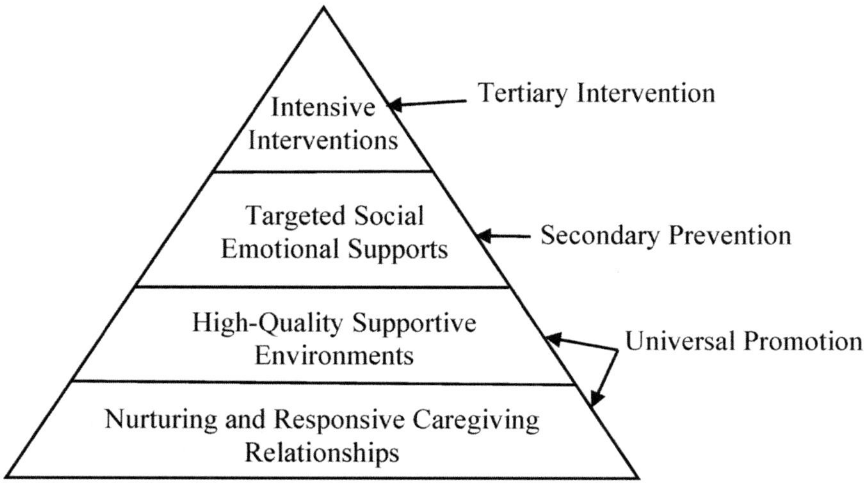

Figure 2. The Pyramid Model for Infants, Toddlers, and Preschoolers. Adapted from Center on the Social and Emotional Foundations for Early Learning (www.vanderbilt.edu/csefel/) and the Technical Assistance Center on Social Emotional Intervention for Young Children (www.challengingbehavior.org).

completed by a 2-hour classroom observation and by teachers' responses to structured interview questions. Demonstrations have shown that the Pyramid Model is associated with improved child social-emotional outcomes, decreased challenging behavior and increased teacher competencies and skills.

Hurley and colleagues (2013) interviewed 25 preschool service providers (i.e., early childhood educators, early childhood special educators, Head Start teachers, and administrators) who were serving recently relocated preschool-age refugee children in a refugee resettlement community in New England. The children in their programs were from families of diverse countries of origin including Bhutan, Burma, Burundi, Dominican Republic of Congo, Ethiopia, Iraq, Kenya, Somalia, and Sudan. The interviews included questions designed to identify the providers' practices recommended as part of the Pyramid Model.

The findings of the interviews indicate that some refugee children experience social isolation and rejection from peers and struggle with the challenges of a foreign language and culture after relocation. The service providers were using many strategies to create the three-tiered support system outlined in the Pyramid Model. They reported on refugee families' perspectives and practices that made implementation of the Pyramid Model challenging. The interview participants expressed frustrations that some refugee families had different expectations for home-school relationships than those of the preschool teachers, and that communication barriers strained collaboration and relationship building. The researchers suggested that community food preparation was a powerful tool for building home-school relationships. In regard to the second level of Tier 1, it was found that the preschool refugee children benefited from a high-quality structured environment with consistent routines and schedules; the teachers stressed the need for predictable routines in helping young refugee children, who are English learners, follow daily routines by using picture schedules.

The teachers in the study also reported that providing focused instruction for children needing the secondary support was sometimes difficult for English learners. They suggested that using peer models and feeling pictures were effective in addressing the children's social and emotional needs. In regard to Tier 3 support, it was found that teachers and families were experiencing cultural dissonance regarding rules of punishment; some families suggested corporal punishment as an acceptable solution for child misbehavior.

Consideration of Cultural and Linguistic Relevance in SWPBIS Implementation

SWPBIS has been described as a promising and culturally responsive set of evidence-based interventions (Muscott et al., 2008). As discussed earlier in this chapter, the system-wide application of PBIS focuses on preventing and addressing behavioral issues early, rather than using reactionary or punishment-based models. This approach has led to decreased exclusionary discipline practices and the increase of other positive outcomes in the general student populations included in various research studies. However, in a study examining the disciplinary exclusion data from 77 schools implementing SWPBIS, Vincent and Tobin (2011) found that African American students remained overrepresented in school exclusion rates, despite the implementation of SWPBIS programs. Although the authors note various limitations to their study and the need for further research, these preliminary results highlight the need for SWPBIS implementation to be culturally sensitive and responsive, particularly for African American students.

In the original development of SWPBIS, Sugai et al. (2000) emphasized the importance of creating procedures that are socially and culturally appropriate with intervention strategies that match the values of families, teachers, schools, support personnel, and community agency personnel. However, much of the original research and development of SWPBIS involved suburban and dominant-culture schools. As further implementation studies have been conducted, researchers and practitioners have called for more "culturally appropriate" SWPBIS models (Utley & Sailor, 2002).

Vincent, Randall, Cartledge, Tobin, and Swain-Bradway (2011) present a model of SWPBIS that focuses on culturally responsive behavioral interventions that build on the literature for culturally responsive academic instruction. They provide an expanded version of Sugai et al.'s (2000) figure of SWPBIS implementation components, including aspects of cultural relevance and validation that mediate the relationship between evidence-based practices and supporting student behaviors (Tobin & Vincent, 2010; Vincent et al., 2011) (see Figure 3 below). The additional considerations include using culturally responsive practices to support student behavior, using data to support culturally valid decision making, creative school-wide systems that support culturally responsive staff behavior, and creating culturally equitable student outcomes. The authors present the following guidelines for teachers to support behavior: (1) enhance staff members' cultural knowledge, (2) enhance staff members' cultural self-awareness, (3) validate others' culture, (4) establish cultural validity, and (5) emphasize cultural equity.

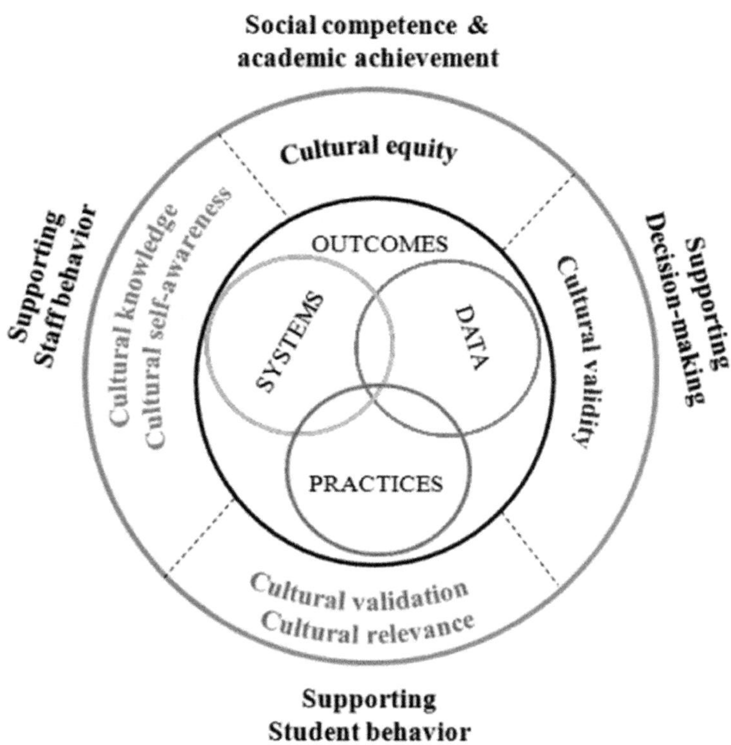

Figure 3. Integrating School-Wide Positive Behavior Support and Culturally Responsive Practices. Adapted from Tobin & Vincent, 2010.

As discussed earlier in this chapter, the achievement gap and discipline gap trends reveal a great need to implement effective interventions that can benefit African American students and other minority groups. For the purposes of this chapter, the guidelines provided by Vincent and colleagues (2011) are applied specifically to African American students, for a closer look at the mediating effect of culturally responsive practices within the PBIS model. First, Vincent et al. suggest that SWPBIS programs should use culturally valid, evidenced-based practices to support student behaviors. More specifically, social-skills instruction should involve teaching and rewarding behaviors that are valid and relevant within the child's culture. For African American students, the delivery and modification of interventions could include input from staff and family members within their culture. Also, students may benefit from discussions about how their family expectations for behavior at home may differ from behavioral expectations at school, allowing students to question perceived unfairness of some rules (Vincent et al., 2011).

Another aspect of the culturally responsive PBIS model calls for staff members to enhance their cultural knowledge and cultural self-awareness. This can be achieved through staff training and consultation that is specifically relevant to the student population (Vincent et al., 2011). For example, teachers of African American students could explore cultural differences and similarities by becoming familiar with Boykin's nine dimensions of African American cultural life (1983). When teachers increase their understanding of their own culture, they can also increase their understanding of the cultural relativity of others' behaviors. It may be helpful for an Asian American teacher to reflect on the information that Asian American culture tends to value the regulation of emotional expressiveness (Kim & Sherman, 2007) while African American culture tends to encourage the direct opposite (Boykin, 1983). This type of awareness could help to increase culturally relevant and valid behavior support practices and decision making.

Next, the data that are collected and reviewed as part of a SWPBIS program should be culturally valid and free of cultural bias. It is important to test data-collection instruments and operational definitions of behavioral violations for validity with African American students and other minority populations (Vincent et al., 2011). When SWPBIS data are disaggregated by student race and ethnicity, researchers have found that African American students continue to have disproportionate rates of disciplinary exclusion (Vincent & Tobin, 2011). Operational definitions may include "talking back" as disrespectful and a violation, while African American students may assume that their communication style is acceptable based on cultural norms (Cartledge & Milburn, 1996). As indicated in Vincent et al.'s model, disaggregation of behavioral data and exploration of cultural validity may be a necessary step to ensure culturally responsive decision making within a PBIS program. In addition, these steps may help to ensure culturally equitable student outcomes, reducing the disproportionate student discipline outcomes as well as increasing the academic achievement and social competence for specific minority groups.

Tobin and Vincent (2011) studied changes in disproportionate exclusion of African American students in relation to implementation of SWPBIS using data from 46 schools and found that certain strategies were associated with reductions in disproportionate exclusions. Although some of the recommended strategies have already been discussed in the model presented by Vincent and colleagues (2011), there are two specific strategies that were found to be significantly associated with reductions in racially disproportionate disciplinary exclusions: (1) acknowledge and reinforce expected student behaviors regularly in the classroom using at least four positive remarks (praise) to one negative remark (reprimand), and (2) use efficient and orderly transitions between instructional and noninstructional activities in the classroom. Other recommended strategies involve the reporting of disaggregated behavioral data, ongoing staff training and support for cultural responsiveness, and the use of local resources to conduct functional behavioral assessments and behavior support planning for students with serious behavior problems.

Conclusion

Approximately 14,000 schools across the United States currently implement SWPBIS. As SWPBIS is implemented nationwide, educators should consider cultural relevance and adjust programs to be developmentally appropriate and culturally valid and responsive. Research on the implementation of the SWPBIS model in schools across the nation shows promising outcomes. The implementation of SWPBIS has resulted in decreases in incidences of problem behavior (Bradshaw, Mitchell, & Leaf, 2010; Carr et al., 2002; Lewis & Sugai, 1999; Sadler, 2000); reduction in office referrals for problem behavior (Bradshaw et al., 2010; Carr et al., 2002; Sadler, 2000); reduction of in-school and out-of-school suspensions (Carr et al., 2002); reduction in school expulsions (Sadler, 2000), and a relationship to increases in the achievement of academic outcomes (Bradshaw et al., 2010; Horner et al., 2005).

Behavioral challenges in young children present major obstacles to the development of social competence. Without early prevention and interventions, many of the young children with social-emotional and behavioral challenges are likely to experience a negative developmental trajectory (Lipsey & Dezon, 1998). Research evidence indicates that PBIS has the potential to decrease challenging behaviors in young children and older students if implemented appropriately. While research evidence is still limited in the success of PBIS with young children and with CLD students, there is a growing emphasis on the system-wide application of PBIS to early childhood programs. The Pyramid Model is a promising approach that provides guidance for the design and delivery of SWPBIS within early childhood programs. Just as the application of PBIS to early childhood programs requires changes suitable to early childhood programs, implementation of the Pyramid Model to support young children with CLD backgrounds requires changes suitable to meeting the needs of these children. There is an urgent need to evaluate implementation of the early childhood Pyramid Model for young children with CLD backgrounds. In early childhood settings where the children are predominantly from CLD backgrounds, challenges and adaptations associated with implementing the culturally responsive Pyramid Model should be identified.

References

Aud, S., Hussar, W., Kena, G., Bianco, K., Frohlich, L., Kemp, J., & Tahan, K. (2011, May). *The condition of education 2011* (NCES 2011–033). Washington, DC: National Center for Education Statistics.

Barbetta, P. M., Norona, K. L., & Bicard, D. F. (2005). Classroom behavior management: A dozen common mistakes and what to do instead. *Preventing School Failure, 49*(3), 11–19.

Benedict, E. A., Horner, R. H., & Squires, J. K. (2007). Assessment and implementation of Positive Behavior Support in preschools. *Topics in Early Childhood Special Education, 27*(3), 174–192.

Boykin, A. W. (1983). The academic performance of Afro-American children. In J. Spence (Ed.), *Achievement and achievement motives* (pp. 324–371). San Francisco, CA: W. H. Freeman.

Boykin, A. W., Tyler, K. M., & Miller, O. (2005). In search of cultural themes and their expressions in the dynamics of classroom life. *Urban Education, 40,* 521–549.

Bradshaw, C. R. S., Mitchell, M., & Leaf, P. (2010). Examining the effects of schoolwide positive behavior interventions and supports on student outcomes: Results from a randomized controlled effectiveness trial in elementary schools. *Journal of Positive Behavior Interventions, 12,* 133–148.

Campbell, S. B. (1995). Behavior problems in preschool children: A review of recent research. *Journal of Child Psychology and Psychiatry, 36,* 113–149.

Campbell, S. B., Spieker, S., Burchinal, M., Poe, M. D., & The NICHD Early Child Care Research Network (2006). Trajectories of aggression from toddlerhood to age 9 predict academic and social functioning through age 12. *Journal of Child Psychology and Psychiatry, and Allied Disciplines, 47,* 791–800.

Carr, E. G., Dunlap, G., Horner, R. H., Koegel, R. L., Turnbull, A. P., & Sailor, W. (2002). Positive Behavior Support: Evolution of an applied science. *Journal of Positive Behavior Interventions, 4*, 4–16.

Cartledge, G., & Kourea, L. (2008). Culturally responsive classrooms for culturally diverse students with and at risk for disabilities. *Exceptional Children, 74*(3), 351–371.

Cartledge, G., & Milburn, J. F. (1996). *Cultural diversity and social skills instruction: Understanding ethnic and gender differences.* Champaign, IL: Research Press.

Crone, D., & Horner, R. (2003). *Building positive support systems in schools: Functional behavioral assessment.* New York: Guilford Press.

Crone, D. A., Horner, R. H., & Hawken, L. S. (2004). *Responding to problem behavior in schools: The behavior education program.* New York: Guilford Press.

Donovan, M. S., & Cross, C. T. (Eds.). (2002). *Minority students in special and gifted education.* Washington, DC: National Academies Press.

Ford, D. Y. (2012). Culturally different students in special education: Looking backward to move forward. *Exceptional Children, 78*(4), 391–405.

Ford, D. Y., & Kea, C. D. (2009). Creating culturally responsive instruction: For students' sake and teachers' sake. *Focus on Exceptional Children, 41*(9), 1–18.

Fox, L., Carta, J., Strain, P. S., Dunlap, G., & Hemmeter, M. L. (2010). Response-to-intervention and the pyramid model. *Infants and Young Children, 23*, 3–14.

Fox, L., Dunlap, G., Hemmeter, M. L., Joseph, G., & Strain, P. (2003). The teaching pyramid: A model for supporting social competence and preventing challenging behavior in young children. *Young Children, 58*, 48–52.

Fox, L., & Hemmeter, M. L. (2009). A program-wide model for supporting social emotional development and addressing challenging behavior in early childhood settings. In W. Sailor, G. Dunlap, G. Sugai, & R. Horner (Eds.), *Handbook of Positive Behavior Support* (pp. 177–202). New York: Springer.

Gilliam, W. S. (2005). *Prekindergarteners left behind: Expulsion rates in state prekindergarten systems.* New Haven, CT: Yale University Child Study Center. Retreived from http://fcd-us.org/resources/prekindergartners-left-behind-expulsion-rates-state-prekindergarten-programs

Gregory, A. & Mosely, P. M. (2004). The discipline gap: Teachers' views on the over-representation of African American students in the discipline system. *Equity & Excellence in Education, 37*, 18–30.

Gregory, J. F. (1997). Three strikes and they're out: African American boys and American schools' responses to misbehavior. *International Journal of Adolescence and Youth, 7*(10), 25–34.

Heller, K. A, Holtzman, W. H., & Messick, S. (Eds.). (1982). *Placing children in special education: A strategy for equity.* Washington, DC: National Academy Press.

Hemmeter, M. L., Corso, R., & Cheatham, G. (2006, February). *Issues in addressing challenging behaviors in young children: A national survey of early childhood educators.* Paper presented at the Conference on Research Innovations in Early Intervention, San Diego, CA.

Hemmeter, M. L., Fox, L., Jack, S., & Broyles, L. (2007). A program-wide model of Positive Behavior Support in early childhood settings. *Journal of Early Intervention, 29*(4), 337–355.

Hemmeter, M. L., Fox, L., & Snyder, P. (2008). *The teaching pyramid observation tool—research edition* (Unpublished assessment instrument). Nashville, TN: Vanderbilt University.

Hemmeter, M. L., Ostrosky, M., & Fox, L. (2006). Social and emotional foundations for early learning: A conceptual model for intervention. *School Psychology Review, 35*, 583–601.

Horner, R. H., Sugai, G., Todd, A. W., & Lewis-Palmer, T. (2005). Schoolwide positive behavior support. In L. M. Bambara & L. Kern (Eds.), *Individualized supports for students with behavior problems: Designing behavior support plans* (pp. 359–390). New York: Guilford Press.

Hurley, J. J., Saini, S., Warren, R. A., & Carberry, A. J. (2013). Use of the Pyramid Model for supporting preschool refugees. *Early Child Development and Care, 183*, 75–91.

Kaiser, B., & Rasminsky, J. S. (2011). *Challenging behavior in young children: Understanding, preventing and responding effectively* (3rd ed.). Upper Saddle River, NJ: Pearson.

Kim, H. S., & Sherman, D. K. (2007). "Express yourself": Culture and the effect of self-expression on choice. *Journal of Personality and Social Psychology, 92*(1), 1–11. doi:10.1037/0022-3514.92.1.1

Krasch, D., & Carter, D. R. (2009). Monitoring classroom behavior in early childhood: Using group observation data to make decisions. *Early Childhood Education Journal, 36*, 475–482.

Lewis, T. J., & Sugai, G. (1999). Effective behavior support: A systems approach to proactive schoolwide management. *Focus on Exceptional Children, 31*(6), 1–24.

Lipsey, M. W., & Derzon, J. H. (1998). Predictors of violent or serious delinquency in adolescence and early adulthood: A synthesis of longitudinal research. In R. Loeber & D. P. Farrington (Eds.), *Serious and violent juvenile offenders: Risk factors and successful interventions* (pp. 86–105). Thousand Oaks: Sage Publications.

Muscott, H., Szczesiul, S., Berk, B., Staub, K., Hoover, J., & Perry-Chisholm, P. (2008). Positive Behavior Interventions and Supports. *Teaching Exceptional Children, 40*(6), 6–14.

Oberg, K. (1960). Adjustment to new cultural environments. *Practical Anthropology, 7*, 170–179.

Ogbu, J. U. (2003). *Black American students in an affluent suburb: A study of academic disengagement.* Mahwah, NJ: Lawrence Erlbaum Associates.

Planty, M., Provasnik, S., & Daniel, B. (2007). *The condition of education 2007* (Report No. NCES 2007–065). Washington, DC: National Center for Education Statistics.

Sadler, C. (2000). Effective behavior support: Implementation at the district level. *Journal of Positive Behavior Intervention, 2*(4), 241–243.

Skiba, R. J., Horner, R. H., Chung, C.-G., Rausch, M. K., May, S. L., & Tobin, T. (2011). Race is not neutral: A national investigation of African American and Latino disproportionality in school discipline. *School Psychology Review, 40*(1), 85.

Skiba, R. J., Simmons, A. B., Ritter, S., Gibb, A. C., Rausch, M. K., Cuadrado, J., & Choong-Geun, C. (2008). Achieving equity in special education: History, status, and current challenges. *Exceptional Children, 74*(3), 264–288.

Squires, J., & Bricker, D. (2007). *An activity-based approach to developing young children's social emotional competence.* Baltimore, MD: Paul H. Brookes.

Stormont, M. (2002). Externalizing behavior problems in young children: Contributing factors and early intervention. *Psychology in the Schools, 39,* 127–138.

Stormont, M., Lewis, T. J., & Beckner, R. (2005). Positive Behavior Support systems: Applying key features in preschool settings. *Teaching Exceptional Children, 37*(6), 42–49.

Stormont, M. A., Smith, S. C., & Lewis, T. J. (2007). Teacher implementation of precorrection and praise statements in Head Start classrooms as a component of a program-wide system of Positive Behavior Support. *Journal of Behavior Education, 16,* 280–290.

Sugai, G., Horner, R. H., Dunlap, G., Hieneman, M., Lewis, T. J., Nelson, C. M., ... Wilcox, B. (2000). Applying Positive Behavior Support and functional behavioral assessment in schools. *Journal of Positive Behavior Interventions, 2*(3), 131–143. doi:10.1177/109830070000200302

Tobin, T. J., & Vincent, C. G. (2010). *Culturally competent School-Wide Positive Behavior Support: From theory to evaluation data* [PowerPoint slides]. Retrieved from http://www.pbis.org/common/pbisresources/presentations/PBS_tobin_vincent.pptx

Tobin, T. J., & Vincent, C. G. (2011). Strategies for preventing disproportionate exclusions of African American students. *Preventing School Failure, 55*(4), 192–201.

Trent, S. C., Kea, C. D., & Oh, K. (2008). Preparing preservice educators for cultural diversity: How far have we come? *Exceptional Children, 74,* 328–350.

Utley, C. A., & Sailor, W. (2002). Positive Behavior Support and urban school improvement/Special section/. *Journal of Positive Behavior Interventions, 4,* 195.

Vincent, C. G., Randall, C., Cartledge, G., Tobin, T. J., & Swain-Bradway, J. (2011). Toward a conceptual integration of cultural responsiveness and Schoolwide Positive Behavior Support. *Journal of Positive Behavior Interventions, 13*(4), 219–229. doi:10.1177/1098300711399765

Vincent, C. G., & Tobin, T. J. (2011). The relationship between implementation of School-Wide Positive Behavior Support (SWPBS) and disciplinary exclusion of students from various ethnic backgrounds with and without disabilities. *Journal of Emotional and Behavioral Disorders, 19*(4), 217–232.

Webb-Johnson, G. (2002). Are schools ready for Joshua? Dimensions of African-American culture among students identified as having behavioral/emotional disorders. *International Journal of Qualitative Studies in Education, 15*(6), 653–671. doi:10.1080/0951839022000014367

Wentzel, K. R. (2002). Are effective teachers like good parents? Teaching styles and student adjustment in early adolescence. *Child Development, 73*(1), 287–301. doi:10.2307/3696445

5. Culturally Relevant Positive Behavioral Interventions and Supports for Promoting School Success of Young Children with Problem Behavior from Culturally and Linguistically Diverse Backgrounds

Kwang-Sun Cho Blair, Chun Zhang, and Angie Chai

Effective interventions for children ages birth to five years are essential to promote their healthy social-emotional development, which is critical for overall health, well-being, and success in school and life. There is growing evidence that early childhood social-emotional development or mental health is associated with positive outcomes for young children with problem behavior (Fox & Hemmeter, 2009). However, despite teachers' efforts to prevent problems using appropriate guidance procedures and social-emotional skill instruction, a small portion of children in early childhood settings continue to exhibit persistent problem behavior (Brauner & Stephens, 2006). These children have difficulty following teacher directions, engaging in classroom routines and activities, and interacting positively with peers. Although they require intensive individualized interventions, many of these children's needs are unmet due to insufficient support within the early childhood programs (Blair, Fox, & Lentini, 2010; Hoover, Kubicek, Rosenberg, Zundel, & Rosenberg, 2012). It is well documented in the literature that young children with problem behavior are unlikely to outgrow their problems (Whitehurst & Fischel, 1994), not being able to acquire school readiness skills that will be fundamental to their success in school. The literature indicates that most preschool children who have externalizing problem behaviors will continue to have problems during their school years (Campbell, 1995; Lavigne et al., 2001).

Educators in early childhood settings are working with increasing numbers of children from minority and non-English-speaking homes. Nearly half of the country's children under age 5 are from racial or ethnic minorities (Cohn & Bahrampour, 2006). Although the demands increase for early childhood professionals to serve culturally and linguistically diverse (CLD) children, the vast majority of the professionals come from the majority Euro-American culture (Voltz, 1998). Children from CLD backgrounds often enter early childhood programs with an increased risk for failure. Identifying these children's needs through a culturally relevant assessment process faces particular challenges. Studies on children with disabilities have consistently indicated that CLD children are overrepresented in early intervention and special education (Yansen & Shulman, 1996). Despite the importance of creating culturally relevant interventions for CLD children, there has been little discussion in the scientific literature about what this entails and how it can be achieved.

The most common approach to addressing problem behavior in schools has been the delivery of punitive consequences (Sugai & Horner, 2002; Walker, Colvin, & Ramsey, 1995). Teachers are likely to reprimand these children and use other reactive strategies to suppress behaviors, thus delivering messages to children that they are not as successful as their peers. Most researchers agree that applying reactive and punitive consequences does little to prevent or remediate problem behavior and may likely exacerbate the behavior (Mayer & Sulzer-Azaroff, 1990; Noguera, 1995; Shores, Gunter, & Jack, 1993). Early educators can significantly reduce the negative effects of problem behavior if properly prepared; however, the literature indicates that rarely do early childhood professional learning programs target persistent problem behavior (Arnold, McWilliams, & Arnold, 1998; Hemmeter, Santos, & Ostrosky 2008).

In recognition of the importance of providing supportive environments to prevent early problem behavior and to promote positive social-emotional development, a growing body of empirical evidence supports the program-wide adoption of a multi-tiered system of supports utilizing the framework of Positive Behavioral Interventions and Supports (PBIS), also called Positive Behavior Support (Carter, Van Norman, & Tredwell, 2011; Hemmeter, Fox, Jack, Broyles, & Doubet, 2007). PBIS is a broad science- and values-driven approach for addressing challenging behavior that employs many of the proactive, non-punitive, evidence-based instructional strategies. PBIS is generally supported by a program leadership team consisting of an administrator, teachers, mental health consultant, family counselor, and a parent. PBIS at the individual level or Tier 3 includes a wide range of systemic and individualized strategies aimed at improving individual quality of life (Blair et al., 2010; Carr et al., 2002). PBIS provides a basis for the collaboration necessary to support young children in struggling programs. Culturally responsive pedagogy can be easily incorporated.

In this chapter, we first describe how to design culturally relevant individualized PBIS plans for young children with problem behavior at Tier 3. We then describe various effective evidence-based intervention strategies that teach new skills and decrease or prevent problem behavior. Third, we present strategies for implementing plans, including monitoring child progress and improving treatment fidelity. We conclude the chapter by discussing ways to sustain effective behavior support systems in early childhood settings, such as public preschools, community childcare, and Head Start programs.

Designing Culturally Relevant Individualized PBIS Plans

PBIS at the individual level provides intensive individualized support that is designed to meet the specific needs of the small percentage of children who did not make adequate progress at Tiers 1 and 2. PBIS at the individual level employs a team-based process of identifying Tier 3 children's needs and goals (Fox & Hemmeter, 2009; Horner, Sugai, & Anderson, 2010). It involves conducting functional behavior assessment (FBA) to identify environmental events and targeted problem behavior, developing and implementing a multi-component behavior support plan based on the FBA results, and monitoring progress of the plan. With ongoing training and support, all classroom staff can learn to implement PBIS. Evidence suggests that when early childhood program staff have access to ongoing consultation support, they can better address challenging behavior and prevent future problems (Gilliam, 2005). It is recommended that a PBIS program identify a leadership team that includes administrators, staff, families, and personnel with expertise in behavior support (Fox & Hemmeter, 2009). A culturally focused PBIS should be culturally appealing; staff buy-in helps to motivate and sustain their participation in the process. Within and across early childhood settings, there is a great deal of variability in program quality, training, and qualifications of staff and resources available to support the implementation of PBIS. The methods described in this chapter for designing and implementing individualized PBIS should be adapted to address the diverse needs of programs, staff, families, and individual children.

Developing a PBIS Team

While the leadership team plays an important role in the program-wide implementation of PBIS, individualized PBIS calls for a team effort involving stakeholders who are responsible for intervention and who exert direct or indirect influence on the life of the child (Fox & Hemmeter, 2009). The behavior support team essentially consists of family members and classroom staff who have an ongoing relationship with the child and who are affected by the child's challenging behavior and support. Therefore, identifying those individuals who can contribute to the PBIS process and building a well-functioning collaborative team is the key to effective PBIS at the individual level (Dunlap et al., 2010; Lucyshyn, Horner, Dunlap, Albin, & Ben, 2002). When considering that PBIS requires resources, commitment, and support, it is also desirable to include program leadership in the team at the Tier 3 level, including administrators who have direct access to program resources and are in a position to facilitate optimal interventions. The number of members will vary from team to team based on the individual needs of the child. Most important, including the family as a full member of the child's support team can lead to successful intervention.

If the family of the target child is not proficient in English and speaks a different language from other team members, implementing the PBIS process becomes more complicated. Therefore, the team should include an interpreter. The interpreter must understand both mainstream and the child's culture well enough to explain cross-cultural variables and anticipate acceptable and expected conventions for interaction. A range of acceptable options should be given to families for their roles and responsibilities in the process of individualized PBIS. Although not all members will be directly involved with implementing the intervention and monitoring its progress, all members should be responsible for helping develop the intervention plan and evaluating the child's progress. Team membership requires a commitment to participate in on-going communication (Dunlap et al., 2010).

Conducting Functional Behavior Assessment

The most crucial part of designing PBIS plans at the individual level is conducting FBA. FBA uses various assessment strategies to identify environmental variables that predict and maintain problem behaviors. After identifying the maintaining variables, hypotheses about the purpose or intended function of the challenging behavior are developed (Crone & Horner, 2003; O'Neill et al., 1997). More specifically, FBA helps examine: (a) when and under what conditions the problem behavior is most and least likely to occur; and

(b) what maintains the behavior, or what outcomes the behavior produces for the child. Functions are broadly categorized as either positive reinforcement or negative reinforcement, falling into one of five general categories: (1) to get attention; (2) to get tangibles; (3) to escape or avoid an aversive task or situation; (4) to get sensory stimulation; and (5) to avoid sensory stimulation. For children with severe disabilities and with limited communication skills, the problem behavior may function to communicate wants and needs (Durand & Crimmins, 1992; O'Neill et al., 1997).

The function of problem behavior is determined by examining the context in which behavior occurs and interpreting the purpose the behavior serves for the child within that context. Children learn to behave in ways that satisfy needs or that result in desired outcomes. As such, FBA should identify what the child gains, avoids, or controls through the behavior. An effective FBA must use multiple sources and multiple methods to gather information (O'Neill et al., 1997). Table 1 describes essential steps, purposes, and methods of conducting FBA. In addition to identifying functions, identifying child-specific communication, social, and environmental factors associated with the occurrence and non-occurrence of problem behavior is important to better understand the child's behavior. Conducting FBA helps the team gather information on what setting variables such as being tired, sick, or hungry occasion the problem behavior and what might trigger the child's behavior.

Table 1. Steps, Purposes, and Methods in Conducting FBA

Steps	Purpose	Methods
1. Review records	To gather initial background information on the child (e.g., current services the child is receiving, history of challenging behavior, child's strengths and weaknesses)	Examination of the child's records: • Developmental profile • Diagnostic and medical records • Assessments from therapists • Previous behavior assessments • Previous intervention efforts • Individualized Education Programs or Individualized Family Service Plan • Behavior incident reports • Teacher notes and home-program communication
2. Conduct interviews	To identify contexts and conditions for direct observations and establish initial hypotheses	Interviews with teachers, family members, and other adults with direct contact using: • Functional Assessment Interview Form (O'Neill et al., 1997) • Functional Assessment Interview-Parent Form (Blair & Fox, 2011)

(Continues)

Table 1. (Continued)

Steps	Purpose	Methods
3. Conduct observations	To identify the events that are antecedent and consequent to child behavior and to confirm hypotheses	Observations of the child within the naturally occurring routines and activities using: • Scatter plot chart (Touchette, MacDonald, & Langer, 1985) • ABC observation (Bijou, Peterson, & Ault, 1968) • Setting event checklist
4. Collect information about classroom and home	To better understand the classroom and home ecologies and child's behavior and to identify potential target family routines	Additional classroom assessments and interviews with family members using: • Classroom Assessment Scoring System (CLASS: Pianta, La Paro, & Hamre, 2008) • Teaching Pyramid Observation Tool (TPOT: Hemmeter, Fox, & Snyder, 2008) • Family Routines and Activities Questionnaire (Blair & Fox, 2011)
5. Summarize assessment results	To develop hypotheses on the problem behavior	Use a visual diagram to depict the setting event, antecedent, behavior, consequence, and identified function

As shown in Table 1, various methods are utilized to conduct FBA, all of which can be grouped into two categories: indirect assessment and direct assessment. Indirect assessment utilizes record reviews to identify relevant background information related to the problem behavior and conducting interviews with people who directly interact with the child. The behavior of young children can only be understood within the context of family and culture. If professionals who conduct FBA are unfamiliar with a child's culture or language, it is especially important that the assessment involve procedures for gathering information about family, language patterns, and conventions for communication and interaction.

Indirect Assessment—Record Review and Interview

A record review will help to identify medical or educational issues that may impact behavior and previous effective strategies that may inform the intervention. Interviews with family members, teachers, and other staff working with the child can provide valuable information regarding the child's behaviors, his or her culture, and values. In general, indirect FBA, employing record review and interview, is not adequate for conducting a comprehensive FBA (Alter, Conroy,

Mancil, & Haydon, 2008; Crone & Horner, 2003). The individual PBIS team members should be cautioned against using indirect assessment as the sole method for identifying the function of problem behaviors. Direct observations lead to more accurate hypotheses. Still, using a variety of indirect methods is important if there are multiple functions for a particular behavior or if the child has differential functioning depending on the environment. O'Neill and colleagues (1997) suggest that the FBA interview address the following areas:

- Description of the problem behaviors (e.g., topographies or forms of the behaviors, frequency, and intensity)
- Identification of immediate antecedent events (e.g., time when the behavior does or does not occur, physical setting, persons present, activity or task demand at hand)
- Identification of setting events that increase the likelihood of the occurrence of target behavior (e.g., medications, medical issues, sleep routines, eating routines, weather, and interactions with others)—these do not necessarily happen immediately before the target behavior
- Identification of items, activities, or events that may be aversive (types of food, certain noises, sensory stimulation)
- Identification of consequence or outcome of the target behavior
- Identification of replacement and other desirable behaviors
- Identification of the child's current methods of communication
- Identification of reinforcement that is specific to the child
- Description of interventions that have been attempted to decrease or eliminate the behavior

For children with CLD backgrounds, careful attention should be given to understand the child's behavior in the context of cultural norms and expectations. The team must determine: (a) how the child's behavior is interpreted in the child's home environment and cultural community; (b) whether the child's behavior is culturally appropriate, and how family members respond; and (c) whether teacher and classmate expectations confuse the child.

Furthermore, it is necessary to identify child-specific social and communication difficulties associated with the occurrence of problem behavior to better understand the function or purpose behind the child's behavior and to design an effective behavior support plan. Team members should use interviews to identify whether the child: (a) has been identified as having developmental delay or disability; (b) has difficulty effectively communicating and interacting with others at home or in the cultural community compared to same-age peers in the classroom; and (c) is failing to learn English.

Direct Assessment—Observation
Following indirect FBA, direct observational FBA should be conducted during naturally occurring routines and activities. Direct FBA can provide accurate, detailed information about the child, and also about the environment. It can provide more causal information as to what triggers and maintains the behavior (O'Neill et al., 1997). The most common method is ABC (Antecedent, Behavior, and Consequence) narrative recording (Bijou et al., 1968). This observational method allows the observer to organize anecdotal or descriptive information regarding the child's interactions with others during observations.

An ABC chart (Figure 1) can be individualized to contain several predetermined categories of antecedent behavior, responses, and consequent events, along with narrative recordings of additional information and observations. During this type of data collection, the observer collects data only when the behaviors of interest occur. Another common direct FBA method is using scatter plot charts. A scatter plot chart is useful in exploring the relationship between time of day or activity and challenging behavior (Touchette et al., 1985). The scatter plot is a graphic inspection technique in which response frequencies are visually depicted on the chart. The chart can be developed to observe and record the relationship between a specific set of classroom variables and behaviors (e.g., transition and child's noncompliance behavior) to analyze a particular situation. An advantage of using the scatter plot is that it is effective for a number of measurement strategies, such as count, frequency, duration, or latency.

Once sufficient amounts of data are available, a decision should be made on whether additional data are needed to clarify or confirm behavior patterns. It is recommended that initial observation data be gathered for two to five days or until a minimum of 15 to 20 occurrences of the behavior of concern have been gathered to determine whether the pattern is consistent with the initial summary statements developed from the initial indirect FBA (O'Neill et al., 1997).

Summarizing the FBA Results.
The information gathered from indirect and direct FBA should be summarized to develop hypotheses by comparing information collected from various FBA methods. The FBA summary is basically a hypothesis statement that includes: (a) immediate antecedents, (b) description of the challenging behavior, (c) function of the behavior, and (d) influential setting events. The following visual diagram is suggested to develop the summary statement (O'Neill et al., 1997). Multiple summary statements should be developed if the child's behavior occurs during multiple situations.

A-B-C Observation Chart

Date: 1/15/2013 Child: Matt Observer: Sara
Target Behavior(s): Scream, say "no," and kick
Reported setting event(s): Did not have breakfast

Observation Start Time: 9:00 a.m. Observation Stop Time: 9:30 a.m.

Time	Context	Antecedent	Behavior	Consequence	Perceived Function
9:03–9:04	Circle	Teacher told Matt to join the circle.	Matt said "no," playing with a toy in the play area.	Teacher let Matt play in the play area.	Get toy
9:10–9:15	Circle	Teacher told him to sit on his spot.	Matt ignored teacher direction and continued playing with a toy.	Teacher let Matt play with the toy.	Get toy
9:25–9:30	Transition	Teacher took the toy Matt was playing with.	Matt started screaming and kicking his teacher.	Teacher gave the toy back to him and told him he could have it for 5 more minutes.	Get toy

Observation Summary:

Target challenging behaviors occur most often when: Matt's preferred toys are removed or he is not allowed to have them, during circle or transition time. Missing breakfast seems to be a setting event that increases the likelihood of the behaviors.
The function(s) of Matt's problem behavior (screaming, saying "no," and kicking) seems to be: To gain access to tangibles.

Figure 1. An example of an ABC observation chart.

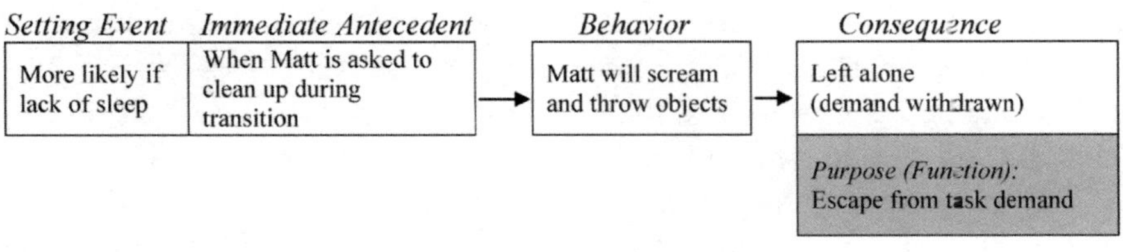

Figure 2. An example of a visual summary statement.

Figure 2 gives an example of a visual summary statement. In this example, Matt's FBA results can be summarized as "When Matt is asked to clean up during transition time, he will scream or throw objects and be left alone, which results in escaping from the task demand. His problem behavior is more likely to occur when he did not eat breakfast."

Collection of Information About the Classroom and Home

As team members gather information about the specific environmental events associated with the child's behavior, collecting further information about the classroom and home might be necessary to better understand the classroom and home ecologies and child's behavior, as well as to identify family routines that might be targeted for intervention. Gathering information about the teacher's general classroom arrangements, instructional practices, and the emotional climate of the classroom would be helpful in understanding how the classroom structure, social emotional climate, classroom rules and expectations, and teacher interaction style affect the child's behavior. Such tools might include the Classroom Assessment Scoring System (CLASS: Pianta, La Paro, & Hamre, 2008) and the Teaching Pyramid Observation Tool (TPOT: Hemmeter, Fox, & Snyder, 2014). These tools will provide information on whether the teacher has practices in place that promote and support the appropriate child behavior.

If supporting the child's behavior at home is recommended, gathering additional information about the home is necessary to identify family routines and activities that were not focused on during FBA and that might be targeted for intervention. The team should focus on identifying the child's engagement, independence, social relationship, and family expectations during family routines. Figure 3 shows an example of a questionnaire designed to collect information on family routines and activities.

Testing Hypotheses

Although indirect and direct FBA methods can help identify functions of behavior, hypothesis testing is necessary when the functions are not clear. In particular, behaviors that serve multiple functions require an experimental analysis or testing of the hypothesis to confirm that the hypothesis is accurate. To do so, the assessor must systematically manipulate certain environmental variables. A procedure known as analog assessment or functional analysis is one way to conduct the experiment. Analog assessment involves the use of a contrived set of controlled conditions to test the accuracy of the hypothesis. The procedure involves testing four conditions: (1) alone, (2) task demand, (3) attention, and (4) free play (Iwata, Dorsey, Slifer, Bauman, & Richman, 1982). While this strategy has proven to be effective in identifying the functions of a behavior, it is most useful in highly controlled settings (O'Neill et al., 1997).

Family Routines and Activities Questionnaire

Child: __________ Person filling out this form: ________ Date: _____

We'd like to learn about your child's daily routines and activities. This helps us understand him or her better.

1. What routines and activities (getting ready for school, taking a bath, eating a meal, chores, watching TV, nap) happen during certain parts of the day?
   Mornings:
   Afternoons:
   Nights:
2. Are there things you do or places you go once a week or maybe once every two weeks?
3. Are there other events that happen fairly regularly or during the weekend (such as shopping, going to church)?
4. Who are important people in your child's life? Who are helpful in your child's care, and who may also have activities and routines with your child (such as grandparents, brother, neighbor)?
5. What routines or activities does your child enjoy doing?
6. Does your child get to spend time with other children?
7. What routine or activity(s) does your child not like or have difficulty with?
   - What does your child usually do during the routine or activity? How does your child take part in the routine or activity? How well does your child take part in the routine or activity?
   - What expectations (such as getting dressed with help, eating breakfast, helping with cleaning up breakfast, brushing teeth during the morning routine) do you have for your child during the routine/activity?

Figure 3. An example of a questionnaire designed to identify family routines and activities. Adapted from Blair & Fox, 2011, p. 97.

A more realistic option is to manipulate specific classroom variables (e.g., complexity of tasks, teacher attention, and physical proximity) by introducing or withdrawing variables that are assumed to trigger the occurrence of problem behavior. For example, when it is hypothesized that a child is more likely to engage in challenging behavior during non-preferred activities, two conditions (preferred and non-preferred) should be organized to test the hypothesis with the child participating in both identified preferred and non-preferred activities. The two conditions can be tested through the use of an alternating treatment design in which the conditions are alternated relatively quickly on a regular schedule (e.g., five minutes for each condition with two or three alterations). This procedure is known as structural analysis (Stitchter, Sasso, & Jolivette, 2004), antecedent-based functional analysis (Hanley, Iwata, & McCord, 2003), or brief intervention testing (Umbreit, Ferro, Liaupsin, & Lane, 2007), and helps determine precisely the conditions under which the child is most and least likely to behave appropriately.

Studies on structural analysis have indicated that conducting the experimental FBA in natural school and early childhood settings was helpful in identifying environmental and instructional variables that support the successful integration of the children into the inclusive settings (Blair, Umbreit, & Bos, 1999; Blair, Umbreit, Dunlap, & Jung, 2007; Stitchter et al., 2004). When conducting the structural analysis, the procedures should not interfere with the classroom routine or ecology. The child should not be removed from usual activities or routines; rather the activity or routine should be modified, or the teacher's behavior should be modified to see its effect on the child's response.

Developing a PBIS Plan

After functions of problem behavior are identified based on the FBA results, the team members can develop a PBIS plan to address the target problem behaviors and to promote alternative behaviors. The key elements of a PBIS plan are a description of target problem behavior, a summary of FBA, goals, and multi-component strategies, and a monitoring plan.

Linking the FBA Results to the PBIS Plan

Linking the FBA results to the PBIS plan is critical to develop a technically sound and effective plan. To link the FBA to the plan or intervention strategies, FBA statements from the FBA should be included in the plan, and the selected strategies should be logically consistent with the statements. It is suggested that a competing behavior model or diagram is used as a way to link the FBA results to the plan and to develop effective intervention strategies (O'Neill et al., 1997). The competing behavior model depicts the FBA summary statements, alternative or competing behaviors, and the contingencies associated with the behaviors, and intervention strategies that address the distant setting events, immediate antecedents, and maintaining consequences.

Development of Behavioral Goals

The successful intervention for children with problem behavior at Tier 3 requires the team members to identify behaviors or skills to target for intervention. The goals must reflect behavior that can be measured and achieved in a reasonable timeframe (e.g., "Matt will use sign language to say 'all done' with verbal prompt when he is finished eating."). The goals should focus on teaching the child alternative, replacement behavior that serves the same function as the problem behavior, decrease future occurrence of the problem behavior, and address any repeated episodes of the problem behavior (Blair et al., 2010; Wood, Ferro, Umbreit, & Liaupsin, 2011).

Replacement behaviors for young children can usually be categorized into three types of behaviors: (1) functionally equivalent communication skills; (2) self-regulation skills; and (3) social skills. Functionally equivalent communication, or functional communication skills, refer to how a child uses language skills to make wants and concerns known (e.g., requesting of attention, turns, objects, help). Self-regulation skills refer to children's capacity for controlling emotions, self-management, and self-relaxation (e.g., expressing feelings, impulse regulation, delay of gratification, anger control, self-soothing, accepting "no"). Social skills include daily interaction skills (e.g., cooperation with peers, taking turns, compliance, participation in activities, and managing relationships). Effective replacement skills have the potential to enhance functional skills that are critical to success in the environment.

When the purpose of the behavior cannot be honored, different alternative behavior that might not serve the same function should be identified and taught. For example, for a child who screams and kicks to escape the car seat, teaching the child to select a toy and play while in his car seat would be more appropriate than teaching him to say "no." One other important consideration in identifying alternative, replacement skill is determining when and where the new skill will be taught. The key to ensuring that the child learns a replacement skill is to make sure that instruction is repetitive and consistent.

Early childhood professionals working with children from CLD families are faced with challenges in determining whether these children's problems are due to deficits in their development, developmental differences resulted from families of CLD backgrounds, or program failure of meeting these children's needs. Families are as diverse within cultural and linguistic groups. Culture and language are critical factors, but many other aspects of family life interact with cultural and linguistic identity (Qi & Kaiser, 2003; Shepard & Dickstein, 2009). Therefore, the most important task for the team is to understand a child within the context of the family and to identify appropriate and meaningful goals for the child. When selecting a replacement behavior, the team should examine whether the child understands multiple directions, single sentences, words, gestures, pictures, or objects and can express needs and wants using verbal language, sign language, gestures, or pictures. Team members should collaborate to identify behavior that is easier and more efficient for the child to engage in than the problem behavior.

Developing Function-Based, Multi-Component Interventions

Developing a plan that is technically sound focuses on selecting strategies that make the problem behavior *irrelevant*, *inefficient*, and *ineffective* (O'Neill et al., 1997). A multi-component PBIS plan that addresses all three areas will be consistent with the basic principles of behavior.

Making the problem behavior *irrelevant* implies changing the environment so that there is no need to use the problem behavior to gain access to reinforcers that maintain problem behavior. Strategies for changing the environment such as changing the physical setting, schedule, activities, materials, and curriculum should be selected to make the problem behavior irrelevant, which will reduce the likelihood that the child will encounter these environmental conditions. For example, if a child engages in off-task behavior by lying on the floor during circle time as a way of getting attention in an otherwise developmentally inappropriate environment, the child's behavior could become irrelevant if active physical activities preferred by the child were developed and provided during the circle time activities. Including such environmental strategies that make problem behavior irrelevant and unnecessary is an essential component of a PBIS plan. Those strategies include altering the physical settings (e.g., creating new activity centers), increasing predictability, providing choices of activities, using visual cues, adjusting seating arrangements, adjusting instructions, and increasing social interactions (Blair et al., 1999, 2010; O'Neill et al., 1997). Researchers suggest that these strategies alone may not eliminate the problem behavior, but can make other teaching and response strategies more effective (O'Neill et al., 1997; Snell & Janney, 2000).

Making problem behavior *inefficient* implies teaching new behaviors that are easier to use than problem behavior for gaining access to reinforcers. The PBIS plan focuses on identifying and teaching alternative, socially appropriate replacement behaviors that are more efficient than problem behavior. Teaching functional communication skills that could replace the problem behavior can provide an immediate mechanism for the child to meet her/his needs. The team must identify the function of the problem behavior in order to teach an efficient functional communication skill (e.g., teaching how to ask for help in receiving the reinforcer that was previously reached through escape or attention-getting behavior). In addition to the functional communication skills, the child should also be taught social skills and other desired behaviors that function more efficiently in the environment.

Another important component of a PBIS plan is to make the problem behavior *ineffective*. Making the problem behavior ineffective implies that the problem behavior no longer works to produce the desired outcome, that is, obtaining reinforcers. Response strategies focus on how to handle target problem behavior if it occurs again and how to reinforce the replacement and desirable behaviors when the child uses the new skills. The plan should include such strategies as managing consequences to reinforce replacement skills and desired behaviors, withholding reinforcement or redirecting the child to the new alternative replacement behavior following problem behavior, and using natural, less intrusive consequences that address the identified function.

Developing a Plan with Contextual Fit

To help CLD children adjust to the classroom environment and to promote their social-emotional development, it is important to address their problem behavior within classroom routines. Providing the opportunity and support to engage in appropriate behaviors within regularly occurring routines can create a positive classroom culture and ecology (Blair et al., 2010). Children who are not familiar with classroom routines are more likely to have difficulty engaging in the routines. Efforts to address problem behavior must focus on three critical areas: (1) creating a positive classroom environment that promotes engagement in routines, activities, and social interactions; (2) teaching desired alternative behavior to meet the child's needs; and (3) altering adult behavior so they are not inadvertently reinforcing problem behavior.

Successful PBIS requires the participation and buy-in of the classroom staff and family members, which requires a contextual fit between the plan and the classroom staff, family members, resources, and environment. The team members should examine whether the developed plan aligns with the goals, the people implementing the plan have the capacity and commitment to do so, and the necessary resources to implement the plan are available. The plan should be effective and easily implementable; the team members should focus on developing a plan that accommodates competing demands on teaching staff, is consistent with the teacher skill levels, and is manageable. Culturally sensitive FBA would be the first step in securing PBIS intervention for CLD children. However, without adequate preparation, early childhood professionals are often not aware of the individual needs of CLD families.

To develop culturally sensitive plans, team meetings should seek to enhance cultural self-awareness; help staff and family members select goals and strategies; identify issues associated with the plan's contextual fit; discuss staff and family values, cultural perspectives, communication, and language backgrounds; adapt the plan based on the family's interaction style; and develop ongoing communication systems (Blair & Fox, 2011). If the family members lack English skills, involving bilingual professionals from diverse backgrounds who are knowledgeable on the customs, values, and cultural differences and who share common characteristics with the family would hasten good rapport and help CLD families feel more comfortable and familiar with the behavior support being provided to their child. Figure 4 is an example of a self-assessment rating scale designed to assess the contextual fit of an individualized PBIS plan.

Self-Assessment of Contextual Fit for Early Educators

This checklist provides a reflection tool for early educators to assess the extent to which the behavior support plan fits with the contextual features of your classroom. It asks you to rate your knowledge of the elements of the plan, the skills that will be needed for plan implementation, and your confidence about if the plan can be implemented with fidelity. This checklist will help you identify potential contextual fit issues prior to plan implementation. After this checklist is completed, discuss the concerns you have about the behavior support plan with the team. The team should discuss each concern and develop potential solutions or strategies to address each issue.

1. I understand all of the elements of the behavior support plan.

1	2	3	4	5
Strongly Disagree	Disagree	Neutral	Agree	Strongly Agree

2. I know what I am expected to do to implement this behavior support plan.

1	2	3	4	5
Strongly Disagree	Disagree	Neutral	Agree	Strongly Agree

3. I have the skills needed to implement this behavior support plan.

1	2	3	4	5
Strongly Disagree	Disagree	Neutral	Agree	Strongly Agree

4. I am comfortable implementing the elements of this behavior support plan.

1	2	3	4	5
Strongly Disagree	Disagree	Neutral	Agree	Strongly Agree

5. The strategies in the plan are consistent with the developmentally appropriate practices I use in my classroom.

1	2	3	4	5
Strongly Disagree	Disagree	Neutral	Agree	Strongly Agree

6. I have the time needed to implement this behavior support plan.

1	2	3	4	5
Strongly Disagree	Disagree	Neutral	Agree	Strongly Agree

7. I have the materials needed to implement this behavior support plan.

1	2	3	4	5
Strongly Disagree	Disagree	Neutral	Agree	Strongly Agree

8. I believe the behavior support plan will be effective in supporting the target child.

1	2	3	4	5
Strongly Disagree	Disagree	Neutral	Agree	Strongly Agree

Figure 4. A self-assessment scale designed to assess contextual fit of a PBIS plan. From Blair & Fox, 2011, p. 136.

Selecting Effective Intervention Strategies

As discusses above, linking the FBA results to the behavior support plan is the key to developing an effective plan. Developing the following intervention strategies that make the problem behavior irrelevant, inefficient, and ineffective should be the focus: (a) prevention strategies that make the problem behavior irrelevant; (b) teaching strategies that make the problem behavior inefficient; and (c) response strategies that make the problem behavior ineffective. Table 2 gives examples of evidence-based intervention strategies that are developmentally appropriate.

Table 2. Evidence-Based Practices.

Prevention Strategies	Teaching Strategies	Response Strategies
❖ Modification of setting events • Reduce environmental stimuli (e.g., lighting, noise, temperature) • Meet physical needs (e.g., food, place to sleep) • Modify routines (e.g., provide a place to calm down) • Create or increase positive setting events (e.g., spending time with parent when arriving at school) • Increase predictability • Eliminate distracting items ❖ During non-preferred activities or task demands • Reduce activity or task duration, or task difficulty level • Alternate less preferred activities with more preferred activities • Embed preference into activities • Reduce steps in routines • Allow flexible seating positions	❖ Teaching functional communication skills • When child wants to escape: Teach to say, "no," "all done" • When child wants attention: Teach to say, "help," "hug" • When child wants tangible item: Teach to say, "toy," "more" ❖ Teaching other replacement or desirable behaviors • Provide direct instruction using systematic prompting • Use pre-correction (e.g., restate rule, redirect behavior when problem behavior is about to start, remind of replacement behavior) • Provide "Calm-down" break • Use peer modeling procedures	❖ When child uses appropriate behavior • Honor child's requests; gradually delay reinforcement • Provide specific verbal praise • Provide social interaction time with adults or peers • Provide appropriate touch (e.g., high five, hug) • Provide special time with adult, activities, or tangibles • Provide privileges (e.g., line leader, office errands) ❖ When child engages in problem behavior • Provide redirection or visual reminder • Provide verbal, gestural, or visual prompt to use alternative behavior • Acknowledge child's feelings • Present choices

(Continues)

Table 2. (Continued)

Prevention Strategies	Teaching Strategies	Response Strategies
• Modify the schedule • Provide activity choices • Use visual schedule or cues ❖ During preferred activities • Provide a warning or signal to prepare for transitions • Offer choices • Remind of upcoming fun activities • Set clear expectations and rules • Offer frequent assistance • Provide activities that require less assistance	• Use role-play • Use task analysis • Use self-monitoring procedures • Use Social Stories	• Provide extinction (e.g., time-out from reinforcers, withdraw attention) • Follow through with consequences (e.g., wait patiently for compliance; help child complete the task)

Implementing PBIS Plans

Implementing the PBIS plan will vary from intervention to intervention in terms of duration, frequency, and intensity. During implementation, monitoring child progress and implementation fidelity are essential to ensure the success of the plan. Progress monitoring provides ongoing assessment data on targeted problem behavior and new skills to determine whether the child is making adequate progress toward goals or whether changes to the plan are needed. Careful monitoring is needed to ensure that the plan is implemented every day with a high degree of fidelity.

Monitoring Child Progress

Monitoring child progress incorporates two critical components: information gathering and decision making. Continuous assessment of child progress improves the quality and efficiency of the decision-making process (Horner, Sugai, & Todd, 2001). Data must be used to assist with decision making on whether to continue, modify, stop, or begin a different plan. Daily recording will provide important information about whether the child's problem behavior is decreasing and whether he or she is learning new skills. However, the literature indicates that many teachers are familiar with daily observation of target behaviors and see little value in collecting data (Alberto & Troutman, 2006). Therefore, teams must determine who on the team will provide the training and consultation on progress monitoring. If a facilitator (e.g., mental health consultant, PBIS coach) outside of the program, who has experience in FBA and PBIS and who can provide support to classroom staff is available, that person can play an important role in supporting the team members, particularly classroom staff by helping monitor progress. The facilitator can help classroom staff understand the importance of tracking child outcomes to make decisions, identify the specific data that will be collected, understand the use of different data-collection methods, and determine how frequently the data will be collected and analyzed. Team members must develop data-collection systems based on the child's behavioral goals and the behavior support strategies. Event and duration recording, task analysis, and momentary time sampling can be used by classroom staff to collect monitoring data. However, most early childhood classrooms do not have the resources to carry out progress monitoring; therefore, the use of indirect recording systems such as rating scales and checklists are recommended in schools and early childhood programs (Blair & Fox, 2011). The data-collection system should fit within the child's natural routines and activities and should not interrupt the instructional or teacher-child interaction flow. In many instances, rating scales can promote communication within the program and between classroom staff and families.

Recently, a five-point behavior rating scale (BRS) with a combination of direct and indirect observations has been recommended in the field as an efficient and reliable instrument to monitor child progress (Dunlap et al., 2010; Strain, Wilson, & Dunlap, 2011). Developing a BRS requires: (a) clearly defining the target behavior; (b) determining the scale for measuring the behavior; and (c) establishing appropriate anchor points for recording behavioral occurrence.

To determine the scale, the team must decide whether to use frequency, duration, or intensity. For example, if the target behavior is aggression toward peers during center time, the first step is to determine the behavior occurrence on a typical day. This typical level of behavior occurrence (e g., 6–7 times, 10 minutes, 20% of center time) can become Anchor Point 4. The goal the team would like to achieve by the end of the intervention period can be set as Anchor Point 1. The interim anchor points for appropriate behavior are Points 2 and 3. An Anchor Point 5 can be set to represent a day that is worse than a typical day.

For a BRS designed to monitor increases in appropriate behavior, the scale is reversed. That is, the most undesirable day is set at Anchor Point 1, the typical day is set at Anchor Point 2, interim anchors set at Points 3 and 4, and the reasonable goal is set at Anchor 5. For example, the team can set Anchor 2 at one or two appropriate behavior events, Anchor 5 at 10 or more, Anchor 1 at zero (extremely bad day), Anchor 3 at three to six times, and Anchor 4 at seven to nine times (Dunlap et al., 2010). Figure 5 gives an example of a BRS for classroom clean-up (an appropriate behavior) with intensity anchor points and a data collection sheet:

5 = Clean up independently without prompt
4 = Clean up with no refusal after being prompted
3 = Initially refused, but began to clean up
2 = Continued to refuse to clean up by ignoring requests
1 = Threw toys or kicked the teacher

Behavior		Date						
Clean up	Clean up independently when the bell rang	5	5	5	5	5	5	5
	Clean up promptly without refusal, being prompted	4	4	4	4	4	4	4
	Initially refused, but began to clean up	3	3	3	3	3	3	3
	Continued to refuse to clean up by ignoring requests	2	2	2	2	2	2	2
	Threw toys or kicked the teacher	1	1	1	1	1	1	1

Figure 5. An example of a BRS.

Once the monitoring system is determined, it is necessary to schedule when data will be collected. There are no preset guidelines on who must monitor or how often to monitor target behaviors. If it is expected that there will be improvement within a month or less, daily measurement can be planned. Weekly monitoring is appropriate if it is likely to take more than a few months. Most of all, monitoring should be consistent and active, and the monitoring schedule should reflect the child's needs and staff's available recourses. It is suggested that consistent data collection is necessary to refine the intervention and increase child success, and data be periodically reviewed by the behavior support team to ensure communication, make any adjustments as needed, and review progress toward short-term and long-term goals.

Improving Implementation Fidelity

Classroom staff who are responsible for implementation often need training and consultation support to implement the plan with fidelity. The literature indicates that the vast majority of effective intervention for problem behavior has been implemented by researchers and highly trained specialists in controlled settings; very few studies report that individualized function-based intervention or PBIS can be carried out by typical school and early childhood program staff (Blair et al., 2010; Lane, Weisenbach, Phillips, & Wehby, 2007). Therefore, teams should develop a plan for implementation and observing fidelity.

Developing a Fidelity Monitoring Tool
To ensure the implementation fidelity, an implementation fidelity checklist, that is, an objective list of behavior-support strategy steps, should be developed by the team. The fidelity checklist can help the classroom staff self-monitor their implementation or it can be used by a facilitator or team member to monitor and provide feedback on the consistency and accuracy with which the intervention plan is implemented. Team members should review implementation progress at team meetings and address any implementation issues of the plan. If implementation fidelity is inconsistent or not as planned, teams must modify strategies to increase the fidelity.

Coaching and Feedback

Effective implementation of PBIS requires that the implementers understand the actions necessary for behavior change, and also that the value of those actions must outweigh their cost in terms of effort (Scott & Martinek, 2006). There is a consensus among researchers and practitioners that training itself has little impact on teacher performance without additional help from the consultant (Hemmeter, Snyder, Kinder, & Artman, 2011; Noell, Witt, Gilbertson, Ranier, & Freeland, 1997). Studies on the Teaching Pyramid Observation Tool for Preschool Classrooms (TPOT; Hemmeter, Fox, & Snyder, 2008) have shown that teachers in early childhood programs implement less than 40% of the Tier 1, Tier 2, and Tier 3 practices included on the TPOT without additional training and support (Hemmeter, Snyder, & Fox, 2010).

Coaching provides a collaborative relationship that offers a unique mechanism for encouraging classroom staff to implement the PBIS plan with fidelity. A recent study on coaching early childhood special educators to implement the Teaching Pyramid model suggests that in addition to training on the model, coaching sessions on goal setting and action planning followed by performance feedback were effective in increasing implementation fidelity (Fox, Hemmeter, Snyder, Binder, & Clarke, 2011). In the study, coaching sessions occurred twice a week and continued until the teachers met criterion levels of implantation. Coaching observations (30–90 minutes) preceded debriefing sessions (30 minutes).

Designated PBIS coaches, often referred to as consultants, technical assistants, or facilitators within PBIS, can work with staff to monitor progress and improve child outcomes. At the system level, the job of a coach involves assisting schools or programs with implementing functional rules, routines, and procedures in a consistent manner (Lewis & Sugai, 1999). Coaches can also help to create measureable goals and monitor progress to evaluate implementation and responses to increase PBIS efficacy (Scott & Martinek, 2006).

Reinke, Herman, and Sprick (2011) introduced the Classroom Check-Up (CCU) as a guide for universal coaching to teachers who need classroom management support. The CCU leads coaches through a series of steps: (1) assessing the classroom through interviews, checklists, and observations; (2) providing the teacher with feedback; (3) collaborating with the teacher to develop an intervention menu; (4) collaborating with the teacher to choose the intervention; and (5) having the teacher self-monitor implementation of the intervention. Teachers are also provided with daily visual performance feedback in the form of graphs that represent teacher performance. Implementation of the CCU was found to result in increased teacher implementation of effective classroom management strategies as well as decreased disruptive behavior from students.

At the individual level, coaching can take place directly in the classroom to help staff acquire, enhance, or refine specific individualized PBIS plan implementation strategy. It is suggested that a team member with expertise or a facilitator conduct fidelity observations each time a coaching or performance feedback session is provided to classroom staff. Meetings with the facilitator can help staff determine whether the plan is being implemented effectively and follows the planned interventions, and identify areas of concern or unanticipated problems with fidelity (Blair & Fox, 2011).

Research demonstrates that performance feedback was the most effective way to increase implementation fidelity by teachers, and there was a correlation between the level of treatment fidelity and positive treatment outcomes (Noell et al., 1997; Reinke, Lewis-Palmer, & Martin, 2007; Reinke, Lewis-Palmer, & Merrell, 2008; Wilder, Atwell, & Wine, 2006). Hagermoser Sanetti and colleagues (2007) found that performance feedback to teachers was most effectively delivered when coaches used forms of visual feedback, such as graphs on treatment integrity data, combined with verbal feedback. Reinke et al. (2007) also found that visual performance feedback for teachers increased treatment integrity, specifically for the use of behavior-specific praise.

There is promising evidence that performance feedback can be effective in increasing early childhood educators' use of specific evidence-based strategies.

Several studies indicated that training combined with email feedback increases preschool teachers' use of evidence-based practices (Barton & Wolery, 2007; Fullerton, Conroy, & Correa, 2009). Hemmeter, Snyder and Fox (2010) found that training combined with email feedback increased early childhood educators' use of descriptive praise. The email feedback included five components: (1) opening comment, (2) supportive feedback, (3) corrective feedback, (4) planned actions, and (5) closing comments.

Sustaining Effective Behavior Support Systems

Sustaining effective behavior support systems requires the building of a sustainable PBIS system through leadership, teamwork, consistent participation, and regular meetings to discuss the progress on the CLD child with problem behavior. A successful team requires administrators who can support the intervention with time, staff, and money to ensure ongoing team commitment. Access to consultation is important to enhance PBIS sustainability over time. The literature indicates that having a universal prevention system is necessary to implement system-wide PBIS, but is insufficient to produce a long-term impact without a secondary level (e.g., targeted group intervention) and a tertiary level (e.g., intensive individualized PBIS). It is a challenge to implement PBIS at the individual level in early childhood settings where there is a significant need for professional development to help teachers and caregivers learn to address young children's challenging behavior (Blair et al., 2010; Dunlap, Ester, Langhans, & Fox, 2006).

Leadership Team

There is a wide consensus that the single most important component of the effective system-wide PBIS model is the formation and maintenance of a leadership team (Colvin & Fernandez, 2000; Hemmeter, Fox, Jack, Broyles, & Doubet, 2007). They can provide leadership for all phases of development and implementation of individualized PBIS plans, assisting with monitoring and troubleshooting, and addressing issues collaboratively with the individual PBIS team. The leadership team should be actively involved with identifying children who need intensive individualized interventions and help the individual PBIS team determine the children's needs and help design and implement the plans. The leadership team can contribute to sustained system-wide PBIS implementation while addressing individual children who require intensive individualized support, as well as the minority of children who engage in little or no problem behavior but who may benefit from universal support.

Administrative Support

Child problem behavior often leads to teacher burnout; thus, sustained PBIS implementation requires administrative support. The lack of administrative support is a potential barrier to teacher involvement in the PBIS process (George, White, & Schlaffer, 2007). If the classroom staff's perception of the work environment is that it offers little support, their PBIS implementation is likely to be poor. Similarly, staff who are satisfied with and committed to their jobs may be more likely to implement the plan with fidelity. Thus, it is critical to provide strong administrative support to staff during implementation of the plan in order to sustain the implementation, which will result in positive outcomes for children. It should be noted that turnover rates in early childhood settings are high. Team members must examine whether administrators are allocating adequate time to address staffing issues and provide necessary support to classroom staff during implementation of the plan. It is important that the administrators be encouraged to participate in team meetings, and that the facilitator or coach provides regular debriefings to the administrators to promote implementation fidelity and sustainability.

Access to Consultation

Another critical component for sustaining effective behavior support is ongoing access to consultation. The individualized PBIS cannot be designed without FBA, which requires extensive teacher training in understanding of problem behavior and designing and implementing evidence-based intervention strategies. Even with implementing Tier 2 interventions, school teams and staff need assistance in identifying and implementing the evidence-based interventions (Hoyle, Marshall, & Yell, 2011; Stormont & Reinke, 2012). Therefore, for early childhood teachers and caregivers to be able to actively participate in the individualized PBIS process, access to ongoing consultation support is critical. As discussed above, provision of coaching with performance feedback is likely to be a key or active ingredient for ensuring fidelity of intervention implementation. A coach, either internal or external to the program, who has advanced training in PBIS and behavior theory and who can attend team meetings and provide consultation support, should be identified at the beginning of the individualized PBIS team building. The coach could be a member of the leadership team and play a large role in all aspects of individualized PBIS in providing support and guidance as the individual PBIS team members work to implement and monitor the intervention plan.

Conclusions

With the increasing number of diverse young children, recognizing how to effectively promote the children's social emotional development becomes a priority. Young children from CLD backgrounds enter early childhood programs with an increased risk for failure, and therefore it is essential to address these children's needs through a culturally relevant assessment and intervention. Positive, proactive interventions are the most beneficial to children from CLD backgrounds. In this chapter, we described how to design culturally relevant individualized PBIS plans for young children with severe problem behavior. Children with severe problem behavior call for the most intensive and individualized interventions. PBIS is a viable and effective approach for early childhood programs to design and implement individualized interventions. Developing a PBIS plan requires a team-based process to assess child behavior, identify goals, select intervention strategies, and monitor child progress and teacher or caregiver implementation of the plan. We have stressed the importance of involving family members, identifying functions of problem behavior and replacement skills, and selecting evidence-based intervention strategies. We also discussed the importance of designing a PBIS plan with contextual fit, improving treatment fidelity, and sustaining effective behavior support systems in early childhood settings. It is important to acknowledge that the majority of problem behaviors in young children can be resolved with less intensive approaches, and there should be a balance between the intensity and severity of the problem behaviors. We discussed the importance of well-trained staff. For early childhood teachers and caregivers to be able to actively participate in the individualized PBIS process, access to ongoing consultation support is critical. A coach, either internal or external to the program, who can attend team meetings and provide consultation support, should be identified at the beginning of the individualized PBIS team building. Finally, the importance of developing culturally sensitive plans cannot be underemphasized. Team meetings should seek to enhance cultural self-awareness, help staff and family members select goals and strategies, identify issues associated with the plan's contextual fit, discuss staff and family values, cultural perspectives, communication, and language backgrounds, adapt the plan based on the family's interaction style, and develop ongoing communication systems.

References

Alberto, P. A., & Troutman, A. C. (2006). *Applied behavior analysis for teachers* (7th ed.). Upper Saddle River, NJ: Pearson Education.

Alter, P. J., Conroy, M. A., Mancil, G. R., & Haydon, T. (2008). A comparison of functional behavior assessment methodologies with young children: Descriptive methods and functional analysis. *Journal of Behavioral Education, 17*, 200–219.

Arnold, D. H., McWilliams, L., & Arnold, E. H. (1998). Teacher discipline and child misbehavior in day care: Untangling causality with correlational data. *Developmental Psychology, 34*, 276–287.

Barton, E. E., & Wolery, M. (2007). Evaluation of e-mail feedback on the verbal behavior of preservice teachers. *Journal of Early Intervention, 30*, 55–72.

Bijou, S. W., Peterson, R. F., & Ault, M. H. (1968). A method to integrate descriptive and experimental field studies at the level of data and empirical concepts. *Journal of Applied Behavior Analysis, 1*, 175–191.

Blair, K. C., & Fox, L. (2011). *Facilitating individualized interventions to address challenging behavior: Toolkit.* Washington, DC: Center for Early Childhood Mental Health Consultation, Georgetown University.

Blair, K. C., Fox, L., & Lentini, R. (2010). Use of Positive Behavior Support to address the challenging behavior of young children within a community early childhood program. *Topics in Early Childhood Special Education, 30*, 68–79.

Blair, K. C., Umbreit, J., & Bos, C. S. (1999). Using functional assessment and children's preferences to improve the behavior of young children with behavioral disorders. *Behavioral Disorders, 24*, 151–166.

Blair, K. C., Umbreit, J., Dunlap, G., & Jung, G. (2007). Promoting inclusion and peer participation through assessment-based intervention. *Topics in Early Childhood Special Education, 3*, 134–147.

Brauner, C., & Stephens, C. (2006). Estimating the prevalence of early childhood serious emotional/behavioral disorders: Challenges and recommendations. *Public Health Reports, 121*, 303–310.

Campbell, S. B. (1995). Behavior problems in preschool children: A review of recent research. *Journal of Child Psychology and Psychiatry, 36*, 113–149.

Carr, E. G., Dunlap, G., Horner, R. H., Koegel, R. L., Turnbull, A. P., Sailor, W., ... Fox, L. (2002). Positive Behavior Support: Evolution of an applied science. *Journal of Positive Behavior Interventions, 4*, 4–16.

Carter, D. R., Van Norman, R. K., & Tredwell, C. (2011). Program-wide Positive Behavior Support in preschool: Lessons for getting started. *Early Childhood Education Journal, 38*, 349–355.

Cohn, D., & Bahrampour, T. (2006). Of U.S. children under 5, nearly half are minorities. *Washington Post*, A101.

Colvin, G., & Fernandez, E. (2000). Sustaining effective behavior support systems in an elementary school. *Journal of Positive Behavior Interventions, 2*, 251–253.

Crone, D. A., & Horner, R. H. (2003). *Building Positive Behavior Support systems in schools: Functional behavioral assessment.* New York: Guilford Press.

Dunlap, G., Ester, T., Langhans, S., & Fox, L. (2006). Functional communication training with toddlers in home environments. *Journal of Early Intervention, 29*, 81–97.

Dunlap, G., Iovannone, R., Kincaid, D., Wilson, K., Christiansen, K., Strain, P., & English, C. (2010). *Prevent-Teach-Reinforce: A school-based model of individualized Positive Behavior Support.* Baltimore, MD: Paul H. Brookes

Durand, V. M., & Crimmins, D. B. (1992). *The Motivation Assessment Scale.* Topeka, KS: Monaco & Associates.

Fox, L., & Hemmeter, M. L. (2009). A program-wide model for supporting social emotional development and addressing challenging behavior in early childhood settings. In W. Sailor, G. Dunlap, G. Sugai, & R. Horner (Eds.), *Handbook of Positive Behavior Support* (pp. 177–202). New York: Springer.

Fox, L., & Hemmeter, M. L., Snyder, P., Binder, D. P., & Clarke, S. (2011). Coaching early childhood special educators to implement a comprehensive model for prompting young children's social competence. *Topics in Early Childhood Special Education, 31*, 178–192.

Fullerton, E. K., Conroy, M. A., & Correa, V. I. (2009). Early childhood teachers' use of specific praise statements with young children at risk for behavioral disorders. *Behavioral Disorders, 34*, 118–135.

George, M. P., White, G. P., & Schlaffer, J. J. (2007). Implementing school-wide behavior change: Lessons from the field. *Psychology in the Schools, 44*, 41–51.

Gilliam, W. S. (2005). *Prekindergarteners left behind: Expulsion rates in state prekindergarten systems.* New Haven, CT: Yale University Child Study Center. Retrieved from http://fcd-us.org/resources/prekindergartners-left-behind-expulsion-rates-state-prekindergarten-programs

Hagermoser Sanetti, L. M., Luiselli, J., & Handler, M. (2007). Effects of verbal and graphic performance feedback on behavior support plan implementation in an inclusion classroom. *Behavior Modification, 31*, 454–465.

Hanley, G. P., Iwata, B. A., & McCord, B. E. (2003). Functional analysis of problem behavior: A review. *Journal of Applied Behavior Analysis, 36*, 147–186.

Hemmeter, M. L., Fox, L., Jack, S., Broyles, L., & Doubet, S. (2007). A program-wide model of Positive Behavior Support in early childhood settings. *Journal of Early Intervention, 29*, 337–355.

Hemmeter, M. L., Fox, L., & Snyder, P. S. (2014). Teaching Pyramid Observation Tool for Preschool Classrooms (TPOT) Manual, Research Edition. Baltimore: Paul H. Brookes.

Hemmeter, M. L., Santos, R. M., & Ostrosky, M. M. (2008). Preparing early childhood educators to address young children's social-emotional development and challenging behavior. *Journal of Early Intervention, 30*, 321–340.

Hemmeter, M. L., Snyder, P., & Fox, L. (2010, June). *Examining the potential efficacy of a model for addressing social-emotional development and challenging behavior.* Poster presented at the Fifth Annual Institute of Education Sciences Research Conference, National Harbor, MD.

Hemmeter, M. L., Snyder, P., Kinder, K., & Artman, K. (2011). Impact of performance feedback delivered via electronic mail on preschool teachers' use of descriptive praise. *Early Childhood Research Quarterly, 26*, 96–109.

Hoover, S. D., Kubicek, L. F., Rosenberg, C. R., Zundel, C., & Rosenberg, S. A. (2012). Influence of behavioral concerns and early childhood expulsions on the development of early childhood mental health consultation in Colorado. *Infant Mental Health Journal, 33*, 246–255.

Horner, R. H., Sugai, G., & Anderson, C. M. (2010). Examining the evidence base for School-Wide Positive Behavior Support. *Focus on Exceptional Children, 42*, 1–14.

Horner, R. H., Sugai, G., & Todd, A. W. (2001). "Data" need not be a four-letter word: Using data to improve schoolwide discipline. *Beyond Behavior, 11*, 20–22.

Hoyle, C. G., Marshall, K. J., & Yell, M. L. (2011). Positive Behavior Supports: Tier 2 interventions in middle schools. *Preventing School Failure, 55*, 164–170.

Iwata, B. A., Dorsey, M. F., Slifer, K. J., Bauman, K. E., & Richman, G. S. (1982). Toward a functional analysis of self-injury. *Journal of Applied Behavior Analysis, 27*, 197–209.

Lane, K. L., Weisenbach, J. L., Phillips, A., & Wehby, J. H. (2007). Designing, implementing, and evaluating function-based interventions using a systematic, feasible approach. *Behavioral Disorders, 32*, 122–139.

Lavigne, J., Cicchetti, C., Gibbons, R., Binns, H., Larsen, L., & Devito, C. (2001). Oppositional defiant disorder with onset in preschool years: Longitudinal stability and pathways to other disorders. *Journal of the American Academy of Child and Adolescent Psychiatry, 40*, 1393–1401.

Lewis, T. J., & Sugai, G. (1999). Effective behavior support: A systems approach to proactive school-wide management. *Focus on Exceptional Children, 31*, 1–24.

Lucyshyn, J. M., Horner, R. H., Dunlap, G., Albin, R. W., & Ben, K. R. (2002). Positive Behavior Support with families. In J. M. Lucyshyn, G. Dunlap, & R. W. Albin (Eds.), *Families and Positive Behavior Support: Addressing problem behavior in family contexts* (pp. 3–43). Baltimore, MD: Paul H. Brookes.

Mayer, G. R., & Sulzer-Azaroff, B. (1990). Interventions for vandalism. In G. Stoner, M. R. Shinn, & H. M. Walker (Eds.), *Interventions for achievement and behavior problems* (Monograph). Washington, DC: National Association of School Psychologists.

Noell, G. H., Witt, J. C., Gilbertson, D. N., Ranier, D. D., & Freeland, J. T. (1997). Increasing teacher intervention implementation in general education settings through consultation and performance feedback. *School Psychology Quarterly, 12*, 77–88.

Noguera, P. A. (1995). Preventing and producing violence: A critical analysis of responses to school violence. *Harvard Educational Review, 65*, 189–212.

O'Neill, R. E., Horner, R. H., Albin, R. W., Sprague, J. R., Storey, K., & Newton, J. S. (1997). Functional assessment and program development for problem behavior: A practical handbook (2nd ed.). Pacific Grove, CA: Brooks.

Pianta, R. C., La Paro, K. M., & Hamre, B. K. (2008). *Classroom Assessment Scoring System (CLASS) manual.* Baltimore, MD: Paul H. Brookes.

Qi, C. H., & Kaiser, A. P. (2003). Behavior problems of preschool children from low-income families: Review of the literature. *Topics in Early Childhood Special Education, 23*, 188–216.

Reinke, W. M., Herman, K. C., & Sprick, R. S. (2011). *Motivational interviewing for effective classroom management: The Classroom Check-Up*. New York: Guilford Press.

Reinke, W. M., Lewis-Palmer, T., & Martin, E. (2007). The effect of visual performance feedback on teacher behavior-specific praise. *Behavior Modification*, *31*, 247–263.

Reinke, W. M., Lewis-Palmer, T., & Merrell, K. (2008). The Classroom Check-Up: A class-wide teacher consultation model for increasing praise and decreasing disruptive behavior. *School Psychology Review*, *37*, 315–332.

Scott, T. M., & Martinek, G. (2006). Coaching Positive Behavior Support in school settings: Tactics and data-based decision making. *Journal of Positive Behavior Interventions*, *8*, 165–173.

Shepard, S. A., & Dickstein, S. (2009). Preventive intervention for early childhood behavioral problems: An ecological perspective. *Child and Adolescent Psychiatric Clinics of North America*, *18*, 687.

Shores, R. E., Gunter, P. L., & Jack, S. L. (1993). Classroom management strategies: Are they setting events for coercion? *Behavioral Disorders*, *18*, 92–102.

Snell, M. E., & Janney, R. (2000). *Social relationships and peer supports* (1st ed.). Baltimore, MD: Paul H. Brookes.

Stitchter, J. P., Sasso, G. M., & Jolivette, K. (2004). Structural analysis and intervention in a school setting: Effects on problem behavior for a student with an emotional/behavioral disorder. *Journal of Positive Behavior Interventions*, *6*, 166–177.

Stormont, M., & Reinke, W. M. (2012). Using coaching to support classroom-level adoption and use of interventions within School-Wide Positive Behavioral Interventions and Support systems. *Beyond Behavior*, *21*, 11–19.

Strain, P. S., Wilson, K., & Dunlap, G. (2011). Prevent-Teach-Reinforce: Addressing problem behaviors of students with autism in general education classrooms. *Behavioral Disorders*, *36*, 160–171.

Sugai, G., & Horner, R. H. (2002). The evolution of discipline practices: School-Wide Positive Behavior Supports. *Child and Family Behavior Therapy*, *24*, 23–50.

Touchette, P. E., MacDonald, R. F., & Langer, S. N. (1985). A scatter plot for identifying stimulus control of problem behavior. *Journal of Applied Behavior Analysis*, *18*, 343–351.

Umbreit, J., Ferro, J., Liaupsin, C., & Lane, K. L. (2007). *Functional behavioral assessment and function-based intervention: An effective, practical approach*. Upper Saddle River, NJ: Pearson.

Voltz, D. L. (1998). Cultural diversity and special education teacher preparation: Critical issues confronting the field. *Teaching Education and Special Education*, *21*, 63–70.

Walker, H. M., Colvin, G., & Ramsey, E. (1995). *Antisocial behavior in school: Strategies and best practices.* Pacific Grove, CA: Brooks/Cole.

Whitehurst, G. J., & Fischel, J. E. (1994). Early developmental language delay: What, if anything, should a clinician do about it? *Journal of Child Psychology and Psychiatry*, *35*, 613–648.

Wilder, D. A., Atwell, J., & Wine, B. (2006). The effects of varying levels of treatment integrity on child compliance during treatment with a three-step prompting procedure. *Journal of Applied Behavior Analysis, 39*, 369–373.

Wood, B. K., Ferro, J. B., Umbreit, J., & Liaupsin, C. J. (2011). Addressing the challenging behavior of young children through systematic function-based intervention. *Topics in Early Childhood Special Education, 30*, 221–232.

Yansen, E., & Shulman, E. (1996). Language assessment: Multicultural considerations. In L. Suzuki, P. Meller, & J. Ponterotto (Eds.), *The handbook of multicultural assessment* (pp. 353–393). San Francisco, CA: Jossey-Bass.

6. *Class-Wide Positive Behavioral Interventions and Supports in the Elementary School*

Su-Je Cho, Kwang-Sun Cho Blair, and Ji-Ryun Kim

American education guidelines are changing how schools respond to students with academic and behavioral difficulties. As a complement to such guidelines, Positive Behavioral Interventions and Supports (PBIS) provides educators with an effective means of addressing students' behavior problems. Approximately 14,000 schools across the United States currently implement School-Wide PBIS (SWPBIS; see www.pbis.org). A growing body of evidence shows SWPBIS as highly effective and practical in both reducing problem behavior and increasing academic performance of primary and secondary school students (Bradshaw, Mitchell, & Leaf, 2010; Horner et al., 2009; Muscott, Mann, & LeBrun, 2008; Safran & Oswald, 2003).

Despite the increased implementation of SWPBIS, many teachers, especially teachers of students from culturally and linguistically diverse (CLD) backgrounds in urban schools, struggle with establishing effective classroom routines and structure. Without that routine and structure, success in managing challenging behaviors displayed by some students in their classrooms is hit or miss (Pavri, 2004). Research shows student behavior problems are more common in urban schools than in suburban or rural schools (Dunbar, 2004). A disproportionately high number of African American students experience office discipline referrals (e.g., Skiba et al., 2011), harsher punishments for behavioral violations (e.g., Skiba, Michael, Nardo, & Peterson, 2002), suspension and expulsion. These behavioral outcomes correlate to poorer academic outcomes. Urban schools often struggle with higher levels of violence, mobility, truancy, under-qualified staff, and staff turnover; thus, they may require intense levels of support for those students as well as comprehensive training and resources for staff (Warren et al., 2003).

SWPBIS should include classroom support; however, the current literature provides little information on effective class-wide PBIS strategies that improve individual student social and academic outcomes. Although targeting the classroom system to increase effective classroom management practices is likely to reduce classroom disruptions and prevent student problems, the majority of the PBIS research has focused on school-wide and individual-level implementation; less attention has been paid to the classroom systems (Sailor, Dunlap, Sugai, & Horner, 2008). This chapter aims to provide educators with practical strategies to implement the three-tier PBIS framework at the classroom level in urban elementary schools. The chapter covers issues related to implementing class-wide PBIS in a way that improves academic and behavioral performance of culturally and linguistically diverse students.

PBIS Model at the Classroom Level

PBIS is a systematic approach (a) promoting socially acceptable behavior by providing students with effective instruction and specific feedback for improving behaviors (Sugai et al., 2000) and (b) enhancing the capacity of schools to educate all children, especially those with challenging behaviors (Kline, Simpson, Blesz, Smith Myles, & Carter, 2001). The assumption behind the PBIS approach is that behaviors are predictable and predictable problems are preventable. The school-system-wide application of PBIS is based on a three-tier prevention model: (a) primary prevention, (b) secondary prevention, and (c) tertiary prevention (Horner, Sugai, Todd, & Lewis-Palmer, 2005). Previous chapters have extensively described this model.

Incorporated within the structure and expectations of school-wide PBIS is the use of class-wide PBIS, which considers the unique needs of a given classroom (Scott, Park, Swain-Bradway, & Landers, 2007). Keeping consistent with SWPBIS, class-wide PBIS aims to create a classroom climate that fosters student social competence, academic engagement and learning while minimizing disruptive behaviors (Hieneman, Dunlap, & Kincaid, 2005). Class-wide PBIS targets the entire classroom and supports student social competence, academic achievement, and behavior as well as decision making and staff behavior (Simonsen, Fairbanks, Briesch, & Sugai, 2006). PBIS at the classroom level necessitates procedures implementing school-wide expectations for student behavior coupled with pre-planned strategies for particular classrooms (George, Harrower, & Knoster, 2003). It is recommended that the class-wide application of PBIS systematically address: (a) classroom ecology; (b) behavior management; and (c) curriculum and instruction (George et al., 2003). Each area should be assessed to identify protocols needing more support, problem areas to target, and what information ought to be captured for specific students.

Classroom Ecology

Various aspects of classroom environment can be modified to prevent or address behavior problems. The classroom ecological factors such as physical setting, scheduling, and social environment should be assessed to elicit appropriate behavior and to minimize crowding and distraction. The literature indicates that the most effective classrooms are those with a well-ordered environment. Good classroom arrangement can decrease student noise and disruption, increase desirable student interaction and on-task behavior, and positively impact teacher efficiency in terms of maximizing direct interaction with students. Before modifying the curriculum and instruction, modifying classrooms to create an orderly learning environment is key to creating appropriate social interaction in the context of an academic setting. Strategies to improve the physical setting in an elementary classroom include: (a) keeping high-traffic areas free of congestion (e.g., trash cans, pencil sharpeners, computer stations); (b) keeping teaching materials and student supplies readily accessible; (c) keeping students spaced apart during teaching demonstrations; and (d) having desks in a circular arrangement (Simonsen, Fairbanks, Briesch, Myers, & Sugai, 2008). It is suggested that all transitions and non-instructional activities are posted and reviewed regularly. Social interaction within a classroom is also an important factor that can optimize student learning. The literature indicates that effective communication among students and between the teacher and the students enhances social and academic engagement among the students (Evertson & Weinstein, 2006).

Behavior System

As with school-wide PBIS, class-wide PBIS emphasizes teaching, modeling, and reinforcing behavioral expectations set for students in the classroom (Shores, Gunter, Denny, & Jack, 1993). In implementing a primary intervention, classroom teachers should consider elements such as (a) identifying and teaching expectations, (b) acknowledging students' appropriate behaviors, and (c) using evidence-based practices (Simonsen et al., 2008).

Classroom Rules

Researchers and practitioners have successfully implemented effective classroom behavior systems. Some of their strategies include (1) efficient classroom management to increase instructional time, (2) effective instruction techniques that keep students engaged in learning, and (3) group contingencies. Developing a set of classroom expectations and rules is fundamental in PBIS. Rules for the classroom should match school-wide expectations, but be tailored to promote behavior specific to the classroom setting. While expectations are generally stated standards of conduct (e.g., "be responsible, be safe, and be respectful"), effective rules are behavior specific to the classroom setting. Following the rules results in order, discipline, and a well-functioning environment. The rules speak to specific actions and observable behaviors that are desired from students (e.g., "keep hands, feet, and objects to yourself," "wash your hands with soap for at least 20 seconds"). Classroom rules should be five or fewer, and be age appropriate (in the context of language and expectations), stated positively, and easy to understand (Burden, 2006; Scheuermann & Hall, 2008). Rules should be specific, observable, and measurable. When students are involved in the development of those rules, which are subsequently taught, modeled, and reinforced, the students will be more likely to comply (Simonsen et al., 2008).

Positive Interaction

How teachers interact with their students constrains classroom management practices. It has been found that students whose teachers practice positive interactions perform better academically and socially than their peers who have teachers with a negative approach to interacting with their students (Reinke, Lewis-Palmer, & Martin, 2007). Researchers also reported an inverse relationship between the level of praise delivered by teachers and a level of off-task or disruptive behaviors exhibited by their students. In other words, more praise yielded more appropriate behaviors of all students including those with disruptive behaviors (Reinke et al., 2007). Kalis, Vannest, and Parker (2007) suggested teachers' interactions with students at a ratio of four positive interactions to one negative interaction effectively manage their classroom (i.e., minimize time getting students to focus and actually instructing them). Equally important, teachers have to acknowledge students engaging in appropriate behaviors (Stormont & Reinke, 2009).

Classroom Reward Systems

Developing a class-wide reward system is necessary to increase the likelihood of repeated desirable behaviors, to foster a positive climate, to reduce the need for engaging in time-consuming disciplinary measures, and to support efforts of the school-wide PBIS. It is suggested that the class-wide reward system be simple and students be frequently rewarded contingent on desired behavior. Threatening to take earned items or rewards away ought to be avoided (Reinke, Herman, & Stormont, 2013).

Curriculum and Instruction

Effective curriculum and instruction simplifies classroom management. When students are engaged in instruction, they are less likely to display disruptive and off-task behaviors, and more likely to have high levels of academic performance (Greenwood, Terry, Marquis, & Walker, 1994). To meet the needs for all students, differentiated instruction has been widely practiced in schools because all students begin at different levels of understanding and familiarity in each subject taught, and thus teachers' expectations of each student's progress must be different. One way of differentiating instruction is to use Universal Design for Learning (UDL) that can be a framework in developing lesson plans. The UDL provides a blueprint for creating instructional goals, methods, materials, and assessments that work for all students. The UDL is a flexible approach that can be adjusted for the needs of individual students (see www.cast.org).

Rigorous and relevant instruction delivered at an appropriate pace is likely to keep all students engaged in learning. Another way of increasing levels of student engagement in instruction is to provide students with opportunities to respond (often called OTR) to academic questions during instruction (Stichter & Lewis, 2006). The OTR varies in type and characteristics, but generally includes the following elements (Stichter & Lewis, 2006):

1. Increasing rates of teacher talk that includes repeated verbal, visual, or verbal and visual types of prompts for responding during instruction.
2. Presenting information in a way that increases student correct responses.
3. Implementing individualized instructional modifications appropriate for the student's level of functioning and frequent checks for understanding and accuracy.
4. Using repeated instructional prompts that incorporate wait time, allowing students to time to consider and make a response.
5. Providing corrective feedback, error correction, and progress monitoring.

Research found that OTR improved student academic performance in reading (Skinner, Smith, & McLean, 1994) and math (Skinner, Belfiore, Mace, Williams-Wilson, & Johns, 1997).

Group contingencies can be effectively used in the implementation of primary prevention of the three-tier PBIS model. Group contingencies rely on peers to function as change agents (e.g., by providing prompts, encouragement, collaboration; Gable, Arllen, & Hendrickson, 1994). Many researchers and practitioners have used various types of group contingencies because these strategies are relatively easy to implement in a classroom and students respond to them well (Baybak, Luze, & Kamps, 2000; Turco & Elliot, 1990). Examples of group contingencies are the Good Behavior Game and Anchor the Boat.

The Good Behavior Game (GBG) has been used for handling disruptive behaviors in classrooms. Barrish, Saunders, and Wolf (1969) coined the GBG. The steps include (1) defining behavioral expectations, (2) establishing criteria for winning, and (3) teaching the student its rules. Because this game is readily implementable, time efficient, and widely applicable, it has been consistently demonstrated to improve teachers' ability to efficiently manage behaviors in classrooms (Tingstrom, Sterling-Turner, & Wilczynski, 2006). Since the 1960s, researchers have used these steps, as they are or with some modifications, in an effort to decrease undesirable behaviors among students. For example, Barrish and colleagues (1969) used the GBG with 24 students in a fourth-grade math class. The result showed that the levels of talk-out and out-of seat behavior of the students decreased after implementing the GBG. In a similar application, Darveaux (1984) found that a modified GBG with a token economy system (the GBG plus merit) was effective at reducing various disruptive behaviors (e.g., tattling, noise making, out-of-seat) and improving assignment completion for two second-grade students, even though they were considered at risk for an emotional and behavioral disorder.

More recently, Wright and McCurdy (2011) compared two types of interdependent group contingencies in two general-education classrooms in an elementary school: the Good Behavior Game and the Caught Being Good Game (CBGG). Those require the teacher to set a timer/buzzer in the classroom to alarm on a schedule. The participants were a kindergarten and fourth-grade class, with 17 and 20 students, respectively, and both versions of the game were implemented in a counterbalanced fashion. Using a withdrawal design, the authors found both games had similar effects in terms of decreasing disruptive behaviors and increasing on-task behaviors. These studies provide evidence that the Good Behavior Game is an effective strategy.

Another type of group contingency is called Anchor the Boat. One article described how the Anchor the Boat steps were implemented for ten students attending a fourth-grade/fifth-grade learning support classroom (Lohrmann & Talerico, 2004). The target behaviors were (1) stay in seat, (2) complete assignments, and (3) talk in turn. To implement the Anchor the Boat steps, the teachers were trained to (1) use operationally defined behavioral expectations with positive language, (b) use teacher-directed instruction and role-playing to teach the expectations, and (c) reinforce the target students when they met the behavioral criteria. A multiple-baseline design across three subject areas (i.e., reading, language arts, and math) was used to evaluate the effects on the target students. The results showed that dedicating time to directly teaching behavioral expectations and reinforcing student positive behaviors significantly reduced the rate and level of talking-out behavior across all three classes. Although the results for incomplete assignments and out-of-seat behavior were inconclusive, it appears that the Anchor the Boat was good for reducing talking-out-of-turn behavior.

"Tootling" is considered another effective strategy for classroom-based PBIS interventions. The term "tootling" was developed by Skinner, Skinner, and Sterling-Turner (2002) to enhance day-to-day social interactions among students. "Tootling" came from the word "tattling" and the expression "tooting your own horn." When tootling, students are taught to catch positive behaviors of their peers (e.g., giving positive comments, helping peers with a difficult task, sharing materials), to write the behavior on a card, and then to submit the card to the teacher or put in a designated box.

The effects of tootling on disruptive behaviors in the classroom were investigated (Cihak, Kirk, & Boon, 2009). The participants were 19 third-grade students including four students with disabilities (i.e., specific learning disabilities and attention deficit hyperactivity disorder); approximately one-fourth of the students were from either an African American or Hispanic background. The students were taught how to report their classmates' positive behaviors using index cards and then to place the cards in a clear container. The teacher displayed a poster in the front of the classroom to provide feedback to the students regarding the daily number of "tootles" peers reported and the total number of "tootles" required to reach the goal set for the entire class.

Prior to the intervention, the researchers trained the classroom teacher how to implement tootling by reviewing the procedures and how to write tootles at the start of the school day. The target behaviors included (a) talking out, (b) out of seat without teacher's permission, and (c) engaging in any motor behavior that interfered with learning in the classroom. The teacher made a mark next to the corresponding student's initials on the poster when a desirable behavior occurred. Tootles were collected throughout the day prior to routine transitions (i.e., lunch, recess, bathroom, or art class). When the class met their cumulative goal (i.e., 100 tootles that met criteria), the entire class received a group reward (i.e., extra recess time). The results showed that the number of disruptive behaviors decreased significantly during the intervention phases. When the teacher rewarded the students for reporting their peers' positive behaviors, concurrent benefits were observed in the students' classroom behavior. However, when the tootling intervention was withdrawn, the disruptive behaviors increased. This result indicates that tootling is an effective group contingency strategy that can be implemented during the universal prevention stage.

Supporting Students Needing Secondary and Tertiary Supports Within the Classroom

Class-wide PBIS can best be considered as a primary prevention strategy that is aligned to the school-wide PBIS. However, the class-wide PBIS is intended to support a group of students or individual students in the classroom who need additional, targeted group interventions or more intensive interventions. Although the majority of students respond well to primary prevention strategies, some students are not successful with only these strategies. To identify and recommend students for secondary or tertiary prevention supports, evidence ought to be provided to support the recommendation (Fairbanks, Simonsen, & Sugai, 2008). When students are identified for secondary or tertiary prevention supports, teachers should develop further strategies to meet the academic and social needs of these students. While some schools give these students small-group support within the classroom (e.g., a quiet corner), other schools designate specialists who provide a similar type of support in another room in the school. When a student is not successful with secondary support, it would be best to continue that support, but involve a behavior interventionist or special educator in working with the student individually for a longer time each day. Strategies for a more focused intervention for these students within the classroom routines and activities have not been well researched. Nevertheless, in this section we will review some effective strategies with good potential. The strategies are (a) check in/check out, (b) social skills instruction, and (c) function-based intervention.

Check In/Check Out (CICO)

An effective secondary support strategy is CICO, referred to as the Behavior Education Program. Benefits of this approach include: (a) increasing antecedent prompts for appropriate (goal) behavior, (b) increasing the daily and weekly amount of adult feedback, (c) providing a more structured daily schedule for students, and (d) improving the school feedback to families with respect to the students behavior goals (Filter et al., 2007). Crone, Horner, and Hawken (2004) developed procedures for implementing CICO in classroom settings as follows.

1. Create the materials required to implement the CICO intervention. The materials may include a CICO point card listing classroom expectations with prompts to rate the student throughout the day;

2. Identify students whose behaviors are not responsive to the universal classroom management system using data (e.g., office discipline referrals, daily behavioral ratings filled out by the teacher);
3. Invite caregivers of identified students to participate in at-home CICO;
4. Teach students on the CICO procedures.

Fairbanks, Simonsen, and Sugai (2008) added a tracking system to collect daily performance data to evaluate student progress, with which teachers are able to make informed decisions about the program effects over time for each student. Fairbanks and colleagues further recommended a standard routine being in place each day. For example, the teacher briefly checks in with each student in the morning by (a) reviewing classroom expectations, (b) providing a CICO point card, (c) setting a daily goal for points to be earned, and (d) ensuring that the student has the required materials. Throughout the day, the teacher gives the target student points and specific feedback based on the student's performance. At the end of the day, the teacher checks out with each student by (a) reviewing the point card, (b) determining whether or not the student met his or her goal for the day, (c) reinforcing goal achievement, and (d) providing a copy of the point card for the student to take home for a parent's review and signature.

Researchers have obtained positive results from implementing class-wide CICO (e.g., Fairbanks et al., 2008; Hawken, MacLeod, & Rawlings, 2007; Kauffman, 2010). For example, Fairbanks et al. (2008) implemented a three-tiered PBIS approach to 12 elementary students, some of whom engaged in disruptive and problem behaviors. Teachers were required to develop their own primary interventions including the following components: (a) identifying expectations, (b) defining expectations, (c) explicitly and directly teaching expectations, (d) posting expectations, and (e) designing a system to encourage, reinforce, and acknowledge appropriate behavior. The teachers also had to create an acknowledgment or reward system (i.e., tokens) for their students. The result revealed that eight of 12 students responded to the primary intervention, but four required additional behavior support. The teachers were then trained to use the CICO procedures developed by Crone et al. (2004) and elaborated by Fairbanks et al. (2008), and then implemented the procedures to the four students over a week-long period. Progress was monitored through observation data, daily points, and teacher feedback. The result of the secondary support intervention revealed that two of the four students responded to CICO while the rest were recommended for a tertiary intervention. Based on the findings of several studies, it is clear that CICO can be readily implemented with a minimal level of training to reduce problem behaviors in classrooms.

Social Skills Instruction

An increasing number of children enter elementary schools without the social-emotional skills needed to succeed in schools, and this deficit concerns teachers (Rimm-Kaufman, Pianta, & Cox, 2000). Professionals claim that social skills are not inherent in the individual, and students' opportunities to learn are greatly diminished without those skills, and thus many educators in the field of special education have argued that social skills should be taught explicitly and systematically. Social skills are defined as a set of competencies that (a) promote positive social relationships, contribute to peer acceptance and friendship development, (b) lead to satisfactory school adjustment, and (c) allow students to cope with and adapt to the demands of the school environment (Gresham, Van, & Cook, 2006).

Four steps have been suggested to consider when implementing social skills instruction in the classroom (Lane, Wehby, Little, & Cooley, 2005; Warger & Rutherford, 1993). The first step is to identify students who exhibit significant deficits in social skills (Lane et al., 2005). The second is to determine desirable social skills. When teachers define social skills that they expect target students to exhibit, factors such as students' characteristics, cultural values, community norms, and parental expectations should be taken into consideration (Kauffman, 2010). Third, it is important to distinguish between students who cannot perform a given skill and those who have the ability to perform the skill but fail or decline to do so (Gresham, Sugai, & Horner, 2001). Finally, the identified social skill should be directly and systematically taught to target students, and their efforts to engage appropriately in the behavior need to be reinforced (Lane et al., 2005).

Numerous studies have applied social skills instruction to students in elementary schools and reported positive results. For example, Dunleavy, Karwowski, and Shudes-Eitel (1997) reported social skills instruction improved conflict resolution skills of fourth-grade students from socially and culturally disadvantaged backgrounds and decreased the amount of time teachers spent correcting problem behaviors. Similarly, Leffert, Brady, and Siperstein (2009) found the value of class-wide implementation of social skills training for at-risk students.

Function-Based Intervention

To ensure that the tiered system of support is in place for addressing the needs of students with persistent problem behavior in the classroom, there must be processes in place for supporting those students with ongoing problem behavior. It is widely accepted that individualized PBIS using a functional approach to problem behavior should be implemented for students with the most challenging behavior. As described in Chapter 5, functional behavior assessment is the critical part of designing a function-based intervention. However, developing a function-based intervention that is technically sound and consistent with the basic principles of behavior is a challenge for school personnel. Researchers have agreed that the field lacks a standardized program model of individualized PBIS suitable for a widespread application by school personnel (Dunlap, Iovannone, Wilson, Kincaid, & Strain, 2010). Furthermore, very little research has focused on implementation of the individualized interventions within a continuum of behavior supports in the classroom.

The literature indicates that most function-based interventions have key features such as: (a) providing frequent teacher attention (Kamps, Wendland, & Culpepper, 2006); (b) reducing task duration and breaking down task steps (Moore, Anderson, & Kumar, 2005); (c) providing choice and preference (Dunlap et al., 1994; Peterson, Caniglia, & Royster, 2001); (d) interspersing instruction between preferred activities (Blair, Liaupsin, Umbreit, & Kweon, 2006; Noell, Whitmarsh, VanDerHeyden, Gatti, & Slider, 2003); (e) using visual cue cards (Conroy, Asmus, Sellers, & Ladwig, 2005); (f) teaching self-management skills, social skills, and other appropriate behaviors (Kamps et al., 2006; Lewis & Sugai, 1996); (g) withholding reinforcement (Asmus et al., 1999). The intervention strategies focus on (a) removing or altering the antecedent conditions that evoke the problem behavior, (b) developing alternative behaviors by providing appropriate reinforcers, and (c) eliminating the consequences that maintain the problem behavior.

Cho and Blair (2013) evaluated a team-based individualized PBIS approach that included a functional behavioral assessment, designing and implementing a multi-component intervention plan, and a technique for monitoring progress. The goal of the intervention was to prevent behavior problems and increase academic engagement of two sixth-grade students with attention deficit hyperactivity disorder attending a highly structured special education school. The researchers trained the classroom teacher to modify activities, provide visual cues, transition activities, and teach self-regulation skills. The results showed that the students' problem behavior decreased while their academic engagement increased during reading, writing, and math instruction. Social validity with the classroom teacher indicated that the PBIS process and outcome were acceptable.

Although selecting evidence-based intervention strategies is critical, implementing a continuum of intervention is needed. The continuum of intervention should include intervention options of varying intensity that can be linked to the specific needs of students with behavioral challenges. Schools should establish a clear process for determining which students are having problem behavior and selecting intervention strategies through a team-based process. Although students who are unresponsive to the continuum of supports available at primary and secondary interventions might be moved to a tertiary intervention to receive more intensive intervention, for some students who are experiencing very severe or significant behavioral and social emotional problems, providing Tier 3 intervention should be considered rather than delaying access to the intervention.

Issues Related to Implementing Class-Wide PBIS and Teacher Training

While special education teachers are adequately prepared to manage behavior problems in the classroom, the majority of teachers in general education enter the teaching profession without taking a single course on behavior management (Barrett & Davis, 1993; Evertson & Weinstein, 2006). This finding is troublesome considering the fast increase of students with disabilities fully or partly included in general education classrooms. As simple as it may sound, implementing a continuum of support in classrooms requires training, coaching, and ongoing support. It is suggested that a SWPBIS team must identify classrooms that continue to struggle with student behavioral issues, using the same problem-solving, behavioral support approach that has been applied to the entire school level.

Classroom Assessments

To determine whether there is a need for classroom support, the school PBIS team needs to determine how indicative office discipline referral (ODR) data are to a school-system-wide issue or just an issue for a few individual teachers. To get a better understanding of the classroom issues, the SWPBIS team should review the ODR data and determine if there is a Pareto Distribution of classrooms generating a large proportion of referrals or specific types of problem behaviors the teachers are referring. A high number of referrals for classroom disruption will indicate a need for additional assessment and intervention at the classroom level, and possibly additional training and support for an individual teacher.

Various instruments have been developed for classroom assessments. First, the *Classroom Management: Self-Assessment Revised* (Simonsen et al., 2006) is used to (a) determine the extent to which effective general classroom management practices are in place and (b) develop an action plan for enhancement/ maintenance based on this information. It is designed for a teacher to rate him- or herself and develop an action plan in the areas of five critical features of effective classroom management: (1) maximize structure in the classroom; (2) post, teach, review, monitor, and reinforce positively stated expectations; (3) activity engage students in observable ways; (4) establish a continuum of strategies to acknowledge appropriate behavior; and (5) establish a continuum of strategies to respond to inappropriate behavior. For example, to maximize structure in the classroom, the classroom teachers should be able to develop predictable routines and design an environment to elicit age-appropriate behavior and to minimize crowding and distraction. Potential action plan items may include rearranging furniture to ensure better supervision and designating staff and student areas. It is recommended that the teachers complete this assessment at least quarterly. The tool may also be used by a supervisor to evaluate a teacher and provide specific and contingent feedback that will assist in the development of an action plan.

Second, the Classroom Assessment Tool (CAT) is an instrument designed to assist the SWPBIS team in identifying areas of strengths or improvement for the classroom (Florida's Positive Behavior Support Project, 2008). The CAT assesses whether certain classroom ecological, classroom behavior systems, and curricular/instructional variables are in place. The CAT can be completed through either an interview or a teacher self-evaluation checklist. Finally, the Classroom Intervention Plan (CIP) helps the SWPBIS team (or a classroom teacher) identify necessary elements and action plan for each element in implementing a class-wide intervention plan (see a blank form of the CAT and CIP at the end of the chapter).

Class-Wide Consultation

Numerous researchers have pointed out that interventions are often implemented without integrity because they are infeasible or perceived by classroom staff as unacceptable (Noell, Witt, Gilbertson, Ranier, & Freeland, 1997; Jensen, Hoagwood, & Trickett, 1999). Therefore, school-based consultation targeting the classroom level should be provided as an efficient method for improving classroom practices. There is a wide consensus on the use of the problem-solving model in providing class-wide consultation (Tilly, Reschly, & Grimes, 1999). The problem-solving model emphasizes team-based decision making.

Reinke and colleagues (2007) developed the Classroom Check-Up (CCU), a class-wide consultation model to provide classroom level support. The model addresses treatment integrity issues common to school-based consultation. CCU focuses on (a) fostering targeting teachers' motivation to maintain current practices important for student success, (b) reducing negative teacher-student interactions that exacerbate problem behaviors, and (c) increasing teacher behaviors that may promote student competence and success. CCU lists various steps that teachers perform, including classroom assessment, performance feedback, intervention menu development, intervention selection, and self-monitoring of implementation. Reinke et al. implemented the CCU with visual performance feedback and found that it increased the number of classroom management strategies that teachers use, which in turn decreased classroom disruptive behavior.

Supporting Students with CLD Backgrounds
As described earlier, CLD students (especially African American students) experience disproportionately high numbers of office discipline referrals, harsher punishments for behavioral violations, suspension and expulsion. A study with 33 elementary teachers working with predominantly African American students found that teachers using high rates of harsh reprimands reported feeling less efficacious and more emotionally exhausted (Reinke, Herman, & Stormont, 2013). The class-wide PBIS has the potential to improve outcomes for students who are CLD and to accurately determine which students need additional secondary and tertiary support interventions. It will take a great deal of professional development and support for classroom staff to implement the class-wide PBIS with fidelity, which has been described in Chapter 3. Before deciding whether or not a student is responding to the universal support, it is essential to assess the classroom using the Classroom Assessment Tool (CAT) and determine how well the class-wide support is being implemented.

Conclusion

It's estimated that more than 14,000 schools in the United States are currently implementing school-wide PBIS, yet teachers (including those of CLD students in urban schools) continue to struggle with establishing effective classroom routines and structure, and managing disruptive behaviors in their classrooms (Pavri, 2004). In this chapter, we have reviewed a variety of strategies effective for implementing the three-tier Positive Behavioral Interventions and Supports at the classroom level. Although more research has to be done on class-wide PBIS, particularly effective strategies for addressing a more individualized intervention for students within the classroom routines and activities, the existing research provides evidence that the class-wide PBIS has great potential to improve educational outcomes for CLD students. Given that students spend a large amount of time at school and likely experience problems in the classroom, pulling students out of class for intervention should be avoided whenever possible. Effectively meeting the social and academic needs of all students in the classroom should be emphasized through a continuum of interventions varying in intensity. Thus, schools serving a large number of CLD students in urban settings are urged to provide professional development workshops and coaching for teachers to implement the class-wide PBIS with fidelity in order for all students to maximize optimal educational outcomes.

References

Asmus, J. M., Wacker, D. P., Harding, J., Berg, W. K., Derby, M., & Kocis, E. (1999). Evaluation of antecedent stimulus parameters for the treatment of escape-maintained aberrant behavior. *Journal of Applied Behavior Analysis, 32,* 495–513.

Barrett, E. R., & Davis, S. (1993). Perceptions of beginning teachers' needs in classroom management. *Teacher Education and Practice, 11,* 22–27.

Barrish, H. H., Saunders, M., & Wolf, M. M. (1969). Good Behavior Game: Effects of individual contingencies for group consequences on disruptive behavior in a classroom. *Journal of Applied Behavior Analysis, 2,* 119–124.

Baybak, A. E., Luze, G. J., & Kamps, D. M. (2000). The Good Student Game: Behavior management for diverse classrooms. *Intervention in School and Clinic, 35,* 216–223.

Blair, K., Liaupsin, C. J., Umbreit, J., & Kweon, G. (2006). Function-based intervention to support the inclusive placements of young children in Korea. *Education and Training in Developmental Disabilities, 41*(1), 48.

Bradshaw, C. P., Mitchell, M. M., & Leaf, P. J. (2010). Examining the effects of School-Wide Positive Behavioral Interventions and Supports on student outcomes results from a randomized controlled effectiveness trial in elementary schools. *Journal of Positive Behavior Interventions, 12*(3), 133–148.

Burden, P. (2006). *Classroom management: Creating a successful K–12 learning community.* Hoboken, NJ: Wiley.

Cho, S., & Blair, K. C. (2013). *Using Positive Behavior Support to increase academic engagement of a student with ADHD.* Manuscript submitted for publication.

Cihak, D., Kirk, E., & Boon, R. (2009). Effects of classwide positive peer "tootling" to reduce the disruptive classroom behaviors of elementary students with and without disabilities. *Journal of Behavioral Education, 18,* 267–278.

Conroy, M. A., Asmus, J. M., Sellers, J. A., & Ladwig, C. N. (2005). The use of an antecedent-based intervention to decrease stereotypic behavior in a general education classroom: A case study. *Focus on Autism and Other Developmental Disabilities, 20,* 223–230.

Crone, D. A., Horner, R. H., & Hawken, L. S. (2004). *Responding to problem behavior in schools: The behavior education program.* New York: Guilford Press.

Darveaux, D. X. (1984). The Good Behavior Game plus merit: Controlling disruptive behavior and improving student motivation. *School Psychology Review, 13,* 510–518.

Dunbar, C. (2004). *Best practices in classroom management.* Michigan State University. Retrieved from https://www.msu.edu/~dunbarc/dunbar3.pdf

Dunlap, G., DePerczel, M., Clarke, S., Wilson, D., Wright, S., White, R., & Gomez, A. (1994). Choice making to promote adaptive behavior for students with emotional and behavioral challenges. *Journal of Applied Behavior Analysis, 27,* 505–518.

Dunlap, G., Iovannone, R., Wilson, K. J., Kincaid, D. K., & Strain, P. (2010). Prevent-Teach-Reinforce: A standardized model of school-based behavioral intervention. *Journal of Positive Behavior Interventions, 12,* 9–22.

Dunleavy, S., Karwowski, S., & Shudes-Eitel, J. (1997). *Improving social interaction among 4th grade students through social skills instruction*. Distributed by ERIC Clearinghouse.

Evertson, C. M., & Weinstein, C. S. (2006). Classroom management as a field of inquiry. In C. M. Evertson & C. S. Weinstein (Eds.), *Handbook of classroom management: Research, practice, and contemporary issues* (pp. 3–15). Mahwah, NJ: Lawrence Erlbaum.

Fairbanks, S., Simonsen, B., & Sugai, G. (2008). Classwide secondary and tertiary tier practices and systems. *Teaching Exceptional Children*, *40*(6), 44–52.

Filter, K. J., McKenna, M. K., Benedict, E. A., Horner, R. H., Todd, A. W., & Watson, J. (2007). Check In/Check Out: A post-hoc evaluation of an efficient, secondary level targeted intervention for reducing problem behaviors in schools. *Education and Treatment of Children*, *30*, 69–84.

Florida's Positive Behavior Support Project (2008). *Classroom Assessment Tool*. University of South Florida. Retrieved from http://www.pbis.org/evaluation/evaluation_tools.aspx

Gable, R. A., Arllen, N. L., & Hendrickson, J. M. (1994). Use of students with emotional/behavioral disorders as behavior change agents. *Education & Treatment of Children*, *17*(3), 267–276.

George, H. P., Harrower, J. K., & Knoster, T. (2003). School-wide prevention and early intervention: A process for establishing a system of school-wide behavior support. *Preventing School Failure: Alternative Education for Children and Youth*, *47*(4), 170–176.

Greenwood, C. R., Terry, B., Marquis, J., & Walker, D. (1994). Confirming a performance-based instructional model. *School Psychology Review*, *23*, 652–668.

Gresham, F. M., Sugai, G., & Horner, R. H. (2001). Interpreting outcomes of social skills training for students with high-incidence disabilities. *Exceptional Children*, *67*(3), 331–344.

Gresham, F. M., Van, M. B., & Cook, C. R. (2006). Social skills training for teaching replacement behaviors: Remediating acquisition deficits in at-risk students. *Behavioral Disorders*, *31*(4), 363–377.

Hawken, L., MacLeod, K., & Rawlings, L. (2007). Effects of the Behavior Education Program (BEP) on problem behavior with elementary school students. *Journal of Positive Behavior Interventions*, *9*, 94–101.

Hieneman, M., Dunlap, G., & Kincaid, D. (2005). Positive support strategies for students with behavioral disorders in general education settings. *Psychology in the Schools*, *42*, 779–794.

Horner, R. H., Sugai, G., Smolkowski, K., Eber, L., Nakasato, J., Todd, A. W., & Esperanza, J. (2009). A randomized, wait-list controlled effectiveness trial assessing School-Wide Positive Behavior Support in elementary schools. *Journal of Positive Behavior Interventions*, *11*(3), 133–144.

Horner, R. H., Sugai, G., Todd, A. W., & Lewis-Palmer, T. (2005). School-Wide Positive Behavior Support. In L. M. Bambara & L. Kern (Eds.), *Individualized supports for students with problem behaviors* (pp. 359–390). New York: Guilford Press.

Jensen, P. S., Hoagwood, K., & Trickett, E. J. (1999). Ivory towers or earthen trenches? Community collaborations to foster real-world research. *Applied Developmental Science, 3*(4), 206–212. doi:10.1207/s1532480xads0304_4

Kalis, T. M., Vannest, K. J., & Parker, R. (2007). Praise counts: Using self-monitoring to increase effective teaching practices. *Preventing School Failure, 51*, 20–27.

Kamps, D., Wendland, M., & Culpepper, M. (2006). Active teacher participation in functional behavior assessment for students with emotional and behavioral disorders risks in general education classrooms. *Behavioral Disorders, 31*(2), 123–146.

Kauffman, J. M. (2010). *The tragicomedy of public education: Laughing, crying, thinking, fixing*. Verona, WI: Attainment.

Kline, S., Simpson, R. L., Blesz, D. P., Smith Myles, B., & Carter, W. J. (2001). School reform and multicultural learners with emotional and behavioral disorders: Issues, challenges, and solutions. In C. A. Utley & F. E. Obiakor (Eds.), *Special education, multicultural education, and school reform: Components of quality education for learners with mild disabilities* (pp. 118–139). Springfield, IL: Charles C Thomas.

Lane, K. L., Wehby, J. H., Little, M. A., & Cooley, C. (2005). Students educated in self-contained classes and self-contained schools: Part II—How do they progress over time? *Behavior Disorders, 30*, 363–374.

Leffert, J. S., Brady, M. E., & Siperstein, G. N. (2009, December). A "Tools for Teachers" approach for infusing social skills instruction into daily teaching activities. *Teaching Exceptional Children Plus, 6*(2). Retrieved from http://journals.cec.sped.org/cgi/viewcontent.cgi?article=1585&context=tecplus

Lewis, T. J., & Sugai, G. (1996). Functional assessment of problem behavior: A pilot investigation of the comparative and interactive effects of teacher and peer social attention on students in general education settings. *School Psychology Quarterly, 11*, 1–19.

Lohrmann, S., & Talerico, J. (2004). Anchor the boat: A classwide intervention to reduce problem behavior. *Journal of Positive Behavior Interventions, 6*(2), 113–120.

Moore, D. W., Anderson, A., & Kumar, K. (2005). Instructional adaptation in the management of escape-motivated behaviors in a general education classroom. *Journal for Positive Behavior Interventions, 7*(4), 216–223.

Muscott, H. S., Mann, E. L., & LeBrun, M. R. (2008). Positive Behavioral Interventions and Supports in New Hampshire: Effects of large-scale implementation of School-Wide Positive Behavior Support on student discipline and academic achievement. *Journal of Positive Behavior Interventions, 10*(3), 190–205.

Noell, G. H., Whitmarsh, E. L., VanDerHeyden, A. M., Gatti, S. L., & Slider, N. J. (2003). Sequencing instructional tasks: A comparison of contingent and non-contingent interspersal of preferred academic tasks. *Behavior Modification, 27*, 191–216.

Noell, G. H., Witt, J. C., Gilbertson, D. N., Ranier, D. D., & Freeland, J. T. (1997). Increasing teacher intervention implementation in general education settings through consultation and performance feedback. *School Psychology Quarterly, 12*(1), 77–88.

Pavri, S. (2004). General and special education teacher's preparation needs in providing social support: A needs assessment. *Teacher Education and Special Education*, *27*, 433–443. doi:org/10.1177/088840640402700410

Peterson, S. M. P., Caniglia, C., & Royster, A. J. (2001). Application of choice-making intervention for a student with multiply maintained problem behavior. *Focus on Autism and Other Developmental Disabilities*, *16*(4), 240–246.

Reinke, W. M., Herman, K. C., & Stormont, M. (2013). Classroom-level Positive Behavior Supports in schools implementing SW-PBIS: Identifying areas for enhancement. *Journal of Positive Behavior Interventions*, *15*, 39–50.

Reinke, W. M., Lewis-Palmer, T., & Martin, E. (2007). The effect of visual performance feedback on teacher behavior-specific praise. *Behavior Modification*, *31*, 247–263.

Rimm-Kaufman, S. E., Pianta, R. C., & Cox, M. J. (2000). Teacher's judgments of problems in the transition to kindergarten. *Early Childhood Research Quarterly*, *15*, 147–166.

Safran, S. P., & Oswald, K. (2003). Positive Behavior Supports: Can schools reshape disciplinary practices? *Exceptional Children*, *69*(3), 361–373.

Sailor, W., Dunlap, G., Sugai, G., & Horner, R. (Eds.). (2008). *Handbook of Positive Behavior Support*. New York: Springer.

Scheuermann, B. K., & Hall, J. A. (2008). *Positive Behavioral Supports for the classroom*. Upper Saddle River, NJ: Pearson/Merrill Prentice Hall.

Scott, T., Park, K. L., Swain-Bradway, J., & Landers, E. (2007). Positive Behavior Support in the classroom: Facilitating behaviorally inclusive learning environments. *International Journal of Behavioral Consultation and Therapy*, *3*(2), 223–235. Retrieved from http://files.eric.ed.gov/fulltext/EJ801199.pdf

Shores, R. E., Gunter, P. L., Denny, R. K., & Jack, S. L. (1993). Classroom influences on aggressive and disruptive behaviors of students with emotional and behavioral disorders. *Focus on Exceptional Children*, *26*(2), 1–9.

Simonsen, B., Fairbanks, S., Briesch, A., Myers, D., & Sugai, G. (2008). Evidence-based practices in classroom management: Considerations for research to practice. *Education and Treatment of Children*, *31*(3), 351–380.

Simonsen, B., Fairbanks, S., Briesch, A., & Sugai, G. (2006). 7r. Positive Behavior Support. Classroom management: Self-assessment revised. University of Connecticut, Center on Positive Behavioral Interventions and Supports.

Skiba, R. J., Horner, R. H., Chung, C. G., Karega Rausch, M., May, S. L., & Tobin, T. (2011). Race is not neutral: A national investigation of African American and Latino disproportionality in school discipline. *School Psychology Review*, *40*(1), 85.

Skiba, R. J., Michael, R. S., Nardo, A. C., & Peterson, R. L. (2002). The color of discipline: Sources of racial and gender disproportionality in school punishment. *The Urban Review*, *34*(4), 317–342.

Skinner, C. H., Belfiore, P. J., Mace, H. W., Williams-Wilson, S., & Johns, G. A. (1997). Altering response topography to increase response efficiency and learning rates. *School Psychology Quarterly*, *12*(1), 54.

Skinner, C. H., Skinner, A. L., & Sterling-Turner, H. E. (2002). Best practices in contingency management: Application of individual and group contingencies in educational settings. In A. Thomas & J. Grimes (Eds.), *Best Practices in School Psychology* (pp. 817–830). Bethesda, MD: National Association of School Psychologists.

Skinner, C. H., Smith, E. S., & McLean, J. E. (1994). The effects of intertrial interval duration on sight-word learning rates in children with behavioral disorders. *Behavioral Disorders, 19*, 98–107.

Stichter, J., & Lewis, T. J. (2006). Classroom assessment: Targeting variables to improve instruction through a multi-level eco-behavioral model. In M. Hersen (Ed.), *Clinician's handbook of child behavioral assessment* (pp. 569–586). Burlington, MA: Elsevier.

Stormont, M., & Reinke, W. (2009). The importance of precorrective statements and behavior-specific praise and strategies to increase their use. *Beyond Behavior, 18*(3), 26–32.

Sugai, G., Horner, R. H., Dunlap, G., Hieneman, M., Lewis, T. J., Nelson, C. M., & Ruef, M. (2000). Applying Positive Behavior Support and functional behavioral assessment in schools. *Journal of Positive Behavior Interventions, 2*(3), 131–143.

Tilly, W. D., Reschly, D. J., & Grimes, J. (1999). Disability determination in problem solving systems: Conceptual foundations and critical components. In D. J. Reschly, W. D. Tilly III, & J. P. Grimes (Eds.), *Special education in transition: Functional assessment and noncategorical programming* (pp. 285–321). Frederick, CO: Sopris West.

Tingstrom, D. H., Sterling-Turner, H. E., & Wilczynski, S. M. (2006). The Good Behavior Game: 1969–2002. *Behavior Modification, 30*, 225–253.

Turco, T. L., & Elliott, S. N. (1990). Acceptability and effectiveness of group contingencies for improving spelling achievement. *Journal of School Psychology, 28*(1), 27–37.

Warger, C. L., & Rutherford Jr., R. B. (1993). Co-teaching to improve social skills. *Preventing School Failure: Alternative Education for Children and Youth, 37*(4), 21–27.

Warren, J., Edmonson, H., Griggs, P., Lassen, S., McCart, A., Turnbull, A., & Sailor, W. (2003). Urban applications of School-Wide Positive Behavior Support: Critical issues and lessons learned. *Journal of Positive Behavior Interventions, 5*, 80–91.

Wright, R. A., & McCurdy, B. L. (2011). Classwide Positive Behavior Support and group contingencies: Examining a positive variation of the Good Behavior Game. *Journal of Positive Behavior Interventions*. doi:10.1177/1098300711421008

Classroom Management: Self-Assessment Revised

Teacher____________________	Rater____________________	Date____________	
Instructional Activity		Time Start________ Time End ________	
Tally each Positive Student Contacts	Total #	Tally each Negative Student Contacts	Total #
Ratio[1] of Positives to Negatives: _____ to 1			

Classroom Management Practice	Rating
1. *I have arranged my classroom to **minimize crowding and distraction***	Yes No
2. *I have **maximized structure and predictability** in my classroom (e.g., explicit classroom routines, specific directions).*	Yes No
3. *I have posted, taught, reviewed, and reinforced 3-5 **positively stated expectations** (or rules).*	Yes No
4. *I provided **more frequent acknowledgement** for appropriate behaviors than inappropriate behaviors (See top of page).*	Yes No
5. *I provided each student with **multiple opportunities to respond** and participate during instruction.*	Yes No
6. *My instruction **actively engages** students in observable ways (e.g., writing, verbalizing)*	Yes No
7. *I **actively supervised** my classroom (e.g., moving, scanning) during instruction.*	Yes No
8. *I provided **quick, direct, explicit reprimands/redirections** in response to inappropriate behavior.*	Yes No
9. *I have **multiple strategies/systems** in place to **acknowledge** appropriate behavior (e.g., class point systems, praise).*	Yes No
10. *In general, I have provided **specific feedback** in response to social and academic behavior errors as well as correct responses.*	Yes No
Overall classroom management score: *10-8 "yes" = "**Super**"* *7-5 "yes" = "**So-So**"* *<5 "yes" = "**Improvement Needed**"*	# Yes________

[1] To calculate, divide # positives by # of negatives.

Action Planning

The purposes of this assessment are to (a) determine the extent to which effective general classroom management practices are in place and (b) develop an action plan for enhancement/maintenance based on this information. This assessment and action plan can be completed as a "self-assessment" or by an observer.

1. Pick a teacher-led/directed activity that has a specific learning outcome/objective.
2. During the activity, count number of positive and negative student contacts that occur during the activity.
3. After the activity,
   a. Sum the number of positive and negative contacts and calculate the ratio of positive to negative contacts.
   b. Assess whether each classroom management practice was evident
   c. Sum the number of "yes" to determine overall classroom management score.
   d. Based upon your score, develop an action plan for enhancement/maintenance.

Action Plan		
#	Current Level of Performance	Enhancement/Maintenance Strategies[2]

[2] What? When? How? By When?

Note. Simonsen, B., Fairbanks, S., Briesch, A., & Sugai, G. (2006). Positive Behavior Support: Classroom management self-assessment revised. http://www.pbis.org/pbis_resource_detail_page.aspx?Type=4&PBIS_ResourceID=174

CLASSROOM ASSISTANCE TOOL

Recorder or Observer:	Date:
School:	Classroom/Teacher:
Comments:	

I. ECOLOGICAL FACTORS: Various aspects of the environment are altered to prevent or address behavior problems.

A.	**Physical Setting-** The physical classroom setting is organized in a manner that promotes learning and independence.	**In place**	**Some what in place**	**Not in place**
A1.	Are unnecessary or distracting items removed from view and reach?	☐	☐	☐
A2.	Are all materials organized and easily accessible?	☐	☐	☐
A3.	Do students have secure and adequate spaces for personal storage?	☐	☐	☐
A4.	Has furniture been placed to decrease traffic flow challenges?	☐	☐	☐
A5.	Do instructional areas have clear visual boundaries for students?	☐	☐	☐
A6.	Are rules posted and written in words that all can read and/or are those rules illustrated with graphics or icons	☐	☐	☐
B.	**Scheduling-** The scheduling of instruction occurs in a manner that optimizes student learning.	**In place**	**Some what in place**	**Not in place**
B1.	Is the daily schedule of activities posted and reviewed regularly?	☐	☐	☐
B2.	Are transitions & non-instructional activities posted and reviewed regularly?	☐	☐	☐
B3.	Does the daily schedule provide each student with regular time for independent work, 1 to 1 instruction, small and large group activities, socialization, and free time?	☐	☐	☐
B4.	Does each student spend most of his/her time engaged in active learning activities, with little or no unstructured downtime?	☐	☐	☐
C.	**Socialization-** Opportunities for social instruction and social environments occur in a manner that optimizes student learning.	**In place**	**Some what in place**	**Not in place**
C1.	Is there an emphasis on the development of individual responsibility for each student?	☐	☐	☐
C2.	Is there a process for regular (at least weekly) communication between the teacher and family?	☐	☐	☐

C3.	Are skills taught in the setting and situation in which they are naturally needed?	☐	☐	☐
C4.	Are friendships between students promoted?	☐	☐	☐
C5.	Are classroom assistants actively involved with students in a manner that promotes independence, learning, and interaction with peers?	☐	☐	☐
C6.	Are effective, efficient communication strategies being used or taught?	☐	☐	☐
C7.	Are students with disabilities given opportunities to interact and socialize with more typical peers?	☐	☐	☐

2. CLASSROOM BEHAVIOR SYSTEM: A behavior system is developed ar d implemented to prevent or address behavior problems.

D.	A. Define and Teach Behavior	In place	Some what in place	Not in place
D1	Are there clearly defined, positively stated expectations and rules for the classroom (2-3 Classroom Expectations)?	☐	☐	☐
D2	Are behavior referrals (those handled by the office as well as ones managed in the classroom) clearly defined and differentiated?	☐	☐	☐
D3	Is there a system for teaching and practicing behavior expectations and rules to students?	☐	☐	☐
D4	Are data collected from classroom settings analyzed frequently and used to guide ongoing behavior support decisions?	☐	☐	☐
	B. Reward System	**In place**	**Some what in place**	**Not in place**
D5	Does a reward/recognition system for appropriate behavior exist in the classroom?	☐	☐	☐
D6	Are there specific criteria in place for earning rewards and are students aware of the specific criteria?	☐	☐	☐
D7	Are students always eligible to earn rewards?	☐	☐	☐
D8	Are rewards that have been earned taken away or threatened to be removed?	☐	☐	☐
D9	Are rewards age appropriate and accessible to a diverse group of students?	☐	☐	☐
D10	Is specific behavioral praise provided at a rate of 4 positives to every 1 corrective statement?	☐	☐	☐
	C. Consequence System	**In place**	**Some what in place**	**Not in place**
D11	Are data on student performance displayed prominently?	☐	☐	☐
D12	Are the consequences for rule violations preplanned?	☐	☐	☐

D13	Are consequences delivered consistently, respectfully, and in a timely manner?	☐	☐	☐
D14	Are students reminded of their choices in a calm, positive manner prior to escalation[???] in behavior?	☐	☐	☐
D15	Is there a formal system for communicating and involving parents that does not rely entirely on students as the messengers?	☐	☐	☐
D16	Are there positive strategies in place to strengthen home/school partnership?	☐	☐	☐
D17	Are there additional strategies for students who do not respond to class wide expectations?	☐	☐	☐

3. CURRICULUM AND INSTRUCTION: Materials and instructional presentation are altered or adapted to prevent or address behavior problems.

E.	**Instructional Planning And Delivery-** Teaching activities are planned and implemented in ways that optimize student learning.	**In place**	**Some what in place**	**Not in place**
E1	Are lesson objectives and materials used appropriate for students' functioning levels?	☐	☐	☐
E2	Are assignments relevant and meaningful to students?	☐	☐	☐
E3	Are a variety of teaching methods and materials used?	☐	☐	☐
E4	Are appropriate lengths of time provided for the tasks assigned?	☐	☐	☐
E5	Are oral directions paired with pictures, icons, or words that students can read?	☐	☐	☐
E6	Is the pace of instruction appropriate for the needs of all students?	☐	☐	☐
E7	Are student checks for understanding conducted frequently both after directions are delivered and while task is being completed?	☐	☐	☐
E8	Are students provided opportunities to make choices within and/or across tasks?	☐	☐	☐
E9	Is specific academic praise provided during guided and independent practice?	☐	☐	☐
E10	Is corrective feedback provided promptly and positively during guided practice?	☐	☐	☐
E11	Are adaptations made to meet individual student needs?	☐	☐	☐

SUMMARY OF POSITIVE BEHAVIOR SUPPORTS IN CLASSROOM SETTINGS

	Total Marked In Place	Total Somewhat In Place	Total Marked Not In Place
1. Ecological Factors	___ of 17 = ___%	___ of 17 = ___%	___ of 17 = ___%
2. Classroom Behavior Systems	___ of 17 = ___%	___ of 17 = ___%	___ of 17 = ___%
3. Curriculum and Instruction	___ of 17 = ___%	___ of 17 = ___%	___ of 17 = ___%

ACTION PLANNING

1. List the major strengths of the system for classroom environments, **(refer to results above rated *In Place*)**	
2. List the major areas in need of improving Positive Behavior Support for the classroom environment. **(refer to results above rated *Not in place* or *Somewhat in place*)**	
3. Identify next steps for making specific changes to areas of concern.	

CLASSROOM INTERVENTION PLAN
Developed from CAT Tool

Date: School:

Classroom/Teacher:

TEACHING BEHAVIOR	**Classroom Expectations & Rules** (3-5 positively stated. Rules must be stated in a way that compliance is observable.)		
	Teaching Behavior (how you will teach, when will you re-teach, how you will remind students, etc.)		
	Classroom Procedures (daily routine, when to sharpen pencils, turn in homework, get a hall pass, etc.)		
REWARD SYSTEMS	**Reward System** (in addition to the school-wide tokens, how will you recognize appropriate behavior)		
RESPONDING	**Responding to Problem Behavior** (system for dealing with students who decline to follow rules and procedures)		
ENVIRONMENT	**Action plan**	**Resources**	**Status** ☐ Initiated ☐ Somewhat in place ☐ In place
CURRICULUM & INSTRUCTION	**Action plan**	**Resources**	**Status** ☐ Initiated ☐ Somewhat in place ☐ In place

Note. Florida's Positive Behavior Support Project: A Multi-Tiered Support System (2008). http://flpbs.fmhi.usf.edu/resources_classroom.cfm

Section III

7. *Culturally Responsive Positive Behavior Intervention and Support for Culturally and Linguistically Diverse Students Suspected of Having Behavior Problems*

TACHELLE BANKS AND FESTUS E. OBIAKOR

The overrepresentation of culturally and linguistically diverse (CLD) students in suspensions and expulsions, office discipline referrals (ODRs), and corporal punishment has been well documented (Raffaele-Mendez & Knoff, 2003; Skiba, Michael, Nardo, & Peterson, 2002; Wald & Losen, 2003). Research suggests that differential expectations between the home and school lives of CLD students may contribute to this disciplinary disproportionality (Cartledge, Tillman, & Talbert-Johnson, 2001; Neal, McCray, Webb-Johnson, & Bridgest, 2003; Perry, Steele, & Hilliard, 2003; Skiba et al., 2002; Townsend, 2000, 2002). Classrooms are not culturally neutral terrains, but rather are constructed around sets of norms, values, and expected behaviors that are culturally bound. Likewise, students bring into the classroom a host of culturally bound expectations about learning and behavior. Classroom norms and expectations often align with White middle-class values and orientations such as individual praise (Lerman, 2000), competition (Boykin, Tyler, & Miller, 2005; Gay, 2000), individualism (Boykin et al., 2005), and linear thinking and communication patterns (Hale-Benson, 1986; Swartz, 2004).

Culturally responsive practices involve utilizing the cultural knowledge, life experiences, and learning styles of CLD students to make learning more relevant and effective for them (Obiakor, 2008). By building on the knowledge and strengths students bring with them to the classroom from their homes and communities, culturally responsive practice can validate who they are and set high expectations for behavior and learning. It works to comprehensively create an environment where diversity is affirmed and to establish a cultural lens for determining normative behavior and learning expectations (Gay, 2000; King, 2004; Nieto, 2004). Typically, Positive Behavioral Interventions and Supports (PBIS) involves individualized and sustained decision-making, planning, and problem solving, which are intertwined with instructional foci directed toward behavioral expectations. Combining PBIS with cultural and linguistic variables will help to enhance the positive behavior of CLD students. This is the premise of this chapter.

Punitive Disciplinary Practices

Punitive measures have often been employed to address behavioral offenses that occur during the school day. Attention has been given to early identification and intervention in young children to prevent the development and intensification of problem behavior. The literature is clear that addressing the social behavioral needs of children in the early developmental and school years is a worthwhile societal investment (Walker, Ramsey, & Gresham, 2004). It is equally important to prevent the occurrence and worsening of problem behavior in preadolescent and adolescent youth (Biglan, 1995). However, high schools tend to respond to persistent and serious problem behavior by adopting a "get tough" approach. This consists of (a) repeating and restating consequences, (b) increasing the aversiveness of consequences, (c) establishing a bottom line or zero-tolerance level, (d) excluding the student from the "privilege" of attending school through suspensions and expulsions, and (e) offering alternative ways of completing the high school degree in another location (e.g., alternative school, community college) (Sugai & Horner, 2002).

Zero-tolerance policies evolved out of state and federal efforts during the "war on drugs" of the 1980s (Rice, 2009; Teske, 2011). The philosophy behind the effort posited that strict punitive measures would prevent crime and protect law-abiding citizens by removing criminal offenders from the general population. Zero tolerance was conceived as a "one strike" measure during an era of heightened security, and was supported by numerous factions as intense punitive measures were associated with a "tough on crime" stance (Swain & Noblit, 2011). The punishment associated with zero tolerance was theorized to be swift, severe, and certain (Rice, 2009).

In 1994, with the passage of the Gun-Free Schools Act (GFSA), the zero tolerance philosophy was expanded to include American schools. Educational funding requirements contained within the GFSA required a mandatory, one-year expulsion for any student caught carrying a firearm on a school campus (Rice, 2009; Teske, 2011). Many school districts embraced the zero tolerance philosophy as a way to remove subjective influences from student disciplinary procedures (American Psychological Association, 2008), relieve educators of the need to exercise deliberation and critical judgment (Giroux, 2003), and remove dangerous students, while simultaneously sending a strong message of deterrence to others (American Psychological Association, 2008; Gregory & Cornell, 2009). By the 1996–1997 school year, 94% of schools had zero-tolerance policies toward firearms, 91% for other weaponry, 88% for drugs, and 87% for alcohol (Dupper, 2010). Zero tolerance policies have recently been applied to non-violent offenses such as insubordination, and have increasingly been used as an authoritarian tool (Gregory & Cornell, 2009) to punish and remove challenging students (Dupper, 2010).

Zero tolerance policies in schools are a reflection of the precedent set by prisons in that the policies disproportionately affect African American and Hispanic students at a rate approximately three times higher than that of their White peers (Dupper, 2010). It also appears that students with emotional and behavioral disorders are being suspended and expelled at a rate that far exceeds their representation in the overall population (American Psychological Association, 2008). School suspensions have mirrored the exponential growth in criminal incarceration—from 1.7 million students suspended annually in 1974 to 3.1 million students suspended in 2001 (Teske, 2011).

The application of zero tolerance policies in schools has increasingly criminalized student behavior (American Psychological Association, 2008; Giroux, 2003; Swain & Noblit, 2011), creating the erroneous impression that violence and crime in schools is increasing, although data consistently indicates that school violence and disruption have remained stable or may even have decreased since 1985 (American Psychological Association, 2008). The increased reliance on law enforcement to handle situations once dealt with by schools themselves may have created a school-to-prison pipeline, removing students from valuable educational time and normalizing punitive behavior (Dupper, 2010; Swain & Noblit, 2011).

The school-to-prison pipeline idea is disconcerting, suggesting that those most affected by the policies and procedures surrounding zero-tolerance disciplinary action in schools are placed on a high-risk path to incarceration (Dupper, 2010). For certain segments of the student population, schools are increasingly implementing prison-style policies and procedures, including armed security guards, surveillance, and random searches (Giroux, 2003). Instead of investing time and personnel in shaping positive behaviors in students, many school districts are implementing measures that criminalize their behavior and facilitate the removal of problematic students (Giroux, 2003). The school may thus be responsible for shaping future inmates through the removal of educational opportunities and the implementation of punitive measures (Giroux, 2003; Swain & Noblit, 2011).

Zero tolerance disciplinary measures for students absolve administrators of the responsibility of examining the causes, effects, and nature of student offenses, allowing them to increasingly rely on an established rulebook for enforcement (Giroux, 2003). Zero tolerance has also incited the public regarding the perceived nature of crime and risk in our nations' schools, and has increasingly criminalized student behavior (American Psychological Association, 2008; Giroux, 2003; Swain & Noblit, 2011), leading to an increased risk of imprisonment for many CLD students (Giroux, 2003; Swain & Noblit, 2011). The school must remain a safe and disciplined environment for learning to take place; however, by simply removing troubling students, we are increasingly limiting the availability of public education to those who have not "crossed the line" into our ever-expanding notion of criminalizing behaviors (Giroux, 2003; Swain & Noblit, 2011). As previously noted, classroom norms and expectations often align with White middle-class values and orientations. Therefore, punitive practices often lead to the exclusion of students who do not conform to these culturally bound norms, values, and expected behaviors.

Unfortunately, such approaches to managing disciplinary problems can actually trigger and reinforce antisocial behavior, foster environments of control, shift accountability and educational responsibility away from the school, devalue the student-teacher relationship, and weaken the link between academic and social behavior programming (Gottfredson, 1987; Gottfredson, Gottfredson, & Hybl, 1993; Mayer, 1995; Mayer, Butterworth, Nafpaktitis, & Sulzer-Azaroff, 1983; Sugai & Horner, 2002).

Legal Basis for Tiered Intervention Models in Special Education

The 2001 No Child Left Behind (NCLB) Act was instituted to correct the most prevalent achievement gaps among students in specific subgroups (e.g., those with disabilities, from CLD backgrounds, and from socioeconomically disadvantaged backgrounds). The reauthorization of federal special education legislation through the Individuals with Disabilities Education Improvement Act (IDEIA; U.S. Department of Education, 2004) moved to align the accountability for learners with disabilities with the guiding principles of NCLB. This federal mandate was a major revision of the Elementary and Secondary Education Act (ESEA) of 1965. The law significantly challenged the status quo of public schools and established the U.S. Department of Education as a responsible party for increasing student achievement in public schools. Turnbull (2005) identified six primary principles of NCLB, namely: accountability, highly qualified teachers, scientifically based instruction, local flexibility, safe schools, and parent participation and choice. Although the individual provisions of IDEIA are different from NCLB, the overall goals of the two are similar. The partnership of NCLB and IDEIA provides the opportunity for students with disabilities to experience successful academic achievement through the implementation of systemic changes. In addition, IDEIA mandates the use of evidenced-based strategies to address concerns associated with the over identification of CLD students and students from low-income families in certain disability categories.

This combined legislation, which applies to both general and special education programs, serves as an acknowledgment of the racial inequities of the educational system. Considering the length of time that these issues have plagued our school systems, it is likely that the solutions will also require time, revision, and careful monitoring. The counter narrative is that the solutions do not honestly speak to an educational system that has been racially inequitable since its inception. In this line of reasoning, by not directly addressing the inherent racial inequities within the educational system, the academic, social, and emotional needs of CLD students suffer; as a result, inequitable educational services and outcomes flourish.

Positive Behavioral Interventions and Supports (PBIS)

In 2001, the United States Surgeon General published a report (U.S. Department of Health and Human Services) on the status of adolescents and antisocial behavior in which it was reported that schools can expect an increasing number of serious problem behaviors if they allow the establishment of antisocial peer networks inside schools, and if deviant youth behavior is reinforced by peers and adults. To affect the rates and prevent the development of antisocial behavior in youth, the Surgeon General report strongly suggests that a prevention-based approach be emphasized. It also suggests that contingencies be arranged in schools to establish an intolerant attitude toward antisocial behavior, actively break up and monitor antisocial networks, provide parents with strategies to increase their efficiency and effectiveness in the home. The goal is to enhance commitment to school, increase academic success, create and foster a positive school climate, and teach and encourage individual social skills and competence across all students.

The application of PBIS aims to improve school safety and climate within districts and campuses. The PBIS approach is a school-wide prevention and intervention model that proactively improves school behavior issues. This approach has been successful, in part due to its whole-school focus. Difficult behavioral issues that impact climate and safety, such as bullying and aggression, have proven difficult to remedy through small-scale interventions limited to a single classroom or subset of students. Figure 1 illustrates the whole-school focus intended by a PBIS.

To a large measure, PBIS is based on the notion that effective behavior change comes not only from a reduction in inappropriate behaviors, but also from the teaching of suitable alternatives. The goals of behavior change should not only be to help the child in the immediate environment or in the short term, but must also consider his or her life after school and in the long term. The key concept of PBIS is to change a problem behavior. In order to implement PBIS, it is therefore first necessary to remediate deficient contexts related to behavior repertoires or environmental conditions. Behavior repertoire refers to lack of competency in a given behavior skill set or combination of behavior skill sets. This means that a student does not know the necessary behaviors to be successful in a given environment. In this instance, students can be taught behavioral skills to increase the likelihood of success in the classroom environment. Communication, social skills, and self-management skills have all been found necessary to meet the demands of day-to-day existence in school, at home, and in the community. Meanwhile, environmental conditions refer to stimuli in a particular environment that are not conducive to eliciting appropriate behavior from an individual, and that contribute to the emergence of problematic behaviors.

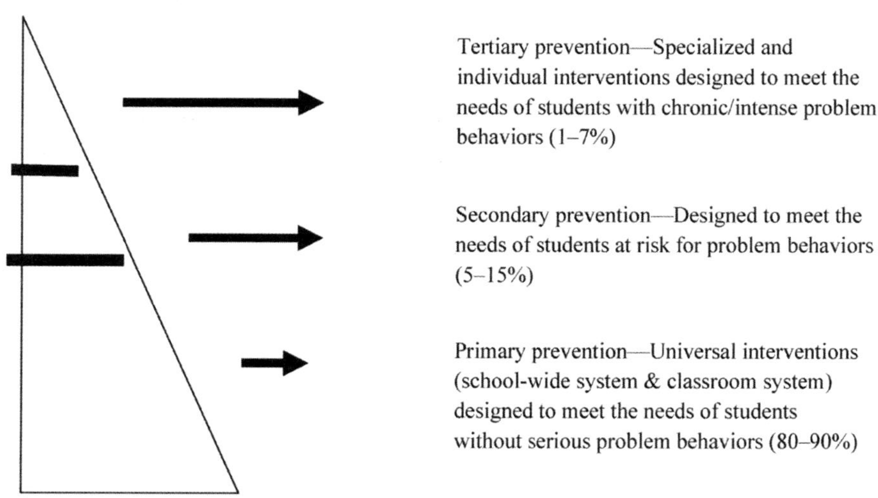

Figure 1. Positive Behavior Intervention Support model.

Approximately 80% of students could comply with primary prevention expectations if (a) they were taught appropriate behaviors, (b) their educators had consistent expectations, and (c) they were provided consistent consequences for those behaviors. Meanwhile, secondary prevention approaches could be developed and implemented for approximately 15% of the school population. Finally, about 5% of the student population would need intensive, individualized behavioral interventions requiring careful planning and documentation. PBIS is a proactive systems approach to school-wide discipline designed to be responsive to current social and educational challenges. Traditionally, PBIS is based on three levels of prevention, namely, primary, secondary, and tertiary. PBIS is not a curriculum, discipline package, or product, but a process for individualized and sustained decision making, planning, and problem solving. As indicated, it has an instructional focus in which emphasis is placed on teaching behavioral expectations directly. The logical extension of this is that PBIS enhances the capacity of schools to educate *all* students, especially students with challenging social behaviors, by establishing (a) clearly defined *outcomes* that relate to academic and social behavior, (b) *systems* that support staff efforts, (c) *practices* that support student success, and (d) *data* utilization that guide decision making (Sugai & Horner, 2005). To make PBIS flourish, general and special education personnel must do the following (Sugai & Horner, 2005):

1. Organize a team.
2. Review data.
3. Analyze, describe, and prioritize problems within a context.
4. Specify measurable outcomes.
5. Select evidenced-based practices.
6. Provide supports for accurate, sustained adoption and implementation.
7. Monitor practice implementation and progress toward outcome.

Finally, in applying PBIS in schools, Carr et al. (1999) found that two categories of intervention worked: that is, stimulus-based and reinforcement-based. Environments are deficient when there are too few stimuli to support positive behavior. Changes in such an environment are necessary as part of the effort to help children with disabilities exhibit more appropriate behavior. On the other hand, from a reinforcement perspective, the existence of positive behaviors competes with or makes negative behaviors unnecessary, because the positive behaviors provide an alternative for accessing the available reinforcement. In the end, PBIS tries to change the environment so that the conditions for appropriate behavior and its reinforcement are available, and to teach in such a way that appropriate behaviors are substituted for problematic ones as a way to access reinforcement in the environment.

While the percentages used in the PBIS model to address student needs are based on theoretical assumptions that most students will respond to evidenced-based practices, what it does not take into account is that a teacher's professional judgment plays a key role in the academic trajectory of the child (Algozzine, Ysseldyke, & Christiansen, 1983; Beswick, Willms, & Sloat, 2005; Leiter & Brown, 1985). For example, Good and Nichols (2001) contend that teachers' beliefs and behaviors are related to student performance. The researchers report on studies that show Black students receive lower teacher evaluations than White students despite higher test scores, as well as studies that indicate Black students, especially males, receive lowered academic scores because of classroom conduct. Sanchez-Fowler, Banks, Anhalt, Devore, and Kalis (2009) found that White teachers rated more children as highly externalizing and less prosocial; whereas African American teachers rated more children as highly externalizing and highly prosocial. The researchers suggested that African American teachers in the study were more culturally aligned to the interpretations of African American student behavior than were their White counterparts. In addition, teachers of students with disabilities are characterized as having low expectations and negative attitudes toward these students, presuming the students will present problem behaviors, and typically attributing lack of progress to the students (Gay, 2000, 2002; Noguera, 2003).

Low tolerance levels and expectations are an indication of the incongruence between the education strategies utilized by teachers and the cultural and linguistic differences of students served in an educational system in which they are required to perform based on standards different from their own. Moreover, lack of tolerance of differences adversely impacts teachers' perceptions of the students they serve in spite of the application of evidenced-based practices, including universal tiered intervention models (Delpit, 1992; Ladson-Billings, 1994). What is needed is an adaptation of the tiered models to better address the needs of all students, including CLD students.

Culturally Responsive Positive Behavioral Interventions and Supports

Culturally Responsive Positive Behavioral Interventions and Supports (CRPBIS) is a system that specifically acknowledges the presence of CLD students and the need for them to find relevant connections among themselves and with the behavioral goals and objectives that schools ask them to perform. CRPBIS attempts to value, consider, and integrate individuals' culture, language, heritage, and experiences in order to facilitate learning and development (Klingner et al., 2005). School-wide behavior supports should therefore be proactive and promote a positive, culturally responsive climate that is conducive to learning by all. Clearly, educators and service providers understand that perceptions of behavioral appropriateness are colored by cultural expectations of what is appropriate and inappropriate across cultures (Obiakor, 2008, 2012). Unlike traditional behavior management, which views the individual alone as the problem and seeks to "fix" him or her by quickly eliminating the challenging behavior, CRPBIS takes a wider view, including such things as setting and lack of skill in the definition of the "problem," and working to change them. As such, PBIS is characterized as a long-term approach to reducing problematic behavior by teaching behavior that is better suited to the given setting, and by providing the contextual supports necessary for successful outcomes (ERIC, 1999). The following components are germane to school-wide CRPBIS models (Klingner et al., 2005):

1. Clearly defined school-wide behavioral expectations
2. Structured plan for the teaching and reinforcing of those expectations
3. Well-defined and consistent adult responsibilities and expectations
4. Established clear system for behavioral infractions and consequences
5. System for monitoring implementation and outcome data

In essence, such plans create the social culture of the school. In acknowledging that there may be gaps between school and home behavior expectations for students, culturally responsive plans must consider the students' home culture in tandem with the school's. In addition, recognizing that behavioral norms are location-specific, the development and teaching of behavioral expectations must clearly delineate and teach expectations for school behaviors while also validating the cultural expectations and ways of being that students bring with them from their homes and communities. This involves incorporating cultural knowledge from students and their families in the development of a school-wide plan and, at times, adjusting school expectations to more closely reflect the values and ways of being that exist within the school community. Further, teams need to support staff in reflecting upon the ways in which their cultural perspectives affect classroom instruction, as well as classroom and school-wide behavioral management. Culturally bound expectations in the classroom and school need to be recognized and acknowledged so that practices can be modified to ensure all students are benefitting equally from school and classroom environments, regardless of gender, ethnicity, socioeconomic status, or disability status. Finally, behavioral interventions must be considered through a culturally responsive lens to ensure that student needs are being addressed and met in a culturally competent manner.

Avoiding "Old" Mistakes: A Critical Look at the Future

Noguera (2003) contended that for many CLD students, especially those with the greatest needs, schools focus so much on behavior control and dispensing punitive consequences that educators fail to realize that these administrative actions are counterproductive and lead students to reject the standards of the school. It should be reiterated that while the percentages used in the tiered models of PBIS are based on theoretical assumptions that students will respond to evidenced-based practices, the model does not consider the professional judgment of the teacher or how the decisions s/he makes affect the academic trajectory of the child and perhaps influence the subsequent need for special education services (Algozzine et al., 1983; Beswick et al., 2005; Leiter & Brown, 1985). For example, educators are more likely to suspend or expel students who demonstrate problematic behaviors, or assign them to more restrictive classroom placements (Lo & Cartledge, 2007; Skiba et al., 2002; Skiba, Poloni-Staudinger, Gallini, Simmons, & Feggins-Azziz, 2006; Skiba et al., 2008). African American children, in particular, receive more disciplinary actions with harsher penalties than White students (Skiba et al., 2002; Verdugo, 2002). These harsh punishments are not productive and relate more consistently than any other factor to the disproportionality in special education (Skiba et al., 2002; Skiba, Poloni-Staudinger, Simmons, Feggins, & Chung, 2005). Moreover, the PBIS model does not explicitly state that as a result of the disproportionality of CLD students receiving special education services, most students receiving tertiary interventions are destined to have continually negative school experiences.

When deciding whether a practice is appropriate for implementation as part of a tiered intervention model, the practice must be validated with the students for whom the intervention is planned. The PBIS model is a promising practice when used with CLD students. Before determining whether a strategy is evidenced-based for these students, the research has to clearly disaggregate CLD variables, as well as additional contextual variables (Klingner & Bianco, 2006). Often, children identified as English language learners (ELLs) are not included in research samples because of their limited English proficiency, which limits the findings in terms of external validity. As a result, prescribed strategies may not be appropriate for CLD students (Klingner & Edwards, 2006). To address the omission of cultural relevance in the tiered behavior model, culturally responsive practices must be integrated in such a way that culture is not viewed as a static set of characteristics located within individuals (e.g., ethnicity and social class), but rather as instrumental and indexed in practice (Gutierrez & Rogoff, 2003). Incorporating culturally responsive practices into the PBIS framework means that both district- and school-level administrators are actively committed to addressing racial/ethnic, socioeconomic, and ability status disparities in office discipline referrals and suspension/expulsion rates. It also means that educators are committed to using their understanding of the experiences lived by students in the design of interventions (Dupper & Bosch, 1996). This active commitment demands sufficient time and planning for professional development to enhance staff members' self- and cultural awareness to increase the use of culturally responsive practices. Further, the district and school must make an open commitment to ensure that all families feel welcome and included in the development of the framework and implementation process.

On the whole, culturally responsive PBIS does not simply involve augmenting PBIS with the addition of culturally responsive practices. Rather, CRPBIS must derive from the infusion of culturally responsive practices throughout the implementation of PBIS. CRPBIS enhances behavioral practices in a school environment by (a) minimizing cultural mismatches in behavioral expectations, (b) creating a cultural lens for viewing behavioral norms, and (c) affirming diversity within the school environment. District- and school-level administrators must make the commitment to addressing issues of equity in order for CRPBIS implementation to be successful. Culturally responsive practices are infused throughout each of the components of school-wide CRPBIS implementation by ensuring families' and students' cultural practices are represented and incorporated when developing school-wide norms, lessons, and reinforcement systems. Further, CRPBIS schools examine and disaggregate disciplinary data by subgroup (i.e., ethnicity, socioeconomic status, and disability status) to examine potential disproportionality in office discipline referrals and, as needed, to modify practices with the goal of equally benefitting all student groups. Armed with this knowledge, general and special educators must examine their current school practices to determine if they accurately reflect the needs of their CLD students and families.

Conclusion

Meeting the needs of students who are different requires professionals to think differently about service provision. Professionals who think differently about their profession and service provision understand the concept that working as servant leaders, contributors, and change agents can positively impact the lives of families and children. In a CRPBIS system, cultural and linguistic differences are not deficits or variables in problematic behavior—such differences are part of the solution. A CRPBIS system will enhance students' behavioral development by constructing a learning environment that reflects their cultural membership in their classes and in their schools. To that end, schools must go beyond mere slogans to develop a proactive environment. Teachers and service providers must attend to all of their students' behavioral needs, and try to incorporate them within the classroom and avoid instances of punishment. Finally, schools must work with communities to examine issues related to classroom discipline, cultural and linguistic differences, and teaching practices so as to further develop successful approaches to teaching positive behavioral skills.

References

Algozzine, B., Ysseldyke, J. E., & Christiansen, S. (1983). An analysis of the incidence of special education placement: The masses are burgeoning. *Journal of Special Education, 17*(2), 141–147.

American Psychological Association. (2008). *Are zero tolerance policies effective in the schools? An evidentiary review and recommendations.* Retrieved from http://www.apa.org/pubs/info/reports/zero-tolerance.pdf

Beswick, J. F., Willms, J. D., & Sloat, E. A. (2005). A comparative study of teacher ratings of emergent literacy skills and student performance on a standardized measure. *Education Journal, 136*(1), 116–137.

Biglan, A. (1995). Translating what we know about the context of antisocial behavior into a lower prevalence of such behavior. *Journal of Applied Behavior Analysis, 28*(4), 479–492.

Boykin, A. W., Tyler, K. M., & Miller, O. A. (2005). In search of cultural themes and their expressions in the dynamics of classroom life. *Urban Education, 40*(5), 521–549.

Carr, E. G., Horner, R. H., Turnbull, A. P., Marquis, J. G., Magito-McLaughlin, D., McAtee, M. L., & Braddock, D. (1999). *Positive Behavior Support for people with developmental disabilities: A research synthesis.* Washington, DC: American Association on Mental Retardation.

Cartledge, G., Tillman, L., & Talbert-Johnson, C. (2001). Professional ethics within the context of student discipline and diversity. *Teacher Education and Special Education, 24*(1), 25–37.

Delpit, L. D. (1992). Education in a multicultural society: Our future's greatest challenge. *Journal of Negro Education, 61*(3), 237–249.

Dupper, D. R. (2010). *A new model of school discipline: Engaging students and preventing behavior problems.* New York: Oxford University Press.

Dupper, D. R., & Bosch, L. A. (1996). Reasons for school suspensions: An examination of data from one school district and recommendations for reducing suspensions. *Journal for a Just and Caring Education, 2*(2), 140–150.

Elementary & Secondary Education Act. (1965). *Elementary & Secondary Education.* Retrieved from http://www2.ed.gov/policy/elsec/leg/esea02/beginning.html

ERIC Clearinghouse on Disabilities and Gifted Education. (1999). *Positive Behavior Support and functional assessment: ERIC/OSEP Digest E580.* Retrieved from http://www.ericdigests.org/2000-2/positive.htm

Gay, G. (2000). *Culturally responsive teaching: Theory, research, and practice.* New York: Teachers College Press.

Gay, G. (2002). Preparing for culturally responsive teaching. *Journal of Teacher Education, 53*(2), 106–116.

Giroux, H. A. (2003). Racial injustice and disposable youth in the age of zero tolerance. *Qualitative Studies in Education, 16*(4), 553–565.

Good, T., & Nichols, S. L. (2001). Expectancy effects in the classroom: A special focus on improving the reading performance of minority students in first-grade classrooms. *Educational Psychologist, 36*(2), 113–126.

Gottfredson, D. C. (1987). An evaluation of an organization development approach to reducing school disorder. *Evaluation Review, 11*(6), 739–763.

Gottfredson, D. C., Gottfredson, G. D., & Hybl, L. G. (1993). Managing adolescent behavior: A multi-year, multi-school study. *American Educational Research Journal, 30*(1), 179–215.

Gregory, A., & Cornell, D. (2009). "Tolerating" adolescent needs: Moving away from zero tolerance policies in high school. *Theory Into Practice, 48*(2), 106–113.

Gutierrez, K. D., & Rogoff, B. (2003). Cultural ways of learning: Individual traits or repertoires of practice. *Educational Researcher, 32*(5), 19–25.

Hale-Benson, J. (1986). *Black children: Their roots, culture, and learning styles* (2nd ed.). Baltimore: Johns Hopkins University Press.

King, K. P. (2004). Both sides now: Examining transformational learning and professional development. *Innovative Higher Education, 29*(2), 153–172.

Klingner, J. K., Artiles, A. J., Kozleski, E., Harry, B., Zion, S., Tate, W., … Riley, D. (2005). Addressing the disproportionate representation of culturally and linguistically diverse students in special education through culturally responsive educational systems. *Education Policy Analysis Archives, 13*(38). Retrieved from http://epaa.asu.edu/epaa/v13n38/

Klingner, J. K., & Bianco, M. (2006). What is special about special education for culturally and linguistically diverse students with disabilities? In B. Cook & B. Schirmer (Eds.), *What is special about special education?* (pp. 37–53). Austin, TX: PRO-ED.

Klingner, J. K., & Edwards, P. (2006). Cultural consideration with response-to-intervention model. *Readings Research Quarterly, 41*(1), 108–117.

Ladson-Billings, G. (1994). *The dreamkeepers: Successful teaching for African-American students.* San Francisco: Jossey-Bass.

Leiter, J., & Brown, J. S. (1985). Determinants of elementary school grading. *Sociology of Education, 58*(3), 166–180.

Lerman, S. (2000). The social turn in mathematics education research. In J. Boaler (Ed.), *Multiple perspectives on mathematics teaching and learning* (pp. 19–44). Westport, CT: Ablex.

Lo, Y.-y., & Cartledge, G. (2007). Office disciplinary referrals in an urban elementary school. *Multicultural Learning and Teaching, 2*(1), 20–38.

Mayer, G. R. (1995). Preventing antisocial behavior in the schools. *Journal of Applied Behavior Analysis, 28*(4), 467–478.

Mayer, G. R., Butterworth, T. W., Nafpaktitis, M., & Sulzer-Azaroff, B. (1983). Preventing school vandalism and improving discipline: A three-year study. *Journal of Applied Behavior Analysis, 16*(4), 355–369.

Neal, L. I., McCray, A. D., Webb-Johnson, G., & Bridgest, S. T. (2003). The effects of African American movement styles on teachers' perceptions and reactions. *Journal of Special Education, 37*(1), 49–57.

Nieto, S. (2004). *Affirming diversity: The sociopolitical context of multicultural education.* Boston: Pearson.

Noguera, P. A. (2003). Schools, prisons, and the social implications of punishment: Rethinking disciplinary practices. *Theory Into Practice, 42*(4), 341–350.

Obiakor, F. E. (2008). *The eight-step approach to multicultural learning and teaching* (3rd ed.). Dubuque, IA: Kendall Hunt.

Obiakor, F. E. (2012). Hobson's choice: Illusory intervention choice for culturally and linguistically diverse learners with problem behaviors. In J. P. Bakken, F. E. Obiakor, & A. F. Rotatori (Eds.), *Behavior disorders: Identification, assessment, and instruction of students with EBD (Advances in Special Education)* (Vol. 22) (pp. 221–231). Bingley, United Kingdom: Emerald.

Perry, T., Steele, C., & Hilliard, A., III. (2003). *Young, gifted, and black: Promoting high achievement among African-American students.* Boston: Beacon Press.

Raffaele-Mendez, L. M., & Knoff, H. M. (2003). Who gets suspended from school and why: A demographic analysis of schools and disciplinary infractions in a large school district. *Education and Treatment of Children, 26*(1), 30–51.

Rice, S. (2009). Education for toleration in an era of zero tolerance school policies: A Deweyan analysis. *Educational Studies: Journal of the American Educational Studies Association, 45*(6), 556–571.

Sanchez-Fowler, L. T., Banks, T., Anhalt, K., Devore, H. H., & Kalis, T. (2009). The effects of externalizing behavior problems on teacher-student relationship quality and academic performance in young African American learners. *Behavioral Disorders, 33*(3), 167–183.

Skiba, R. J., Michael, R. S., Nardo, A. C., & Peterson, R. (2002). The color of discipline: Sources of racial and gender disproportionality in school punishment. *Urban Review, 34*(4), 317–342.

Skiba, R. J., Poloni-Staudinger, L., Gallini, S., Simmons, A. B., & Feggins-Azziz, L. R. (2006). Disparate access: The disproportionality of African American students with disabilities across educational environments. *Exceptional Children, 72*(4), 411–424.

Skiba, R. J., Poloni-Staudinger, L., Simmons, A. B., Feggins, L. R., & Chung, C. G. (2005). Unproven links: Can poverty explain ethnic disproportionality in special education? *The Journal of Special Education, 39*(3), 130–144.

Skiba, R. J., Simmons, A. D., Ritter, S., Gibb, A., Rausch, M. K., Cuadrado, J., & Chung, C. G. (2008). Achieving equity in special education: History, status, and current challenges. *Exceptional Children, 74*(3), 264–288.

Sugai, G., & Horner, R. H. (2002). The evolution of discipline practices: School-Wide Positive Behavior Supports. *Child and Family Behavior Therapy, 24*(1/2), 23–50.

Sugai, G., & Horner, R. H. (2005). School-Wide Positive Behavior Supports: Achieving and sustaining effective learning environments for all students. In W. H. Heward (Ed.), *Focus on behavior analysis in education: Achievements, challenges, and opportunities* (pp. 90–102). Upper Saddle River, NJ: Pearson Prentice-Hall.

Swain, A. E., & Noblit, G. W. (2011). Education in a punitive society: An introduction. *The Urban Review, 43*(4), 465–475.

Swartz, E. (2004). Casing the self: A study of pedagogy and critical thinking. *Teacher Development, 8*(1), 45–65.

Teske, S. C. (2011). A study of zero tolerance policies in schools: A multi-integrated systems approach to improve outcomes for adolescents. *Journal of Child and Adolescent Psychiatric Nursing, 24*(2), 88–97.

Townsend, B. (2000). The disproportionate discipline of African American learners: Reducing school suspension and expulsions. *Exceptional Children, 66*(3), 381–391.

Townsend, B. (2002). "Testing while black": Standards-based school reform and African American learners. *Remedial and Special Education, 23*(4), 222–230.

Turnbull, H. R. (2005). Individuals with Disabilities Education Act reauthorization: Accountability and personal responsibility. *Remedial and Special Education, 26*(6), 320–326.

U.S. Department of Education. (2002). *No Child Left Behind: A desktop reference.* Retrieved from http://www2.ed.gov/admins/lead/account/nclbreference/reference.pdf

U.S. Department of Education. (2004). *Building the legacy: IDEA 2004.* Retrieved from http://idea.ed.gov/

U.S. Department of Health and Human Services. (2001). *Youth violence: A Report of the Surgeon General.* Rockville, MD: Office of the Surgeon General. Retrieved from http://www.ncbi.nlm.nih.gov/books/NBK44294/

Verdugo, R. R. (2002). Race-ethnicity, social class, and zero-tolerance policies. *Education andUrban Society, 35*(1), 50–75.

Wald, J., & Losen, D. J. (2003). Defining and redirecting a school-to-prison pipeline. In J. Wald & D. J. Losen (Eds.), *New directions for youth development (No. 99; Deconstructing the school-to-prison pipeline)* (pp. 9–15). San Francisco: Jossey-Bass.

Walker, H. M., Ramsey, E., & Gresham, F. M. (2004). *Antisocial behavior in school: Evidence-based practices* (2nd ed.). Belmont, CA: Wadsworth/Thomson Learning.

8. *Promoting Socio-Cultural Justice for Culturally and Linguistically Diverse Secondary School Students*

Floyd D. Beachum and Gina L. Gullo

There never was in the world two opinions alike, no more than two hairs or two grains; the most universal quality is diversity.

— Michel Eyquem

The universal quality of diversity is becoming more apparent in K–12 education. Current demographic trends and future projections indicate that the student population of the United States is becoming increasingly diverse, especially racially and ethnically. The U.S. Census Bureau indicated that by the year 2050, people of color will constitute more than 50% of the population (U.S. Census Bureau, 2011). In reference to schools, "While children of color constituted about one-third of the student population in 1995, they are expected to become the numerical majority by 2035. This change will render the expression 'minority students' statistically inaccurate" (Villegas & Lucas, 2002, p. 3). At the same time, most school leaders and teachers are White, middle class, and monolingual, which may result in cultural misunderstandings, cultural mismatch (Delpit, 2006), and/or cultural collision (Beachum & McCray, 2004, 2011). These problems will inevitably force school leaders and the core of teachers in America to reassess their pedagogical approaches and leadership strategies, and result in a deeper look at students, their behaviors, and their academic performance. A promising solution may very well be what is known as School-Wide Positive Behavioral Interventions and Supports (SWPBIS).

SWPBIS is "a systems approach to promoting evidence-based practices to affect important social and academic outcomes for all students" (Sugai, O'Keeffe, & Fallon, 2012, p. 197). The purpose of this chapter is to examine relevant literature on SWPBIS, incorporate culturally relevant insight infused with principles of social justice, and to make recommendations for practice in secondary schools.

As the demographic forecast predicts a more diverse future, the current educational context for students of color is troubling to say the least. These students are plagued by a host of educational issues that are well known by most scholars and practitioners. The achievement gap usually refers to the gap in scores (on a multitude of indicators) between students of color and their White peers (Martinez & Woods, 2007). According to a 2004 report from the National Center for Educational Statistics (NCES), the achievement gap was reflected in math and reading achievement, the taking of advanced courses in high school, Advanced Placement (AP) exam performance, and college entrance exam performance. Similarly, English language learners (ELLs) also had suboptimal educational experiences compared to their monolingual counterparts (Zehler et al., 2003). Furthermore, "students from culturally and linguistically diverse backgrounds experience disproportionate disciplinary consequences compared to White students" (Sugai et al., 2012, p. 198). According to Peterson (2003), these students are suspended and expelled at higher rates than their White peers. In addition, the office referrals that these students receive lead to the loss of precious time in which they could be learning. Scott and Barrett (2004) indicated that one of these office referrals could result in a student spending 20 to 40 minutes out of class. In addition, culturally and linguistically diverse students are frequently overrepresented in special education. In many cases they are misidentified, misassessed, mislabeled, miscategorized, and/or misplaced (Obiakor, 2001, 2007). At the same time, these students are underrepresented in gifted and talented programs (Gordon & Bridglall, 2005; Harry, 1992; Kunjufu, 2005). Overall, the preceding discussion leads one to the conclusion that culturally and linguistically diverse (CLD) learners are faced with more challenges in their educational experience, which can lead to more negative educational outcomes.

Many agree that one of the greatest problems in education today is the negative behaviors of students. One study found that one in five students exhibit disruptive/off-task behaviors as determined by general education teachers (Myers & Holland, 2000). Kunjufu (2002) described a situation in the classroom when a teacher confronts a student regarding negative behavior, and it turns into a standoff, which tends to escalate from there. Beachum and McCray (2011) expanded on this confrontation and named the negative outcome "cultural collusion." When cultural collusion happens, the teacher (or even school leader) reacts in a negative fashion when confronted by the student, which usually leads to an office referral or suspension. In these scenarios, the student loses valuable class time. If this happens repeatedly, the student may decide to only come to school sporadically, decrease her or his academic engagement, and possibly drop out altogether. This could be an implicit collusion between the student and teacher that results in a negative outcome for the student. The road is paved with markers of behavior and all behaviors serve a purpose. The teacher can de-escalate the confrontation in various ways, especially if he or she understands the culture of students and the reasons for certain behaviors. Therefore, an important aspect of student success in schools is an emphasis on their behaviors.

Integrating Positive Behavior Support

A growingly popular strategy for student success with a heavy focus on behavior lies in the Positive Behavior Support model. Positive Behavior Support combines the ideologies of the inclusion movement, person-centered planning, and applied behavior analysis into a simple model for investigating problem behaviors and planning for better outcomes (Bambara & Kern, 2002; Carr et al., 2002). The model breaks all behaviors down into a four-stage contingency where setting events make way for antecedents that cause behaviors (good or bad) that are followed by consequences. Restated, pre-existing conditions, such as illness or hunger, combine with events just prior to the onset of a behavior, such as being given a test or listening to lecture, which together lead to a behavior. This behavior serves a purpose, usually escape or access, which maintains, or reinforces, the exhibited behavior. Together, all these elements occur within the confines of the individual's quality of life (QOL) as displayed in Figure 1. As a result, the student exhibiting problem behaviors often experiences negative interactions with school professionals, which ultimately decrease his or her QOL.

Positive Behavior Support continues to define a structure for how to effectively use the foretasted model to plan for behavior interventions. The first strategy is to make an antecedent intervention, or a change to the setting events or antecedents (Bambara & Knoster, 2009). Antecedent interventions usually allow students a choice of instructional delivery (read or listen to a book), a schedule or routine change (lunch before science or nap

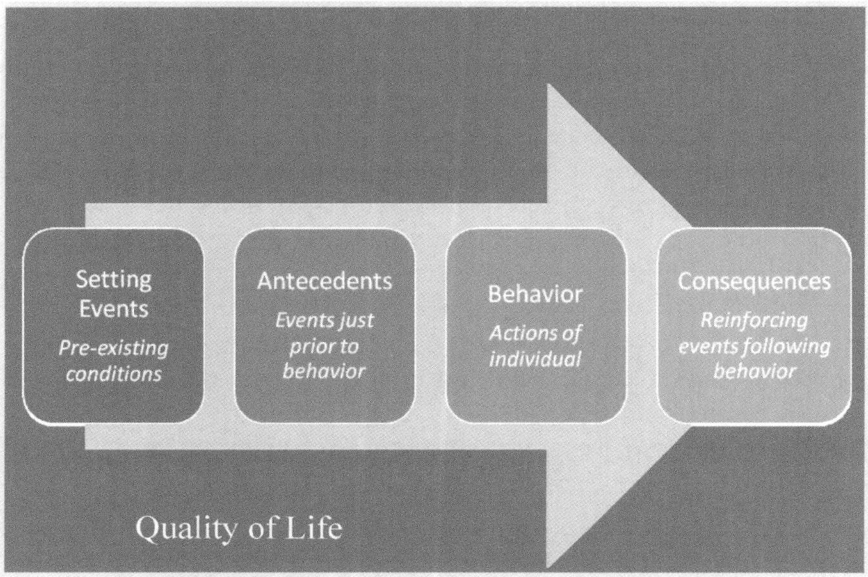

Figure 1. The four-term contingency is set within the improvement of an individual's quality of life in the Positive Behavior Support model.

before school), incorporation of a preference into tasks (listen to music during test taking), or an opportunity for increased participation (calling on student every third question) (Kern, Choutka, & Sokol, 2002). Teachers simply determine what conditions are occurring directly before the problem behavior or what underlying conditions exist and work toward eliminating these conditions or lessening their adversity to the target student.

The next method of Positive Behavior Support intervention is to teach alternate behaviors (Bambara & Knoster, 2009). This method focuses on identifying the inappropriate behavior, determining the socially acceptable behavior, and teaching the student to use the preferred behavior (Rutherford, Quinn, & Mathur, 2004). For example, a student might throw a book on the floor when she does not need it any longer. The teacher would then watch how other students discard their books and see that they tuck it under their desk chairs. Then, the teacher would teach the target student to put his or her book under his chair in the same manner as the other students and reinforce this behavior until it becomes commonplace. Often, students simply do not know what the correct or preferable behavior is, or may not know how to exemplify this behavior. Teaching alternative behaviors works efficiently to guide the student to perform the desired behavior and replaces the problem behaviors.

The third method of Positive Behavior Support intervention focuses on changing the consequences of challenging behaviors (Bambara & Knoster, 2009). At first, one might think this refers to zero-tolerance policies or strict school-suspension systems, but it is much the opposite. In Positive Behavior Support, consequences simply refer to events that occur after behaviors that maintain them. For instance, a student gets an exam and has a tantrum. A teacher would usually send the student to the office, where the student would escape having to take the exam at that time. Here, the student is avoiding an undesirable event (the exam) through the usual "punishment" of being sent to the office. In a consequence intervention, the teacher might have the student bring the exam with him to the office to continue, work on the test in the hallway, or simply do nothing and refuse to attend to the student's tantrum. These interventions deny the student escape from the undesirable task by changing the consequences of the tantrum behavior and are often extremely effective, but challenging to implement (Bambara & Kern, 2002).

The final Positive Behavior Support intervention strategy is a long-term or a QOL change (Bambara & Knoster, 2009). These interventions include acquiring a preferred occupation, teaching life skills, managing home environments, or developing social skills (Bambara & Kern, 2002). Here, students are given supports they need outside of their problem behaviors that will increase their overall QOL, usually in a long-term manner. For instance, a student who has exhibited tantrums through eighth grade may have suffered socially. School professionals might set this student up with a peer buddy who has a large social network and explicitly teach the target student social skills. With this toolkit, the student can develop his or her own social network, which may result in a better QOL for that student and lessen the probability of future problem behaviors.

Together these four interventions strategies (antecedent, alternative skills, consequence, and long-term/QOL) are implemented to most effectively provide supports and interventions for target students. Each works on a different aspect of the undesired behavior in order to fully develop appropriate behaviors in a manner that best fits the student's individual requirements. Although a considerable amount of time is used to collect data on the student's distinct needs, the resulting intervention and support plan provide an individualized approach that meets the particular needs of the target student. Furthermore, the plan allows for inclusion of culturally relevant supports to meet the unique needs of the increasingly diverse student population of today. Unfortunately, schools often do not have the time or resources to implement Positive Behavior Support plans for every student and must take a school-wide approach.

School-Wide Positive Behavioral Intervention and Support

In SWPBIS, students receive supports and interventions in a style similar to that of Positive Behavior Support in a group setting employed through a three-tiered model as displayed in Figure 2 (Lewis & Sugai, 1999; Sugai & Horner, 2002). In this model, all students receive universal supports such as clear expectations and school-wide reinforcement economies. These supports are usually sufficient for 80–90% of the student population. Students who are not succeeding with Tier 1 supports alone are given Tier 2 supports such as check in/check out (CICO) systems or mentoring programs with teachers or staff. This additional level of support often meets the needs of 5–15% of the school population. Finally, students who continue to struggle are provided with Tier 3 supports such as individualized Positive Behavior Support plans or wraparound services. These students usually make up 1–7% of a school's population. Together, these three tiers of support work to facilitate success for all students in a school population.

The first tier of SWPBIS meets the needs of most with implementation for all students across all settings (Horner, Sugai, & Anderson, 2010). Schools implement three to five clear rules and behavioral expectations for maximum efficacy, which are taught using direct instruction and positive reinforcement (Horner et al., 2010; Sugai, Horner, & Gresham, 2002). Each rule is written in a manner that emphasizes what the student should be doing and refrains from using negative words such as "no" or "don't." In practice, schools will post rules visibly throughout the school paired with expectations

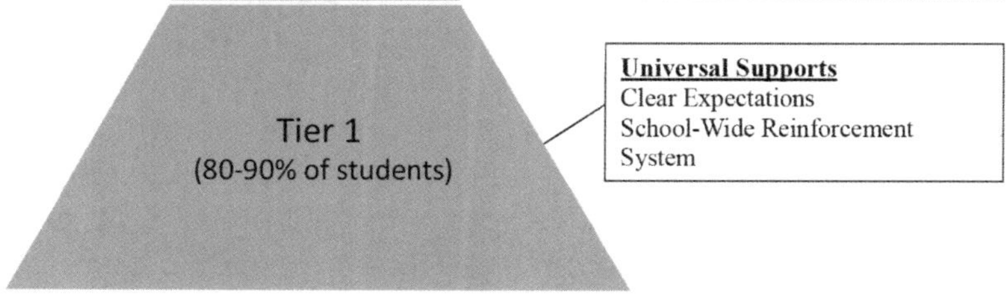

Figure 2. School-Wide Positive Behavior Support is a multi-tiered system.

for how each rule looks when practiced in that particular setting. For example, the following rules may be combined with the behavioral expectations noted when presented in the hallway: Be kind (speak positively to peers, keep hands and feet to self), be ready (be quick in the hallway, get only what you need for class from your locker), and be respectful (use manners, maintain personal space). These rules and expectations are explicitly taught and subsequently reinforced using a school-wide ticket system, pep-rallies, and/or positive feedback. Data are collected to reflect both positive and negative behavioral responses exhibited by students using these supports, and only students who are unable to succeed at the Tier 1 level are moved on to Tier 2 SWPBIS interventions.

The second tier of SWPBIS offers small groups of students extra support interventions that allow them to achieve behavioral success in school (Horner et al., 2010). There are many popular methods for Tier 2 interventions with the following as the most widely used: CICO systems, social skills training, mentoring programs and "think time" (Hoyle, Marshall, & Yell, 2011). CICO systems give students a "point sheet" that they carry to each class. At the start of the class, the student "checks in" and teachers review behavior and academic expectations. At the end of the class, the student "checks out" and teachers award the student points for proper adherence to the previously reviewed expectations. Social skill training is explicit instruction of strategies and techniques for social interactions and anger management. Mentoring programs often employ a check-and-connect paradigm where students have a mentor teacher who takes time to check in with the student daily or weekly and discusses how the student is doing and/or what life factors are affecting his or her performance. "Think time" provides the student with a quiet space or accepted break (put head down during class unquestioned) in order to gather his or her emotions and think rationally before reacting to unpleasant or challenging situations. These interventions are often sufficient to help the remaining students succeed in the school setting; however, a small number of students require tertiary supports.

In the third tier of SWPBIS, students who are failing to succeed or who are unlikely to succeed with all previous supports are provided with individualized interventions (Horner et al., 2010). Most often, students receive a functional behavior analysis (FBA) to break their behaviors into the four-term contingency discussed previously and develop a subsequent individualized Positive Behavior Support plan. Many times students will require multiple Positive Behavior Support plans to address a variety of challenging behaviors. Furthermore, students in this tier are provided with wraparound services that can help them achieve success outside of the school setting and ideally improved their overall QOL (Eber, Hyde, & Suter, 2011). Wraparound services integrate mental health, physical health, occupational, family, and academic services to maximize the efficacy of each element of the partnership. With this final tier of SWPBIS, nearly all students are able to succeed in the school setting.

The SWPBIS framework provides a structural mold in which educators and school leaders can implement a variety of educational strategies from those based in behaviorism to those reflective of culturally relevant learning practices. Incorporation of meaningful behavioral expectations and pertinent interventions that are reflective of students' diverse attributes and lifestyles into SWPBIS systems can develop highly effective school communities (Fallon, O'Keeffe, & Sugai, 2012). Similarly, individualized Positive Behavior Support plans can meet the unique needs of a particular student and highly reflect a student's cultural and linguistic distinctiveness in order to better fit his or her needs. Clearly, Positive Behavior Support and School-Wide Positive Behavioral Interventions and Supports are both areas where research evaluating the efficacy and most appropriate culturally relevant educational practices for CLD learners is necessary.

The Importance of Connecting Culture

While SWPBIS holds much promise for K–12 education, it is also subject to justifiable critique. In its application, it could be utilized in a one-size-fits-all fashion that may do more harm than good. "Behavioral supports cannot be universally applied without attention to culture and context" (Fallon et al., 2012, p. 211). Connecting culture is an important aspect of almost any educational intervention or approach. At the same time, the discussion of culture in K–12 education can be confusing and complex. It brings to mind various questions: How is culture defined? Whose culture is dominant? Why does culture matter when all we have to do is treat everyone with respect? These answers are worth exploring in order to allow educators to successfully implement SWPBIS systems.

Culture is diverse, dynamic, and complex. In psychology, culture has been defined as "a configuration of learned behaviors and results of behavior whose component elements are shared and transmitted by the members of a particular society" (Linton, 1945, p. 32). In anthropology, it has been defined as "The manifestations of social habits of a community, the reactions of the individuals as affected by the habits of the group in which he lives, and the product of human activities as determined by these habits" (Boas, 1966, p. 60). In education, James Banks (1989) stated that culture "is the values, symbols, interpretations, and perspectives that distinguish one people from another in modernized societies" (p. 8). All of the definitions are useful for information, instruction, and interpretive purposes when planning effective and culturally sensitive SWPBIS systems.

Building on these insights, Sugai, O'Keeffe, and Fallon (2012) recommended a behavioral perspective while understanding culture in the context of SWPBIS. They further asserted that SWPBIS is grounded in an analytic tradition based on behavior (Sugai & Horner, 2002) and that applied behavioral analysis (ABA) offers empirical and practical evidence for success in changing the human condition for the better (Alberto & Troutman, 2006; Cooper, Heron, & Heward, 2007; Skinner, 1953). ABA advances our knowledge of behavioral theory into (1) the application to socially distinct problems, (2) continuous close assessment of observable behaviors, and (3) acknowledgement of the connection between behaviors and the environment in which they take place (Baer, Wolf, & Risley, 1968; Cooper, Heron, & Heward, 2007). Within this behavioral framing, Sugai, O'Keeffe, and Fallon (2012) defined culture as follows:

> The extent to which a group of individuals engage in overt and verbal behavior reflecting shared behavioral learning histories, serving to differentiate the group from other groups, and predicting how individuals within the group act in specific setting conditions… [culture] reflects a collection of common verbal and overt behaviors that are learned and maintained by a set of similar social and environmental contingencies (i.e., learning history), and are occasioned (or not) by actions and objects (i.e., stimuli) that define a given setting or context. (p. 200)

This guiding definition clearly identifies a behavior emphasis that connects to group learning histories and common experiences, which can be informative and sometimes predictive. Sugai et al. (2012) also cautioned that behavioral approaches, like SWPBIS, should be tempered with flexibility, uniqueness, and careful use of language. "Flexibility should be used in interpreting and applying this behavior analytic perspective of culture to education. We acknowledge that individuals may have much in common culturally in some situations, but not in others" (p. 200). While understanding culture can be helpful, it does not mean that all groups will always behave in the same manner in every situation. For instance, we cannot assume that African American students will always react the same way to a certain stimulus. In terms of uniqueness, while groups may share learning histories and cultural experiences, individuals are unique within these groups (Skinner, 1971). Thus, it can be difficult to predict individual behavior.

While behavior analytic perspectives can be educative and informative, they are not constant across all groups or individuals. Practitioners must incorporate flexibility, understand uniqueness, and consider that language is not only important with regard to communication, but it also allows people to determine value. According to Sugai et al. (2012), "people may arbitrarily associate different values with different cultural expressions" (pp. 201–202). Thus, some individuals may highly value certain forms of language while denigrating others. For instance, a racially and ethnically diverse school may send out all communications in English only, not realizing that many families may primarily speak Spanish. In another case, a student may be reprimanded in class for speaking slang, or Ebonics, but if the teacher carefully considered culture, they could help the student recognize how to master standard English and become a cultural translator (Beachum & McCray, 2011), and could empower the student to maneuver better in both their own community and the school. This discussion of culture, group and individual needs, and flexibility, uniqueness, and language is well-aligned with the principles of social justice.

Infusing Social Justice with Cultural Considerations in School-Wide Positive Behavior Support

The notion of social justice is becoming more prevalent in educational research and practice. In educational leadership, this notion is beginning to impact research and practice. Currently, scholars have provided multiple definitions for social justice. Goldfarb and Grinberg (2002) stated that social justice is "the exercise of altering these [institutional] arrangements by actively engaging in reclaiming, appropriating, sustaining, and advancing inherent human rights of equity, equality, and fairness in social, economic, educational, and personal dimensions" (p. 162). Theoharis (2007) defined social justice as an approach that has educational leaders place "issues of race, class, gender, disability, sexual orientation, and other historically and currently marginalizing conditions in the United States central to their advocacy, leadership, practice, and vision" (p. 223). Bogotch, Beachum, Blount, Brooks, and English (2008) described social justice as "an optimal belief system that emphasizes equal recognition of all groups and individuals along with redistribution to address social inequity, while emphasizing virtues such as liberation, empowerment, and uplift" (p. 60). In short, social justice is anti-oppression, recognizes all groups equally, and reaffirms human rights. When applied to a school context, social justice works to integrate these elements into educational systems for the betterment of all students. In this spirit, Dantley, Beachum, and McCray (2008) proposed a framework for the examination of social justice where they advised that social justice theory and practice should be relationship driven, holistic, and morally based.

Relationships are a critical aspect of human social interaction. "The power of relationships cannot be underestimated as it is in relationships that we are equipped to come to engage others' perspectives and predispositions which have a monumental impact on our own" (p. 128). Fullan (2004) underscored the importance of relationships when he noted, "The single factor common to every successful change initiative is that relationships improve. If relationships improve, things get better. If they remain the same or get worse, ground is lost" (p. 77). In schools, relationships can be the key to the teaching and learning process. Kunjufu (2002) indicated that no significant learning occurs without a significant relationship and that social justice should be holistic. In other words, "social justice cannot be viewed as ahistorical or acontextual" (Dantley et al., 2008, p. 129). Meanwhile, social justice approaches must keep the entire student in mind, including each student's academic, social, cognitive, and emotional needs.

Finally, social justice should have a moral foundation. Fullan (2001) called for leaders to have a moral purpose when guiding their organizations. He noted that "Moral purpose is about both ends and means. In education, an important end is to make a difference in the lives of students. But the means of getting to that end are also crucial. If you don't treat others fairly, you will be a leader without followers" (Fullan, 2001, p. 13). Beyond treating others fairly, others have called for school leaders to have more of a critical perspective (Beachum & McCray, 2011; Dantley, 2004; Starratt, 1991). Ryan (2006) expounded upon this perspective when he wrote:

> Being critical means becoming more skeptical about established truths. Being critical requires skills that allow one to discern the basis of claims, the assumptions underlying assertions, and the interests that motivate people to promote certain positions. Critical skills allow people to recognize unstated, implicit, and subtle points of view and the often invisible or taken-for-granted conditions that provide the basis for these stances. (p. 114)

Therefore, the moral approach advocates not only equal treatment of all people, but the insight to ask questions and challenge the status quo. There is great theoretical and practical potential when combining the cultural considerations explained above with these elements of social justice. Together, they form the socio-cultural justice framework as displayed in Table 1.

Table 1. The Socio-Cultural Justice Framework.

Cultural Consideration	Social Justice Leadership Frame	Socio-Cultural Justice Framework
Flexibility	Relationship-driven pedagogy	Flexible relationships
Uniqueness	Holistic pedagogy	Holistic uniqueness
Language	Morally-based pedagogy	Moral language

The Socio-Cultural Justice Framework for Practice in Secondary Schools

Flexible Relationships

In secondary schooling (primarily grades 7–12), relationships with families and communities are important. In many ways, local communities and schools are interconnected through sports, community events, public meetings, etc. Thus, relationships between school leaders and educators and the external community need to be flexible. School leaders cannot afford to simply sit within the walls of the school and wait for parents and others to come to the building for parent-teacher conferences and/or graduations; they must make efforts to reach out and forge genuine bonds. Beachum and McCray (2012) agreed, "Educational leaders should create opportunities for dialogue, invite speakers, host events, and build coalitions with the external community" (p. 241). Swaminathan (2005) reminded us that "Schools can never divorce themselves from the communities where they exist" (p. 195). Some tangible suggestions for practice given by McCray, Grant-Overton, and Beachum (2010) are applicable in this case. These suggestions include creating a school-community committee and offering community nights to build relationships between schools and families. Socio-cultural justice is incorporated into the long-term/QOL level of Positive Behavior Support interventions. Building school-community relationships that will facilitate communication and integration between the two entities provides for a long-term support system that can develop consistency in behavioral expectations and cultural sensitivity of these expectations by both family and school personnel.

Holistic Uniqueness

The notion of holistic uniqueness suggests that students should be educated and developed in ways that benefit them cognitively, emotionally, and socially. At the same time, it recognizes the uniqueness of individuals and cultural groups. In the secondary school classroom, this means that teaching approaches are interactive, dynamic, reflective, and/or interdisciplinary. Simultaneously, it promotes equity by utilizing relevant classroom examples, reflects the students' cultures in the lessons, and "gives voice to marginalized populations" (Dantley et al., 2008, p. 131). This means that teachers should be given the space to investigate, inspire, experiment, reflect, revise, relearn, and change with the approval of administration (Beachum & McCray, 2012, p. 241). A practical example of a teaching strategy that exemplifies holistic uniqueness is universally designed learning

(UDL), which focuses on designing instruction that fits the needs of a large variety of learners (Santovec, 2005; Thousand, Villa, & Nevin, 2007). This strategy is holistic because it takes the individual needs of learners and creates a lesson that meets all needs in an assortment of ways. Simultaneously, it is unique because this series of integrations for diverse learning can be used by students to differentiate their own education by enhancing material for extra growth or by adapting or accommodating material to make it accessible to all learners. This level of malleability gives educators room to address cultural issues and unique learning styles. Another area of education where holistic uniqueness thrives is in SWPBIS, where educators use behavioral learning to develop students in emotional, social, and cognitive domains as described earlier.

Moral Language

Moral language proposes that the words used with students and between educators should be grounded in ethics. This tenet suggests that language is used not only for communication between and among individuals, but also as a means for transmitting values. In secondary schools, the language around critique could be powerful in classrooms as well as in faculty discussions. An ethic of critique forces students and teachers to deal with bigger questions of who has power and why; how did things get to be this way; who benefits; and how can we change these arrangements (Starratt, 1991). This language can be controversial, volatile, and stressful, but it also can unleash powerful learning opportunities. Educators have to be very skillful with the aspect of moral language. Another example of moral language is presented in the ethic of caring, which is grounded in relationships (Starratt, 1991). Starratt (1991) indicated that caring "recognizes that it is in the relationship that the specifically human is grounded; isolated individuals functioning only for themselves are but half persons. One becomes whole when one is in relationship with another and many others" (p. 195). Therefore, in secondary schools, it is incumbent upon teachers and administrators to utilize a language of caring that invites students to participate in caring relationships.

When students are cared for, they then learn how to care about others. Moral language around caring also includes sincere dialogue (Freire, 1973). This kind of open discussion should be honest and reflective. In classrooms, it allows students to think about themselves in the context of the lesson and connect the seemingly abstract to their real lives. Among faculty, it can cause a real conversation around difficult educational issues such as the achievement gap, overrepresentation in special education, underrepresentation of female students in science courses, unfair disciplinary practices, and more. These issues could be emotionally charged, thus sincere dialogue keeps the focus on what is best for students. Wheatley (2002) agreed: "Human conversation is the most ancient and easiest way to cultivate the conditions for change—personal change, community, and organizational change" (p. 3). In practice, Singleton and Linton (2005) suggested that when engaging in difficult discussions, participants stay engaged, speak their truths, experience discomfort, and expect and accept non-closure (p. 17). These conversations are important for all educators. "When one group feels marginalized, everybody is affected—including those who are in positions of power and privilege, who often perceive themselves to be unaffected by the experiences of the underserved" (p. 29). The underserved and the privileged are caught in a system of mutual oppression (see Harro, 2000), in which they both are consistently taught to play their unequal roles. This is antithetical to a free, equal, and democratic society.

In terms of SWPBIS, moral language also takes a pertinent role. When presenting expectations, praise, and feedback to students, it is vitally important to use positive language that highlights what behaviors students should exhibit rather than simply noting those that are unwelcomed (Horner et al., 2010; Sugai et al., 2002). Furthermore, Tobin and Vincent (2011) found that inclusion of positive, specific reinforcement lessened the overrepresentation of African American students in disciplinary referral data. With positive language that helps students understand desired behaviors, which is relevant both culturally and linguistically, students are offered more opportunities to succeed in the modern classroom. The Socio-Cultural Justice framework is a way to put equity in action toward the goal of equal educational opportunities and experiences.

Conclusion

In this chapter, we examined Positive Behavior Support and specifically School-Wide Positive Behavior Support. We also argued for the incorporation of cultural relevance in conjunction with SWPBIS, while recognizing the importance of social justice in this endeavor. The result was the development of the Socio-Cultural Justice Framework. It is founded on three pillars: flexible relationships, holistic uniqueness, and moral language. We also addressed the practical implications for the use of the Socio-Cultural Justice Framework in secondary schools. The challenges facing today's schools are no doubt daunting, but educational equity and excellence undergird American society. New thinking, approaches, practices, and frameworks are needed to keep moving in the direction of a more socially just society (Beachum, McCray, Yawn, &

Obiakor, 2012). We should be guided by the words of Cornel West (2001) who wrote:

> To establish a new framework, we need to begin with a frank acknowledgement of the basic humanness and Americanness of each of us. And we must acknowledge that as a people—E Pluribus Unum [out of many, one]—we are on a slippery slope toward economic strife, social turmoil, and cultural chaos. If we go down, we go down together. (p. 4)

References

Alberto, P., & Troutman, A. C. (2006). *Applied behavior analysis for teachers* (7th ed.). Upper Saddle River, NJ: Pearson/Merrill/Prentice Hall.

Baer, D. M., Wolf, M. M., & Risley, T. R. (1968). Some current dimensions of applied behavior analysis. *Journal of Applied Behavior Analysis, 1*, 91–97.

Bambara, L., & Kern, L. (2002). *Individualized supports for students with problem behaviors: Designing positive behavior plans.* New York: Guilford Press.

Bambara, L., & Knoster, T. (2009). *Designing Positive Behavior Support plans* (2nd ed.). Washington, DC: American Association on Intellectual and Developmental Disabilities.

Banks, J. (1989). Multicultural education: Characteristics and goals. In J. Banks & C. McGee Banks (Eds.), *Multicultural Education: Issues and Perspectives* (7th ed.) (pp. 3–32). Hoboken, NJ: John Wiley & Sons.

Beachum, F. D., & McCray, C. R. (2004). Cultural collision in urban schools. *Current Issues in Education, 7*(5). Retrieved from http://cie.asu.edu/volume7/number5/

Beachum, F. D., & McCray, C. R. (2011). *Cultural collision and collusion: Reflections on hip-hop culture, values, and schools.* New York: Peter Lang.

Beachum, F. D., & McCray, C. R. (2012). The fast and the serious: Exploring the notion of culturally relevant leadership. In J. Moore & C. W. Lewis (Eds.), *African American students in urban schools: Critical issues and solutions for achievement* (pp. 231–247). New York: Peter Lang.

Beachum, F. D., McCray, C. R., Yawn, C. D., & Obiakor, F. E. (2012). Multidimensional leadership in urban schools. *National Journal of Urban Education and Practice, 5*(3), 300–314.

Boas, F. (1966). *Race, language, and culture.* New York: The Free Press.

Bogotch, I., Beachum, F., Blount, J., Brooks, J. S., & English, F. W. (2008). *Radicalizing educational leadership: Toward a theory of social justice.* Netherlands: Sense.

Carr, E., Dunlap, G., Horner, R., Koegel, R., Turnbull, A., Sailor, W., … Fox, L. (2002). Positive Behavior Support: Evolution of an applied science. *Journal of Positive Behavior Interventions, 4*(1), 4–16, 20.

Cooper, J. O., Heron, T. E., & Heward, W. L. (2007). *Applied behavior analysis* (2nd ed.). Upper Saddle River, NJ: Pearson/Merrill/Prentice Hall.

Dantley, M. E. (2004). Moral leadership: Shifting the management paradigm. In F. English (Ed.), *Handbook of educational leadership* (pp. 34–46). Thousand Oaks, CA: Sage.

Dantley, M., Beachum, F. D., & McCray C. R. (2008). Exploring the intersectionality of multiple centers within notions of social justice. *Journal of School Leadership, 18*(2), 124–133.

Delpit, L. (2006). *Other people's children: Cultural conflict in the classroom.* New York: The New Press.

Eber, L., Hyde, K., & Suter, J. (2011). Integrating wraparound into a schoolwide system of Positive Behavior Supports. *Journal of Child & Family Studies, 20*(6), 782–790.

Fallon, L. M., O'Keeffe, B. V., & Sugai, G. (2012). Consideration of culture and context in School-Wide Positive Behavior Support: A review of current literature. *Journal of Positive Behavior Interventions, 14*(4), 209–219.

Freire, P. (1973). *Pedagogy of the oppressed.* New York: Seabury Press.

Fullan, M. (2001). *Leading in a culture of change: Personal action guide and workbook.* San Francisco, CA: Jossey-Bass.

Fullan, M. (2004). *Leading in a culture of change: Personal action guide and workbook.* San Francisco: Jossey-Bass.

Goldfarb, K. P., & Grinberg, J. (2002). Leadership for social justice: Authentic participation in the case of a community center in Caracas, Venezuela. *Journal of School Leadership, 12,* 157–173.

Gordon, E. W., & Bridglall, B. L. (2005). Nurturing talent in gifted students of color. *Conceptions of Giftedness, 2,* 120–146.

Harro, B. (2000). The cycle of socialization. In M. Adams, W. J. Blumenfield, R. Castaneda, H. W. Hackman, M. L. Peters, & X. Zuniga (Eds.), *Reading for diversity and social justice: An anthology on racism, anti-Semitism, sexism, heterosexism, ableism, and classism* (pp. 79–82). New York: Routledge.

Harry, B. (1992). *Cultural diversity, families, and the special education system: Communication and empowerment.* New York: Teachers College Press.

Horner, R. H., Sugai, G., & Anderson, C. M. (2010). Examining the evidence base for School-Wide Positive Behavior Support. *Focus on Exceptional Children, 42*(8), 1–14.

Hoyle, C. G., Marshall, K. J., & Yell, M. L. (2011). Positive Behavior Supports: Tier 2 interventions in middle schools. *Preventing School Failure, 55*(3), 164–170.

Kern, L., Choutka, C., & Sokol, N. (2002). Assessment-based antecedent interventions used in natural settings to reduce challenging behavior: An analysis of the literature. *Education and Treatment of Children, 25*(1), 113–130.

Kunjufu, J. (2002). *Black students. Middle-class teachers.* Chicago, IL: African American Images.

Kunjufu, J. (2005). *Keeping Black boys out of special education.* Chicago, IL: African American Images.

Lewis, T., & Sugai, G. (1999). Effective behavior support: A systems approach to proactive schoolwide management. *Focus on Exceptional Children, 31*(6), 1–24.

Linton, R. (1945). *The cultural background of personality.* New York: Appleton-Century-Crofts.

Martinez, L. M., & Woods, D. A. (2007). Closing the racial/ethnic gaps. In M. C. Brown & R. D. Bartee (Eds.), *Still not equal: Expanding educational opportunity in society* (pp. 29–37). New York: Peter Lang.

McCray, C. R., Grant-Overton, C., & Beachum, F. D. (2010). Pedagogy of self-development: The role the Black church can have on African American students. *Journal of Negro Education, 79*(3), 233–248.

Myers, C. L., & Holland, K. L. (2000). Classroom behavioral interventions: Do teachers consider the function of the behavior? *Psychology in the Schools, 37*(3), 271–280.

Obiakor, F. E. (2001). *It even happens in "good" schools: Responding to cultural diversity in today's classrooms.* Thousand Oaks, CA: Corwin Press.

Obiakor, F. E. (2007). *Multicultural special education: Culturally responsive teaching.* Thousand Oaks, CA: Corwin Press.

Peterson, R. L. (2003). Teaching the social curriculum: School discipline as instruction. *Preventing School Failure, 47*(2), 66–73.

Rutherford, R., Quinn, M., & Mathur, S. (2004). *Handbook of research in emotional and behavioral disorders.* New York: Guilford Press.

Ryan, J. (2006). *Inclusive leadership.* San Francisco, CA: Jossey-Bass.

Santovec, M. (2005). Accessibility and universal design. *Distance Education Report, 9*(9), 3–7.

Scott, T., & Barrett, S. (2004). Using staff and student time engaged in disciplinary procedures to evaluate the impact of school-wide PBS. *Journal of Positive Behavior Interventions, 6*, 21–27.

Singleton, G., & Linton, C. (2005). *Courageous conversations about race: A field guide for achieving equity in schools.* Thousand Oaks, CA: Sage.

Skinner, B. F. (1953). *Verbal behavior.* Acton, MA: Copley.

Skinner, B. F. (1971). *Beyond freedom and dignity.* New York: Knopf.

Starratt, R. J. (1991). Building an ethical school: A theory of practice in educational leadership. *Educational Administration Quarterly, 27*(2), 185–202.

Sugai, G., & Horner, R. H. (2002). The evolution of discipline practices: School-Wide Positive Behavior Supports. *Child and Family Behavior Therapy, 24*, 23–50.

Sugai, G., Horner, R. H., & Gresham, F. M. (2002). Behaviorally effective school environments. In M. R. Shinn, H. M. Walker, & G. Stoner (Eds.), *Interventions for academic and behavior problems II: Preventative and remedial approaches* (pp. 315–350). Bethesda, MD: National Association of School Psychologists.

Sugai, G., O'Keeffe, B. V., & Fallon, L. M. (2012). A contextual consideration of culture and School-Wide Positive Behavior Support. *Journal of Positive Behavior Interventions, 14*(4), 197–208.

Swaminathan, R. (2005). Building community in urban schools: Promises and challenges. In F. E. Obiakor & F. D. Beachum (Eds.), *Urban education for the 21st Century: Research, issues, and perspectives* (pp. 187–197). Springfield, IL: Charles C Thomas.

Theoharis, G. (2007). Social justice educational leaders and resistance: Toward a theory of social justice leadership. *Educational Administration Quarterly, 43*(2), 221–258.

Thousand, J., Villa, R., & Nevin, A. (2007). *Differentiating instruction: Collaborative planning and teaching for universally designed learning*. Thousand Oaks, CA: Corwin Press.

Tobin, T. J., & Vincent, C. G. (2011). Strategies for preventing disproportionate exclusions of African American students. *Preventing School Failure*, *55*(4), 192–201.

U.S. Census Bureau. (2008). *Percent of the projected population by race and Hispanic origin for the United States: 2010 to 2050* (NP2008-T6). http://www.census.gov/population/projections/data/national/2008.html

U.S. Census Bureau. (2011). *90+ in the United States: 2006–2008* (ACS-17). Washington, DC: U.S. Government Printing Office.

Villegas, A. M., & Lucas, T. (2002). *Educating culturally responsive teachers*. Albany, NY: SUNY Press.

West, C. (2001). *Race matters*. Boston, MA: Beacon Press.

Wheatley, M. (2002). *Turning to one another: Simple conversations to restore hope to the future*. San Francisco: Berrett-Koehler.

Zehler, A., Fleischman, H., Hopstock, P., Stephenson, T., Pendzick, M., & Sapru, S. (2003). *Policy report: Summary findings related to LEP and SPED-LEP students*. Report submitted to U.S. Department of Education, Office of English Language Acquisition, Language Enhancement, and Academic Achievement of Limited English Proficient Students. Arlington, VA: Development Associates.

9. *A School-Wide Positive Behavior Support Model in Middle and High School*

CHRISTOPHER D. YAWN AND LENWOOD GIBSON JR.

Teachers often find themselves in the undesirable and precarious position of having to address problematic student behaviors (Gibson, 2013). School violence and lack of administrative response are the reasons many teachers have given for leaving their school or even the teaching profession as a whole (Smith & Smith, 2006). While there have indeed been instances of teachers "crying wolf" or magnifying minor offenses, the fact is that many teachers are faced with behavioral issues that they are not adequately trained to handle (Obiakor, 2004). Conversely, many students find themselves in schools where they would like to see (a) more structure, (b) adults showing them there are boundaries, and (c) adults demonstrating care for students by stopping and correctly addressing self-destructive behavior. Across many school districts, the focus is on exerting control and enforcing draconian disciplinary methods that ultimately cause students more harm than good. There is an overreliance on ineffective measures that simply punish and remove students from the learning environment, instead of teaching them appropriate replacement behaviors (Sugai & Horner, 2008). For example, the American Psychological Association has investigated the use of zero tolerance and found that it has not yielded the expected results in curtailing school violence (2008); yet it remains a widely adopted policy. Sanctioned methods of punishment have often resulted in the prejudicial treatment of students from culturally and linguistically diverse (CLD) backgrounds (Losen & Gillespie, 2012). Furthermore, students who are the most vulnerable and disenchanted with school are the most likely recipients of punitive disciplinary actions (Krezmien, Leone, & Achilles, 2006).

The ineffective and disproportionate use of punitive disciplinary measures has been written about extensively and gained national attention (Fabelo, et al., 2011; Losen & Gillespie, 2012; Skiba, Michael, Nardo, & Peterson, 2002). For example, the offices of the Attorney General Eric Holder and Secretary of Education Arne Duncan collaborated to form the Supportive School Discipline Initiative, in an effort to curtail what is commonly referred to as the school-to-prison pipeline (U.S. Department of Justice, 2011). The stated goals of this initiative are to:

> Build consensus for action among federal, state and local education and justice stakeholders; collaborate on research and data collection that may be needed to inform this work, such as evaluations of alternative disciplinary policies and interventions; develop guidance to ensure that school discipline policies and practices comply with the nation's civil rights laws and to promote positive disciplinary options to both keep kids in school and improve the climate for learning; and promote awareness and knowledge about evidence-based and promising policies and practices among state judicial and education leadership. (U.S. Department of Justice, 2011, para 4)

This is certainly a necessary move in the right direction to bring an end to school policies that have no place in the educational system. Additionally, such a highly publicized initiative is likely to bring about funding to support research that disseminates knowledge about best practices. Such practices should (a) reduce and prevent problematic behaviors, (b) build students' academic and social skills, and (c) increase instructional capacity (Carr et al., 2002; Coffey & Horner, 2012; Sugai & Horner, 2008). These key qualities, together with contextual considerations, are necessary for the successful implementation of School-Wide Positive Behavior Support (SWPBS); they will be examined in this chapter.

Conceptualizing School-Wide Positive Behavior Support

Responding to individual student infractions is traditionally how school personnel implement disciplinary measures. Therefore, a student must commit an inappropriate action in order to elicit a staff reaction. This type of reactionary behavior management is often ineffective, and does nothing to teach offending students more desirable behaviors. Often, students engaging in inappropriate behaviors have an appropriate goal in mind; it is their strategy for achieving the goal that is flawed. If students are not taught how to correctly reach their objectives, it is highly likely that they will repeat the inappropriate behaviors. Explicitly teaching students what is expected of them will help prevent and/or eliminate many of the common disruptions that occur in schools. Thus, a systematic approach is necessary to reduce confusion and ensure that all students, faculty, and staff are on the same page.

The use of school-wide approaches to prevent and address problem behaviors began more than two decades ago, has increasingly been implemented in school districts across the nation, and has consistently been found to be effective (Colvin, Kame'enui, & Sugai, 1993). School-Wide Positive Behavior Support (SWPBS) is a systematic approach to preventing and/or decreasing problematic behaviors and increasing effective teaching and learning. It is accomplished by directly teaching and publicizing expectations and consequences; consistently rewarding positive behaviors; making decisions based on data analyses; and providing multi-tiered systems of support for students (Sugai & Horner, 2002, 2006). The multi-tiered systems of support consist of three levels:

1. Primary level of support (Tier 1) includes evidence-based teaching strategies, positive reinforcement, and data-driven decision making (Ervin, Schaughency, Matthews, Goodman, & McGlinchey, 2007). Supports at this level are universal, and most students typically respond well to them.
2. Secondary level of support (Tier 2) is more focused systems of support that are intended for students who do not respond to Tier 1 supports. This level includes interventions such as small-group instruction, data-based decision making about specific student behavior, and explicit feedback on behavioral progress toward goals (Ervin et al., 2007).
3. Tertiary level of support (Tier 3) is designed for students who do not respond to Tier 1 and 2 interventions and exhibit the most extreme and frequent problematic behaviors (Walker, Cheney, Stage, & Blum, 2005). At this level, individualized interventions are provided, including wraparound services, one-on-one social skills training, and data-based decision making and planning teams (Eber, Hyd, & Suter, 2011).

Across all tiers, data collection and data-based decision making are evident. Likewise, evaluation of the effectiveness of a SWPBS system is determined by an analysis of the data. Often, such data consist of office referrals (Sprague, Sugai, Horner, & Walker, 1999).

Office referrals can provide a quick snapshot of data such as rates of suspension, expulsion, and tardiness. However, a more expansive and valuable use of office-referral data would include the locations within the school where there are frequent occurrences of problematic behaviors, the time of day most problematic behavior occurs, and specifics (e.g., fighting, physical and/or verbal teacher-student altercation) about the most frequent problem behaviors (Sprague et al., 1999). Having access to such detailed data provides administrators with: (a) the information they need to strategically plan everyday routines, (b) an awareness of the areas where increased supervision is necessary, and (c) a better grasp of the necessity and/or level of need for security personnel. Subsequently, routines such as switching classes between periods can be effectively modified to ensure that an appropriate amount of time is allocated and that traffic flow patterns are established to help reduce confusion, increase safety, and eliminate congestion in hallways and stairwells. Additionally, increased school personnel can be shifted to areas of the school where and/or when problematic behaviors are known to consistently occur. Finally, the frequency of severe student behaviors (e.g., physical fighting) can help administrators determine if school security officers are needed, and if so, how many.

For SWPBS to be effective, it is critical that a majority of school personnel actively support all the measures to help create a sustainable system. Specifically, it has been reported that at least 80% of school staff must support the implementation of SWPBS for it to be effective (Handler et al., 2007). The success of SWPBS is heavily dependent on consistency across settings and individuals. Expectations and consequences cannot vary. When students know there is a uniform system in place, it can reduce confusion and increase compliance, because rules and consequences are conspicuous throughout the entire school.

Keys to Reducing and Preventing Problematic Behavior

SWPBS is derived from applied behavior analysis. As such, the most basic principle of behavior modification, positive reinforcement, is the underlying mechanism for sustaining an effective SWPBS system. From a behavior analyst perspective, behavior consists of an individual's observable and measurable interactions with the environment (Johnston & Pennypacker, 1980). Positive reinforcement dictates the probability of a specific behavior occurring (Cooper, Heron, & Heward, 2007). Many of our actions are determined by what we perceive to be their result (i.e., our return). For example, if we do exceptional work at our job, we expect to receive a bonus, some type of recognition, or simply to have good feelings about it. That *return* heavily influences whether or not we will do exceptional work in the future (Skinner, 1953). In school, if a student raises his/her hand during class and is called on by the teacher, receiving such attention increases the probability that s/he will raise his/her hand in the future. In this example, raising the hand was the behavior and the teacher's attention (calling on the student) was the positive reinforcer. Often, attempts at changing problem behaviors are unsuccessful because a replacement behavior does not produce the same level of reinforcement as the problem behavior. Using the aforementioned hand-raising example, a student may revert to calling out if hand-raising does not solicit the desired response, immediately or at all. Thus, if the student receives immediate attention when s/he calls out, but is forced to wait or not receive attention at all when s/he raises a hand, s/he will quickly revert to calling out.

An often overlooked rule is that the effectiveness of a reinforcer can only be determined by the individual exhibiting the behavior. Therefore, school personnel should not make assumptions about what they think might motivate a student from a particular group. Two of the simplest methods for figuring out what students find acceptable as reinforcers is to simply ask them or observe what they do when given free time (Scheuermann & Hall, 2012). Understanding basic principles of behavior plays a critical role in responding to individual student needs and successfully implementing SWPBS.

As mentioned, SWPBS is a multi-tiered support system. Tier 1 supports are in place to prevent or decrease the occurrence of problematic behavior. Positive reinforcement occurs for students when they adhere to school rules, perform well in class, and appropriately interact with each other. Commonly, schools with a SWPBS system will have tangible items or activities such as a student store, a pep rally, trips, and/or certificates as a way of rewarding (i.e., positively reinforcing) good student behavior. Most students will respond well to this type of reward system—and thereafter, refrain from engaging in problem behavior. Students requiring Tiers 2 and 3 levels of support engage in disruptive behaviors more frequently. Depending on the severity of the student's behaviors, a support team may need to develop a behavioral intervention plan (BIP) (Buck, Polloway, Kirkpatrick, Patton, & Fad, 2000). Ultimately, a BIP is put in place to reduce and eliminate problem behaviors. The most effective BIPs are developed based on a functional behavior assessment (FBA) of the student (Vollmer & Northup, 1996). Fully detailing how to conduct a FBA and develop a BIP is beyond the scope of this chapter; an FBA will simply be described as a multi-step method used to determine why a particular behavior is occurring. Once the team completes an FBA, they will be able to develop a BIP that equips the student and staff with a strategy for addressing, avoiding, and eliminating the occurrence of problematic behaviors.

Keys to Building Students' Academic and Social Skills

Students who frequently engage in problematic behaviors often demonstrate poor academic and social skills (Algozzine, Wang, & Violette, 2010). Avoidance and escape are common reasons for problematic behavior (Cooper et al., 2007). For example, when students know the teacher is going to ask them to complete a task (e.g., read aloud) that they struggle with, they will engage in some type of behavior that will either cause them to be removed from the classroom or avert the teacher's attention so they no longer need to comply with the direction. Struggling students often present themselves as tough, trouble-making individuals to avert attention away from their academic shortcomings. A significant number of students lack the academic skills necessary to be successful in school; therefore, increasing their academic and social skills not only benefits them in the classroom, but also serves as a preventative mechanism.

Building students' academic and social skills requires well-thought-out interventions that are aligned with individual students' skill deficits. Schools should engage in universal screenings to identify students who exhibit problem behaviors and/or are at risk of failing academically (Walker et al., 2005). Subsequently, an FBA should be conducted with these students and function-based supports should be put in place. Effectiveness of this strategy was demonstrated in a study conducted by Burke, Hagan-Burke, and Sugai (2003). They conducted an FBA on a student and found that the target student engaged in problematic behaviors when presented with reading tasks that required comprehension. With the teacher, the researchers developed an intervention that focused on pre-teaching vocabulary concepts. As a result, the target student's off-task behavior decreased. In a different study that focused on strengthening students' social skills, Lo, Loe, and Cartledge (2002) assessed the effects of social-skills instruction for a group of middle school students. During the first phase of the intervention, a social-skills curriculum was taught to small groups of three or four students. In the next phase, the same social-skills curriculum was also taught to the whole class. Overall, the targeted students' antisocial behaviors decreased in the classroom and the lunchroom (Lo et al., 2002).

The Burke et al. study (2003) is an example of how a simple investigation to discover the root of a problem can avert patterns of inappropriate behaviors demonstrated by students. More important, students benefit from such individualized interventions to address their academic and social needs. A significant implication of the Lo et al. study (2002) is that some students require explicit instruction regarding appropriate behaviors, and need to be prompted by teachers and parents to practice the newly learned behaviors. Furthermore, both studies demonstrate the inverse relationship between academic performance and problematic social behavior. Specifically, the more time students are actively engaged in academic tasks, the less time they have to engage in disruptive behavior. Conversely, the more time students engage in disruptive behavior, the less time they engage in and are exposed to academic tasks. Consequently, much of the onus falls on teachers to deliver lessons that do more than align with the scope and sequence and address standards. Moreover, lessons need to include the perspectives of CLD groups and exclude culturally insensitive viewpoints.

Keys to Increasing Instructional Capacity

Establishing a well-run SWPBS requires the efforts of a variety of individuals beyond the classroom teacher. These individuals include family, peers, and other school community members. Individual students who demonstrate problematic behaviors must be taught replacement behaviors in multiple ways, from multiple instructors, and in multiple settings. A target behavior may be said to have generalized when at least one of the following has occurred: (a) the replacement behavior is exhibited in an environment different from the one in which it was taught, (b) the replacement behavior is exhibited when prompted by an individual different from the one who taught it to the target student, and/or (c) the replacement behavior is exhibited as a result of various prompts (e.g., verbal direction, written direction) different from those to which the target student was taught to respond (Cooper et al., 2007). Arguably, generalization is the most important feature of any behavior change, because a student must advance from being taught and reminded to use a replacement behavior to habitually demonstrating it on his/her own.

All students benefit from generalization, and most demonstrate it seamlessly. However, it is particularly important that students in need of Tier 2 and 3 levels of support be given interventions that program for generalization. Programming for generalization can be as easy as posting signs in the classroom and/or home to remind students to use the replacement behavior and, if necessary, listing the steps for correctly completing it. Assistance from others is crucial, and there must be open communication between the student(s) and the instructor. If a behavioral intervention is clearly communicated to a peer, that student can model correct use of the replacement behavior and even prompt the target student to use it when appropriate. Involving a target student's family can allow an intervention to take place in both the school and home settings. This will help increase the number of times that the student can practice the replacement behavior and will help speed along the student's ability to master it.

Effective communication between school personnel and families is essential for the vitality of any SWPBS system. Unfortunately, this does not always take place, and many CLD parents are purposely or unconsciously excluded from collaborative efforts because they are viewed as complacent or uncaring about their child's education (Boyd & Correa, 2005; Harry, 2002). The significance of this misperception should not be overlooked; it could be one of the variables contributing to the disproportionate number of punitive actions taken against CLD students. Programming for generalization is extremely important for all students, and need not be an onerous task burdening school personnel only. Opportunities for student learning can increase the instructional capacity of SWPBS when multiple members of the team and beyond collaborate to develop and implement strategies that promote generalization.

Contextual Considerations for SWPBS at the Middle and High School Levels

There are a number of contextual factors at the middle and high school levels that should be considered when implementing SWPBS. Some can be easily mitigated while others require a considerable amount of effort to overcome. Nevertheless, students will follow the staff's lead. In that regard, the adults within the school building—no matter at what level—dictate the success or failure of SWPBS.

Children often enter school with excitement and wonderment about the unknown. The novelty and fascination of school can carry children for many years. Unfortunately, for many students with academic and behavior problems, the positive effects of first entering school wanes quickly, and the school environment comes to be viewed as a place where inadequacies are highlighted, and a sense of failure is reinforced. We have discussed the relationship between student behavior and academic achievement; many students who exhibit problematic behaviors are failing academically (Torres, Nordness, Pierce, & Epstein, 2003). It is extremely important to work with children in their early school years, when they first begin to fail academically and to demonstrate problematic behaviors. Conversely, if the need is not apparent, preventative measures should be put in place.

School staff must make a concerted effort to screen for children at risk for problematic behavior. Subsequently, supports must be put in place for those children who need them. Without early identification and proper intervention, a cycle of school failure and harsh disciplinary measures (e.g., suspension, expulsion) are the likely result (Fox, Dunlap, & Powell, 2002). Additionally, as students get older they become more susceptible, because the use of punitive measures such as suspension and expulsion increases exponentially from elementary school to middle school (Losen, 2011). Despite common rhetoric, research shows that without intervention, children will not simply "grow out of" deviant behavior, and those who demonstrate problematic behaviors early have an increased probability of later maladjustment (Campbell, Shaw, & Gilliom, 2000).

Despite the noted effectiveness of SWPBS, its implementation has mostly occurred in elementary and middle schools, as opposed to high schools (Flannery, Sugai, & Anderson, 2009). That some of the underlying principles of SWPBS do not align with the objectives of high school helps explain why this effective system has not gained traction there. For example, implementing an effective SWPBS demands the support and collaboration of most staff. In many high schools, teachers and administrators are fragmented according to departments. An embedded school culture of polarization runs counter to the necessary collaboration of SWPBS. To establish teams that will assess student behavior and create effective interventions, members must come from multiple environments that the student frequently interacts with.

Another example of high school misalignment with SWPBS is positive reinforcement of appropriate behavior. In many high schools there is a struggle with publicly acknowledging students who exhibit appropriate behavior. In some instances, difficulty arises because high school staff is of the belief that students should not be rewarded for simply doing what they are expected to do. However, even though high school students have been in school for a number of years, it should not be assumed that they know what is expected of them. Some students may come from schools where disruptive behavior was the norm because school personnel lacked behavior management skills. Therefore, no assumptions should be made regarding students' notions of expected behavior. At any level, if students demonstrate appropriate behavior, age-appropriate positive reinforcement should follow.

Culture and SWPBS

When data are disaggregated by race and ethnicity, as well as by disability and non-disability status, Black students and students with disabilities are subjected to traditional methods of discipline (e.g., suspension, expulsion) at an increased rate (Losen, 2011). It should be noted that students who have a history of being suspended are more likely than others to be suspended again, experience academic failure, drop out, and be incarcerated (Fabelo et al., 2011; Losen & Gillespie, 2012). Therefore, lopsided administering of punitive disciplinary measures against Black students and students with disabilities should not only be viewed as discriminatory, but also as a violation of their civil rights. The overarching premise of *Brown v. Board of Education* (1954) was educational equality, deliberate action toward the provision of quality education for all, and an end to government- and school-sanctioned segregation (Blanchett, Mumford, & Beachum, 2005). Ironically, many school districts are actively engaged in de facto segregation that results in an exorbitant number of CLD students who are removed from the general-education setting. Additionally, Cartledge (2005) found that CLD students who are placed in these segregated and restrictive environments are unlikely to return to the general-education setting. An effective SWPBS system should help combat unfair treatment. However, no system is foolproof and all systems are susceptible to human error.

The student population has fundamentally changed over the last 50 years. Cultural disconnects between students and teachers likely exist in many schools across the United States. It has been projected that in less than a decade, White students will no longer comprise the majority in the nation's schools (Hussar & Bailey, 2011). While the student population has changed significantly, the teachers charged with educating them have remained the same (Snyder & Dillow, 2011). Additionally, multiple sources have documented the disproportionate representation of minority students in special education (Artiles & Ortiz, 2002; Artiles, Trent & Palmer, 2004; Gardner & Miranda, 2001; Harry, 2002; Skrtic, 2003). Ironically, as is the case with general educators, only 14% of special educators are from CLD groups (National Clearinghouse for Professions in Special Education, 2002). Student behavior is often used as a factor in identifying a student as emotionally disturbed. Undoubtedly, personal sensitivities about behaviors affect whether or not a teacher believes a particular behavior to be appropriate. As a result, behaviors exhibited by CLD students are often misinterpreted and undervalued (Cartledge, Kea, & Ida, 2000). For example, a White female teacher may view dialogue between African American males as aggressive and misuse her position of authority and discipline over the students (e.g., detention, principal's office, etc.), instead of making inquiries about what was being discussed. This briefly exemplifies how a teacher can misread cultural characteristics, such as styles of talking, and miss an opportunity to bridge CLD student interests with academic content. Academic engagement is a critical component of effective instruction, which is vital to the overall success of a SWPBS system. Therefore, teachers must seize teachable moments and provide lessons that are highly engaging and culturally relevant.

Relationships between students and teachers are arguably the most significant factor in determining the success of SWPBS. If these relationships are fractured, it is almost guaranteed that the SWPBS will not work. If teachers lack respect for students' cultures, and make no effort to learn about them, students will neither respect nor adhere to any system teachers try to put in place. A teacher who is better prepared to work with CLD students and their families will be less intimidated by cultural differences, able to build a good rapport, and more able to assist in establishing an effective SWPBS system. Therefore, it is crucial that all teachers be equipped with strategies to learn more about the various cultures of his/her students, and moreover, how to foster positive relationships with CLD students and their families.

Cultural identity formation truly takes root during the influential years one spends in middle and high school. Multiple factors such as peers, family, and community play a significant role in the development of a young person's identity. It is a unique process, undergone by all but varied among individuals. We all carry this historical process within us. Unfortunately, CLD students often find themselves at odds with the traditions of their school in that they were established by individuals with a Eurocentric perspective. While acculturation has always been one of the objectives of our schools, given the current and rapidly shifting makeup of our school populations, there needs to be a paradigm shift in terms of what students are expected to acculturate to. Administrators and teachers are charged with this unique challenge and should recruit the assistance of key stakeholders. Ultimately, schools should take on a true community form that celebrates cultural differences and provides opportunities that promote success for all students. Beachum, Yawn, McCray, and Obiakor (2012) contend "[school] leaders should envision a school environment that promotes both intellectual engagement as well as moral astuteness. These leaders should have a heightened understanding of the moral mission of schools; this mission helps to support American democracy" (p. 307).

Conclusion

It is a commonly held belief that every student deserves a chance to succeed. However, subjecting students to disciplinary actions that are reactive and do not include a teaching component is irresponsible, and places those students at increased risk for negative school outcomes including academic failure, school dropout, and alternative placement (Raffaele Mendez, 2003). The temporary or permanent removal of a student who is deemed problematic is essentially a placebo treatment that fails to solve schools' underlying problems with behavior management and classroom instruction. Hopes that traditional disciplinary measures will prove a point to other students is misguided for a number of reasons; these include (a) such measures are unlikely to resonate with students who do not respect the school or do not deem it to be an environment that will lead them to self-enrichment, (b) the removal of one "problem" student often leads to increased disruptions from students who did not previously display such behaviors (Noguera, 2003), and (c) authoritarian rule over students will only create an "us versus them" school culture and erode student morale and pride in their school.

All too often, neighborhood schools carry with them a history of disappointment and disenfranchisement. For the newly entering, high-hope-carrying teacher or administrator, this is almost certain to be more than s/he bargained for. However, across many school districts, officials are beginning to realize that traditional approaches to discipline do not work and disproportionately affect CLD students and students with disabilities. As a result, more proactive approaches such as SWPBS have been deemed necessary to effectively manage the behaviors of all students. School professionals must understand that an essential characteristic of SWPBS is the provision of quality curriculum and instruction that helps to curtail inappropriate behavior and is intertwined with culture. Cultural relevance must be present in all aspects of teaching and learning to help bridge barriers between students and teachers and families and schools. It is imperative that teachers take on the responsibility to educate themselves about the various cultures of their students and continue to build their cultural competence. This responsibility is a teacher's professional duty, because when teachers bring prejudice and unfounded biases into schools, CLD students experience negative educational outcomes. Finally, it is essential to the success of SWPBS that the vast majority of staff is on board. Belief in the mantra "it takes a village" must ring loud for SWPBS to have a positive effect. If the adults take the lead, the children will follow.

References

Algozzine, B., Wang, C., & Violette, A. S. (2010). Reexamining the relationship between academic achievement and social behavior. *Journal of Positive Behavior Interventions, 13*, 3–16.

American Psychological Association Zero Tolerance Task Force. (2008). Are zero-tolerance policies effective in the schools? *American Psychologist, 63*, 852–862.

Artiles, A. J., & Ortiz, A. (2002). *English language learners with special education needs: Identification, assessment, and instruction*. McHenry, IL: Center for Applied Linguistics, Delta Systems.

Artiles, A. J., Trent, S. C., & Palmer, J. (2004). Culturally diverse students in special education: Legacies and prospects. In J. A. Banks & C. M Banks (Eds.), *Handbook of research on multicultural education* (2nd ed., pp. 716–735). San Francisco: Jossey-Bass.

Beachum, F. D., Yawn, C. D., McCray, C. R., & Obiakor, F. E. (2012). Multidimensional leadership in urban schools. *National Journal of Urban Education & Practice*, *5*(3), 300–316.

Blanchett, W. J., Mumford, V., & Beachum, F. (2005). Urban school failure and disproportionality in a post-*Brown* era. *Remedial and Special Education*, *26*, 70–81.

Boyd, B. A., & Correa, V. I. (2005). Developing a framework for reducing cultural clash between African American parents and the special education system. *Multicultural Perspectives*, *7*, 3–11.

Brown v. Board of Education, 347 U.S. 483 (1954).

Buck, G. H., Polloway, E. A., Kirkpatrick, M. A., Patton, J. R., & Fad, K. M. (2000). Developing behavioral intervention plans: A sequential approach. *Intervention & School Clinic*, *36*, 3–9.

Burke, M. D., Hagan-Burke, S., & Sugai, G. (2003). The efficacy of function-based interventions for students with learning disabilities who exhibit escape-maintained problem behaviors: Preliminary results from a single-case experiment. *Learning Disability Quarterly*, *26*, 15–25.

Campbell, S. B., Shaw, D. S., & Gilliom, M. (2000). Early externalizing behavior problems: Toddlers and preschoolers at risk for later maladjustment. *Development and Psychopathology*, *12*, 467–488.

Carr, E., Dunlap, G., Horner, R., Koegel, R., Turnbull, A., Sailor, W,…Fox, L. (2002). Positive Behavior Support: Evolution of an applied science. *Journal of Positive Behavior Interventions*, *4*, 4–16.

Cartledge, G. (2005). Restrictiveness and race in special education: The failure to prevent or return. *Learning Disabilities: A Contemporary Journal*, *3*, 27–32.

Cartledge, G., Kea, C. D., & Ida, D. J. (2000). Anticipating differences—celebrating strengths: Providing culturally competent services for students with serious emotional disturbance. *Teaching Exceptional Children*, *32*(3), 30–37.

Coffey, J. H., & Horner, R. H. (2012). The sustainability of schoolwide positive behavior interventions and supports. *Exceptional Children*, *78*, 407–422.

Colvin, G., Kame'enui, E., & Sugai, G. (1993). Reconceptualizing behavior management and school-wide discipline in general education. *Education and Treatment of Children*, *16*, 361–381.

Cooper, J. O., Heron, T. E., & Heward, W. L. (2007). *Applied behavior analysis* (2nd ed.). Upper Saddle River, NJ: Pearson Prentice Hall.

Eber, L., Hyde, K., & Suter, J. C. (2011). Integrating wraparound into a schoolwide system of Positive Behavior Supports. *Journal of Child & Family Studies*, *20*, 782–790.

Ervin, R. A., Schaughency, E., Matthews, A., Goodman, S. D., & McGlinchey, M. T. (2007). Primary and secondary prevention of behavior difficulties: Developing a data-informed problem-solving model to guide decision making at a school-wide level. *Psychology in the Schools*, *44*, 7–18.

Fabelo, T., Thompson, M. D., Plotkin, M., Carmichael, D., Marchbanks, M. P., & Booth, E. A. (2011, July). *Breaking schools' rules: A statewide study of how school discipline relates to students' success and juvenile justice involvement*. New York: Council of State Governments Justice Center. Retrieved from http://csgjusticecenter.org/youth/breaking-schools-rules-report/

Flannery, K. B., Sugai, G., & Anderson, C. M. (2009). School-Wide Positive Behavior Support in high school: Early lessons learned. *Journal of Positive Behavior Interventions, 11*, 177–185.

Fox, L., Dunlap, G., & Powell, D. (2002). Young children with challenging behavior: Issues and considerations for behavior support. *Journal of Positive Behavior Interventions, 4*, 208–217.

Gardner, R., & Miranda, A. H. (2001). Improving outcomes for urban African American students. *Journal of Negro Education, 70*(4), 255–263.

Gibson, L., Jr. (2013). Culturally relevant behavior management strategies. In C. D. Yawn & F. E. Obiakor (Eds.), *Urban special education: The New York experience* (pp. 91–110). Debuque, IA: Kendall Hunt.

Handler, M. W., Rey, J., Connell, J., Their, K., Feinberg, A., & Putnam, R. (2007). Practical considerations in creating School-Wide Positive Behavior Support in public schools. *Psychology in the Schools, 44*, 29–39.

Harry, B. (2002). Trends and issues in serving culturally diverse families of children with disabilities. *Journal of Special Education, 36*, 131–138.

Hussar, W. J., & Bailey, T. M. (2011). *Projections of Education Statistics to 2019* (NCES 2011–017). Washington, DC: National Center for Education Statistics, Institute of Education Sciences, U.S. Department of Education.

Johnston, J. M., & Pennypacker, H. S. (1980). *Strategies and tactics for human behavioral research*. Hillsdale, NJ: Lawrence Erlbaum.

Krezmien, M. P., Leone, P. E., & Achilles, G. M. (2006). Suspension, race, and disability: Analysis of statewide practices and reporting. *Journal of Emotional and Behavioral Disorders, 14*, 217–226.

Lo, Y.-y., Loe, S. A., & Cartledge, G. (2002, August). The effects of social skills instruction on the social behaviors of students at risk for emotional or behavioral disorders. *Behavior Disorders, 27*, 371–385.

Losen, D. J. (2011, October 5). *Discipline policies, successful schools, and racial justice*. Boulder, CO: National Education Policy Center. Retrieved from http://nepc.colorado.edu/publication/discipline-policies

Losen, D. J., & Gillespie, J. (2012, August). *Opportunities suspended: The disparate impact of disciplinary exclusion from school*. The Civil Rights Project/Proyecto Derechos Civiles. Retrieved from http://civilrightsproject.ucla.edu/resources/projects/center-for-civil-rights-remedies/school-to-prison-folder/federal-reports/upcoming-ccrr-research/losen-gillespie-opportunity-suspended-2012.pdf

National Clearinghouse for Professions in Special Education. (2002). *Just the facts: Percent of special education teachers by racial group 1999–2000*. Retrieved from http://cecp.air.org/teams/stratpart/ncpse.asp

Noguera, P. A. (2003). Schools, prisons, and social implications of punishment: Rethinking disciplinary practices. *Theory Into Practice*, *4*, 341–350.

Obiakor, F. E. (2004). Impact of changing demographics on public education for culturally diverse learners with behavior problems: Implications for teacher preparation. In L. M. Bullock & R. A. Gable (Eds.), *Quality personnel preparation in emotional/behavioral disorders: Current perspectives and future directions* (pp. 51–63). Denton, TX: University of North Texas, Institute for Behavioral and Learning Differences.

Raffaele Mendez, L. M. (2003). Predictors of suspension and negative school outcomes: A longitudinal investigation. In J. Wald & D. L. Losen (Eds.), *New directions for youth development* (no. 99: Deconstructing the school-to-prison pipeline) (pp. 17–34). San Francisco: Jossey-Bass.

Scheuermann, B. K., & Hall, J. A. (2012). *Positive Behavioral Supports for the classroom* (2nd ed.). Columbus, OH: Pearson.

Skiba, R. J., Michael, R. S., Nardo, A. C., & Peterson, R. L. (2002). The color of discipline: Sources of racial and gender disproportionality in school punishment. *Urban Review*, *34*, 317–342.

Skinner, B. F. (1953). *Science and human behavior.* New York: Macmillan.

Skrtic, T. M. (2003). An organizational analysis of the overrepresentation of poor and minority students in special education. *Multiple Voices*, *6*(1), 41–57.

Smith, D. L., & Smith, B. J. (2006). Perceptions of violence: The views of teachers who left urban schools. *High School Journal*, *89*(3), 34–42.

Snyder, T. D., & Dillow, S. A. (2011). *Digest of Education Statistics 2010* (NCES 2011–015). Washington, DC: National Center for Education Statistics, Institute of Education Sciences, U.S. Department of Education.

Sprague, J. R., Sugai, G., Horner, R. H., & Walker, H. M. (1999). Using office discipline referral data to evaluate school-wide discipline and violence prevention interventions. *Oregon School Study Council Bulletin*, *42*(2). Eugene, OR: University of Oregon, College of Education.

Sugai, G., & Horner, R. H. (2002). Introduction to the special series on Positive Behavior Support in schools. *Journal of Emotional and Behavioral Disorders*, *10*, 130–135.

Sugai, G., & Horner, R. H. (2006). A promising approach for expanding and sustaining School- Wide Positive Behavior Support. *School of Psychology Review*, *35*, 246–259.

Sugai, G., & Horner, R. H. (2008). What we know and need to know about preventing problem behavior in schools. *Exceptionality*, *16*, 67–77.

Torres, C., Nordness, P. D., Pierce, C. D., & Epstein, M. H. (2003). Research on the academic status of children with emotional and behavioral disorders: A review of the literature from 1961 to 2000. *Journal of Emotional and Behavioral Disorders*, *11*, 198–210.

U.S. Department of Justice. (2011, July 21). *Attorney General Holder, Secretary Duncan announce effort to respond to school-to-prison pipeline by supporting good discipline practices* [Justice news]. Retrieved from http://www.justice.gov/opa/pr/2011/July/11-ag-951.html

Vollmer, T., & Northup, J. (1996). Some implications of functional analysis for school psychology. *School Psychology Quarterly*, *11*, 76–92.

Walker, B., Cheney, D., Stage, S., & Blum, C. (2005). Schoolwide screening and Positive Behavior Supports: Identifying and supporting students at risk for school failure. *Journal of Positive Interventions*, *7*, 194–204.

Section IV

10. *Common and Unique Themes of Positive Behavior Interventions and Supports Across Grade/Age Levels*

CARLOS R. MCCRAY, CHUN ZHANG, SU-JE CHO,
AND SAMUEL MARTIN

Positive Behavioral Interventions and Supports (PBIS) has received a tremendous amount of attention from scholars since its inception in the 1990s. In light of this increased interest, some researchers (Filter, Tincani, & Fung, 2009) have asked whether PBIS has helped with regard to the myriad behavioral issues some students bring to the educative process. Unfortunately, many students continue to display disruptive behavior, which has the potential to completely shut down a classroom and prevent other students from learning (Duran, Zhou, Frew, Kwok, & Benz, 2011; Goh & Bambara, 2012). Beachum and McCray (2011) proposed the theory of *cultural collision and collusion* as one of the main antecedents to "disruptive behavior" in culturally and linguistically diverse student populations. According to their theory, in many instances there is a mismatch of cultures between student and educator. As a result, many educators are not adequately prepared to deal with the behavior of students whose culture is completely different from their own. This is cultural collision. The notion of cultural collusion is the corollary of cultural collision. Because of the cultural clash that occurs between culturally and linguistically diverse (CLD) students and teachers, students can become aware of the deficit thinking of educators and begin to act out even more as a result of feelings of inadequacy.

Beachum and McCray's theory has merit and is worthy of consideration. Regardless of the reasons for students' acting out, however, the reality is that educators and school officials must become more proactive in preventing and curbing potential outbursts, aggressive behaviors, and acts of non-compliance among students (Duran et al., 2011; Goh & Bambara, 2012). The concept of PBIS offers educators an entirely new direction in terms of how to deal with disciplinary infractions, as well as prevent violations of school rules. Alas, PBIS has not become as institutionalized in schools as many proponents had hoped it would. Educators today are still using antiquated disciplinary measures to "deal" with students who, for whatever reason, are not behaving appropriately (Lindle, 2008). For instance, a December 2010 article in the *New York Times* (Tavernise, 2010) reported that the Baltimore School System had handed out 26,000 school suspensions in 2004. Thus, upon taking the job, the new Baltimore School superintendent made it his top priority to reduce school suspensions. Clearly, some form of alternative disciplinary measures could have been used to reduce the number of school suspensions in the Baltimore school system that year.

The Baltimore School system is not alone in having an excessive number of school suspensions and expulsions each year. In many urban school districts across the nation with high percentages of students of color, there are also high percentages of suspensions and expulsions, strategies that are used to "maintain control" (Welch & Payne, 2012). It seems, therefore, that for many urban school districts, the modus operandi for dealing with disciplinary infractions is to simply jettison both behavioral issues and student from the classroom and school (Beachum & McCray, 2011; Duran et al., 2011; Lindle, 2008; Peterson, 2003; Skiba & Peterson, 1999; Welch & Payne, 2012). Fortunately, PBIS offers educators and school officials an alternative to this antiquated and nonegalitarian way of enforcing school rules and disciplinary practices (Goh & Bambara, 2012).

The purpose of this chapter is to examine the common themes of PBIS across different grade levels. The chapter is divided into five sections. The first looks at how PBIS can be used in preschool and the elementary grade levels (i.e., grades pre-K–5); the second looks at PBIS in the middle grades (i.e., grades 6–8); and the third section will take an in-depth look at PBIS at the high school level (i.e., grades 9–12). In the fourth and fifth sections, we address the implications of using PBIS across grade levels, and draw some conclusions for educators and school administrators to enhance their praxis.

We believe it is crucial to ascertain how educators are utilizing PBIS across grade levels in order to solidify best practices. There is a misconception among some educators that what works for one group of students (i.e., age/grade level) will not work for another (Masten, Juvonen, & Spatzier, 2009). We readily acknowledge that there is some validity to this. Far too often, school officials select programmatic resources based on the notion that

such programs worked for one group of students; consequently, they must work for other students as well. Intellectual and pedagogical certitude in either direction can lead to miseducation of students. Thus, we offer this critique of PBIS at different age/grade levels in order to identify common themes and, hopefully, inspire educators and school officials to think outside the box in its implementation.

PBIS Across Age/Grades Levels

Early Childhood Through Elementary Grade Levels

PBIS models can be utilized across all grade levels to help ensure students are engaged in positive social and academic behaviors, both inside and outside the classroom (Masten et al., 2009). Goh and Bambara (2012) found that the most common use of PBIS in elementary schools is the Individual Positive Behavioral Interventions and Supports (IPBIS) model. According to Bambara (2005), IPBIS is designed to help educators in an array of categories concerning students' behavior. IPBIS is a behavior approach that relies on multiple data sources to determine the best course of action for a student, while contextualizing the student's behavior. In addition to promoting contextualization, IPBIS is a proactive approach designed to prevent negative behavior before it occurs (Bambara, 2005). Goh and Bambara (2012) also found IPBIS to be a "multi-component behavioral intervention plan" that makes no assumptions concerning the student's behavioral issues or disposition (p. 272). Moreover, IPBIS ensures easy transitions in the implementation of the plan from the teacher to others (i.e., parents and paraprofessionals) who are there to assist the student. In fact, Goh and Bambara (2012) indicated that a truly attractive aspect of IPBIS is that it allows parents to be involved in both the generating and intervention phases of the plan.

At the early childhood level, helping young children develop social and emotional skills, identify and express feelings, and form positive relationships with peers and adults will help them build a solid social and emotional foundation. Teaching young children to use words, objects, toys, and real-life experiences and interactions to understand and express feelings and solve problems should be a major part of the early childhood curriculum. In early childhood classrooms, young children use daily routines and activities to learn and practice these skills with peers and adults, while they are also learning other important pre-academic skills (i.e., cognitive, adaptive, language and communication) across domains. Learning about positive behaviors and PBIS can be naturally embedded in large-group and small-group daily routines and activities. More important, families and professionals can use regular home-school communication notebooks or other approaches to support young children in developing appropriate and positive behaviors and social skills across settings. Educators should use developmentally appropriate strategies to help young children learn the behavioral expectations emphasized in an early childhood PBIS program (Stormont, Lewis, & Beckner, 2005). These strategies include, but are not limited to, using praise, pictures and other visual representations of behavioral expectations; puppet shows; taking photographs of students who are exhibiting the highlighted behaviors and posting them in classroom and home settings; and describing expectations using words and actions that young children can understand (Hemmeter, Fox, Jack, & Broyles, 2007).

Another form of PBIS used at the elementary level is the check in/check out (CICO) model (Todd, Campbell, Meyer, & Horner, 2008). The CICO model is geared more toward targeted interventions, and has been proven effective with students at this level. According to Todd et al. (2008), "the value of targeted interventions had gained more attention as educators search for highly efficient strategies for preventing and addressing problem behavior (Crone, Horner, & Hawken, 2003; Fairbanks, Sugai, Guardino, & Lathrop, in press; Filter et al., in press; Hawken & Homer, 2004; Lewis & Sugai, 1999; March & Horner, 2002" (p. 46). The purpose of targeted interventions is to help students who are bordering on displaying behavioral issues. They are designed to give such students continuous feedback and adjustments. The CICO model is fairly simple for educators to develop and use. The components undergirding the CICO model are organizational systems, intervention practices, and data use (Todd et al., 2008). Each helps the educator structure the educational organization so as to assist the student with behavior modification specifically related to his or her displayed behaviors. But what truly undergirds the CICO model is the report card system (Davies & McLaughlin, 1989; Dougherty & Dougherty, 1977; Hawken & Horner, 2003). The report card system allows teachers to establish structure, intervention practices, and data collection.

Indeed, without the report card system, the CICO model would not be as effective in modifying students' behavior. The report card system allows educators to structure behavior modification interventions so as to directly address students' needs. Also, as the educator observes a child matriculate through his or her school day, the educator can take pertinent notes to provide to the student. Such feedback is crucial in modifying students' behavior.

At points throughout the day, a student may experience a minor—or even major—collapse in his or her progress toward achieving the desired targeted goals. When this occurs, it is the teachers' obligation under the report card system to remind the student of the behavioral objectives he or she is expected to reach. And as the school day draws to a close, the educator, through observation and intervention, should have collected sufficient data to share with the child and his or her parents. The CICO report card system requires that parents be updated on the day-to-day data the educator collects on the child's behavior (Todd et al., 2008). According to Todd et al. (2008), "The home report include[s] documentation of points earned and comments about what went well and things the student should work on the next day" (p. 51). Parents are also obligated to correspond with the school by indicating that they have received the report of the child's behavior for the previous day (Crone, Horner, & Hawken, 2003).

Another instrument strongly associated with PBIS that is used at the early childhood and elementary levels is the systematic screening tool. According to Lane et al. (2011), the purpose of the systematic screening tool is to help educators gain an overall assessment of the school culture and climate with regard to the level of threat posed by student behavior. In addition, systematic screening tools help educators to recognize students who might need extra support "in the form of secondary and tertiary prevention" (p. 39). Lane et al. (2011) have posited that systematic screening tools are comparable with the three-tier system of PBIS (i.e., primary prevention [preventive], secondary prevention [reversal], and tertiary prevention [supporting]). In their research, Lane et al. (2011) "explore data-driven approaches to interpreting systematic screening data collected as regular school practices ... to (a) measure the overall level of risk present in a school over time, and (b) identify students who may require more targeted supports in the form of secondary and tertiary preventions efforts" (p. 40). Although Lane et al. (2011) conducted their research over multiple grade levels (i.e., early childhood, elementary, middle, and high school), they indicated that systematic screening tools were initially designed for educators at the elementary level to reduce behavioral problems through the three-tier prevention methods.

Middle Grade Level

As students move from the elementary grades into middle and junior high grades, existing or undiagnosed problem behaviors may begin to intensify. At this level, educators are indeed one of the last lines of defense to help students with problematic behaviors alter their conduct. Caldarella, Young, Richardson, Young, and Young (2008) found that students whose behavioral problems continued into their middle and junior high years were gravely at risk of not succeeding in school. Similarly, Caldarella et al. (2008) found that students with emotional behavior disorders (EBD) had the greatest risk of dropping out of the educative process altogether. According to Caldarella et al. (2008):

> ... about half (51%) [of students with EBD] drop out of high school, which is the highest dropout rate of any educational disability category. Youth with EBD have lower grades and fail more classes. For secondary school students with EBD, 73% have a history of suspension or expulsion from school compared with only 22% of students in the general population. (p. 105)

Researchers (Caldarella et al., 2008; Lane, Rogers, et al., 2007) have been adamant that in order to ameliorate or reduce these outcomes in students classified as EBD, educators must utilize effective screening, especially at the middle-school and junior-high levels.

Kauffman (1999) also found that effective screening is crucial if educators are to deal appropriately with students with EBD or other inappropriate behaviors. But unfortunately, Caldarella et al. (2008) found that at least 10–20% of students with "mental health concerns" had not received the appropriate "interventions" (p. 105). Meanwhile, Lane, Parks, Kalberg, and Carter (2007) reported that "although researchers and practitioners are clear on the importance of early screening and intervention at the elementary level (Newcomer, Lewis, & Powers, 2002), little attention has been devoted to developing systematic screeners for use at the middle school level" (p. 210). Ironically, as mentioned previously, middle school and junior grade levels can be the most challenging time for educators in dealing with students experiencing severe behavior disorders. It would be a mistake for educators to assume that effective screening has been completed at the elementary level and that students have been diagnosed for all behavioral issues. Thus, Caldarella et al. (2008) posited the Systematic Screening for Behavior Disorders (SSBD) as an effective way to identify students with behavioral disorders at the middle grade levels, and advocate strongly for its use in tandem with PBIS.

In order for SSBD to work effectively, educators have to maintain constant observation with regard to students' risk status. It takes educators away from the business-as-usual model where, in many instances, teachers are unconsciously waiting for students to fail from a behavioral standpoint (Glover & Albers, 2007). When students reach the point where they are beginning to display certain EBD characteristics, it becomes even more difficult to stage an intervention. Such educational malpractice by educators and school leaders winds up doing severe damage to students who might otherwise have been able to matriculate through the educative process (Obiakor, Beachum, & Harris, 2010). According to Caldarella et al.

(2008), SSBD consists of three stages. In stage one, educators attempt to identify students displaying possible signs of EBD in either the internalizing or externalizing categories. Internalizing behaviors are those in which the student displays antisocial behavior, whereas externalizing behaviors include dispositional displays such as aggression and non-compliance (Lane, Parks et al., 2007; Lane, Rogers et al., 2007). Caldarella et al. (2008) further defined internalizing and externalizing behaviors, stating that internalizing behaviors include "painful shyness, [being teased, neglected and avoided by other students, and having] severely restricted activity levels" (p. 109). In contrast, examples of externalizing behaviors in his definition include situations where a student "steals" from others, "physically assaults an adult," and "damages others' property" (p. 109).

The second stage of SSBD consists of educators rating students' behavior on a specified scale to ascertain their particular risk. Finally, stage three "consists of obtaining independent classroom observations of behaviors for students who meet or exceed normative criteria on the SSBD Stage 2" (Caldarella et al., 2008, p. 109). When used properly, SSBD can enhance the success of PBIS (Nelson, Benner, Reid, Epstein, & Currin, 2002). In essence, SSBD is designed to help educators screen students who are at risk of EBD. "Effective screening and early identification of at-risk students may help to decrease the chances that EBD will develop and worsen over time" (Caldarella et al., 2008, p. 107).

Although SSBD has been mainly used in elementary schools over the last few years, studies (Caldarella et al., 2008; Lane, Parks et al., 2007; Lane, Rogers et al., 2007) have shown that it is also effective when used at the middle and junior grade levels. Such studies are vitally important because they give middle school and junior grade teachers the opportunity to identify those students who are potential threats to both the school culture and to themselves. As stated earlier, many educators seem to subscribe to the notion that once students have made it to the middle and junior grade levels, not much can be done for them in terms of intervention. On the contrary, research has shown that educators can still have a major impact on young adolescents at these grade levels (Caldarella et al., 2008; Lane, Parks et al., 2007; Lane, Rogers et al., 2007).

High School Level

If some educators are apprehensive about PBIS at the middle and junior grade levels, their misgivings must increase exponentially at the high school level (Bohanon et al., 2006). Bohanon and colleagues conducted a study in an urban high school in Chicago to ascertain how educators and school officials were utilizing the school-wide application of PBIS. According to Lane, Wehby, Robertson, and Rogers (2007), however, few researchers have engaged in studies dealing with PBIS at the high school level:

> To date, the majority of studies examining the efficacy of primary preventions plans—the foundation of the thee-tiered model—have been conducted at the elementary level (Hunter, Elias, & Norris, 2001; Lane & Menzies, 2003; Netzel & Eber, 2003; White, Marr, Ellis, Audette, & Algozzine, 2001). Far less evidence has been acquired as to the efficacy of primary prevention plans in … high schools. (p. 4)

We suspect that part of the reason why researchers—and perhaps even educators—have given less consideration to PBIS at the high school level is the ingrained notion that it becomes more difficult to address and correct students' behaviors once they reach a certain age (Bohanon et al., 2006). This acquiescence on the part of educators to the notion that it is extremely problematic to control older students is supported by the overwhelmingly exclusionary disciplinary measures imposed on students at the high school level compared to students at the middle and elementary grade levels (McCray & Beachum, 2006). Bohanon et al. (2006) caution that neither educators nor researchers should abandon the principles of PBIS simply because students have reached a certain age. In fact, they argue that the principles of PBIS work across age groups and grade levels, and can be effective with children, adolescents, and even adults.

PBIS is a multifaceted approach designed to improve the overall school climate and culture by helping teachers, students, and parents (Bohanon et al., 2006). It is designed to incorporate universal strategies for all students (primary intervention), as well as targeted interventions for those who need extra help (secondary intervention), and to provide very intense support (tertiary prevention, i.e., mental health support services and intensive curricular modifications) for those students who are struggling mightily with compliance. Lane, Wehby et al. (2007) indicated that "approximately 5% to 7% of the student body may need this level of prevention" (p. 4). They also estimated that 10% to 15% of a student population will need support at the secondary intervention stage (Lane, Wehby et al., 2007). Beachum and McCray (2011) challenged educators at the high school level; they asked why the number of students suspended and expelled from school on a daily basis due to the ineptitude of educators in dealing with students who come from a different cultural background does not cause more cognitive dissonance. Meanwhile, Bohanon and colleagues found that a school-wide PBIS plan could remedy the exclusionary measures that educators so often use for student infractions at the high school level.

According to Bohanon et al. (2006), one of the main criteria for implementing a school-wide PBIS (SWPBIS) plan entails educators laying out a rationale for the plan. Oftentimes, school leaders embark on a goal or objective without first clearly justifying it to the stakeholders. This is one of the main reasons why SWPBIS programs have failed to become institutionalized (Kaufman, 1995), especially at the high school level. School leaders need to be clear on the need and the goals for successful implementation. Bohanon et al. (2006) also found that it is important for school leaders and educators to be "on the same page" as it relates to the expectations of the school-wide behavior plan. And once expectations have been clearly established, the "structure" must be set in place for teaching expected behaviors (Bohanon et al., 2006). In many instances, this is where the leadership of the school breaks down. School leaders fail to communicate clearly the conditions under which something will occur. This can undermine the SWPBIS model.

The next criterion of SWPBIS is of vital importance for school leaders and educators. We mentioned earlier that high school students are subjected to many more suspensions and expulsions than elementary and middle school students. Thus, a major criterion for SWPBIS is for the leadership team to spell out specifically which behaviors are to be dealt with by faculty and which by the administration. This criterion of SWPBIS should mitigate the daily distraction of trivial office referrals to school leaders and ultimately provide the chance for educators to brainstorm as to how to deal with minor behavioral issues (Warren et al., 2003).

Lane, Wehby et al. (2007) have argued that many of our schools face serious behavioral issues, and that this is not something to be taken lightly. We completely agree that not all office referrals are trivial, and readily acknowledge that some behaviors must be dealt with in a cogent manner by school officials. Thus, SWPBIS also provides structures "to address serious office referral behavior" (Bohanon et al., 2006, p. 132). This key component of a SWPBIS assures educators that the leadership team will support them when the behavior of a student gets completely out of control. However, the fact remains that many office referrals to the principal's office are for infractions that would be better dealt with by the educator at the classroom level. To reiterate, we agree with Lane, Wehby et al. (2007) that there are students with serious and chronic behavioral issues within our schools; we argue, however, that SWPBIS equips educators and school leaders to work with those students displaying chronic misbehavior.

Finally, the last important component of SWPBIS is keeping an accurate record of how students are behaving, especially at the secondary and tertiary levels. If school officials do not keep an accurate record of students' behaviors, it could invalidate the entire premise of SWPBIS. Even though this is the final step, it is a vital one in SWPBIS (Warren et al., 2003).

Bohanon et al. (2006) discovered five specific challenges that high schools face in implementing SWPBIS. They are: (1) the school-wide acknowledgment system, (2) teaching behaviors in a high school setting, (3) logistics of implementation, (4) enacting consistent policies to address behavioral issues, and (5) modifying office disciplinary referrals (ODR) forms to track data (Bohanon et al., 2006). The challenge of the school-wide acknowledgement system deals with educators' struggle to find the right way to recognize positive behavior in high school students. Many teachers feel that students at this level have outgrown the need for recognition of positive behavior. Bohanon et al. (2006) disagree, claiming that high school students can benefit from educators' acknowledgement of good behavior. The challenge of teaching behaviors in high school is also undergirded by educators' beliefs and expectations regarding high school students. As mentioned earlier, many educators do not believe it is possible to teach corrective behaviors to high school students. This probably explains why we see so many suspensions and expulsions at the high school level. Once again, Bohanon et al. (2006) have found that corrective measures by caring teachers can be taught to high school students. The challenge of the logistics of implementation is essentially the challenge of creating school-wide structures to edify students on positive behaviors. Again, such structures and resources are critical to a successful SWPBIS. Bohanon et al. found that complaints about inadequate resources and structures often arose during educators' efforts to implement a SWPBIS model effectively.

The fourth challenge that Bohanon et al. (2006) identified in implementing SWPBIS at the high school level was enacting consistent policies to address behavioral issues. It is imperative for school leaders and educators to formulate consistent policies for addressing school infractions and problematic behavior. When some students are treated differently from others as a result of their behavior, they become quickly cognizant of the disciplinary inequity. We are not suggesting that schools implement zero-tolerance policies! What we are suggesting is that educators and school leaders make a concerted effort to be consistent in how they treat students. In other words, educators should resist the temptation to show favoritism.

Finally, the fifth and last challenge Bohanon et al. (2006) discovered in their research was that of modifying ODR forms. ODR are another way in which teachers and administrators can develop records of students' behavior. However, the recordkeeping has to be meaningful. According to Bohanon et al. (2006), meaningful record keeping includes "teachers providing data about the location and time of referrals. Also, [it provides] consideration for teachers about the possible motivation of behavior" (p. 143). In order for SWPBIS to flourish within a school, teachers and school administrators must be diligent in meeting these challenges, and not simply give in to the premise that PBIS is more appropriate for elementary and middle grade students.

Discussion and Implications

Throughout this chapter, we have tried to give an overview of different forms of PBIS models and structures used at the early childhood, elementary, middle school, and high school grade levels. We found that there are many similarities and common themes in PBIS across grade levels. However, the actual implementation of PBIS across grade levels may differ, and educators and school leaders will need to be diligent, especially at the high school level. PBIS is a student behavioral model that has proven effective for all students across all grade levels. It seems that the only drawback to the utilization of PBIS in many instances is in its implementation. We found that educators at the elementary and middle school level (i.e., grades 1–5 and 6–8) have a clearer understanding of the utilization of PBIS than teachers at the high school grade levels (i.e., grades 9–12).

At the early childhood, elementary, and middle school grade levels, research has shown that educators and school officials have been diligent in the use of PBIS in various forms. For instance, many educators at the elementary level have begun to use the Individual Positive Behavioral Interventions and Supports (IPBIS) model to contextualize students' behavior. Contextualizing the behavior of students is something that educators have not always readily done. As with Beachum and McCray's theory of cultural collision (2011), this speaks to the fact that educators at times may not understand that students bring their own set of problems and cultures with them to the educative process. However, the cultural collision between students and educators is one of the main reasons why educators should contextualize the behavior of their students.

Often, what educators believe to be willful disobedience may simply be a cultural mismatch between student and educator; this mismatch can lead to what Obiakor, Harris-Obiakor, Garza-Nelson, and Randall (2005) called the misidentification, misassessment, miscategorization, and/or misplacement of students. In addition to Beachum and McCray's cultural collision argument (2011), the contextualization of behavior is vitally important in relation to Abraham Maslow's hierarchy of needs. According to Maslow, certain needs must be met in order for an individual to reach self-actualization. These needs are: physiological, safety, belongingness or social, and esteem. Contextualization of behavior allows the educator to take into account those needs that are not met in children and that might serve as a catalyst for non-compliance and disruptive behavior.

With regard to the middle school grade levels, we found that educators are beginning to use PBIS tools to identify students with emotional behavior disorders (EBD). Teachers are using sophisticated screening techniques such as the Systematic Screening for Behavior Disorders (SSBD) to proactively identify those students who display symptoms of EBD (i.e., internalizing and externalizing behaviors). In the middle school grade levels, being proactive in identifying these students is crucial. Being proactive entails educators having a keen understanding of students who are potential bullies or victims of bullies. Oftentimes, educators overlook the aggressive behavior of students, attributing it to draconian rites of passage, and assuming that all students, especially boys, engage in aggressive behavior at some point during the educative process. However, the "rites of passage" argument makes no sense to parents of students who have committed suicide because of being bullied at school. SSBD is a worthy tool that can be used by educators to identify those students who have aggressive tendencies toward others in the building.

For teachers to be proactive in identifying students with potential EBD tendencies, they must adhere to the data as the basis for informed decisions. SSBD demands this of educators, especially at the middle school level. Franzen and Kamps (2008) provided a wonderful illustration of teachers using PBIS proactively during recess. According to Franzen and Kamps (2008), if educators begin to pay close attention to the number of office "referrals from the playground," they can make modifications to decrease the number of students visiting the school nurse or school administrator (p. 160). SSBD—together with PBIS—is designed to reduce the number of students who matriculate to the principal's office, but educators must be willing to adhere to the data being collected.

Finally, one of the more surprising aspects of this chapter was how PBIS is being utilized at the high school level. Bohanon et al. (2006) conducted a study on high schools using a SWPBIS model. Unfortunately, they found that school leaders had not been thorough in their rationale for using such a model. As indicated earlier, implementing a school-wide behavior plan consists of at least six specific components, ranging from precisely stating the rationale for the plan, to developing the appropriate structure and resources to implement it, cultivating a sense of fairness with regard to disciplining students, and developing a system to record and track the behaviors of students. Bohanon et al. (2006) concluded that each of the steps or components in a SWPBIS plan is crucial, and neglecting one or more could compromise the entire plan. Thus, Bohanon and colleagues found that teachers were unsure about the SWPBIS model due to the fact that school leaders had not done the proper preparation. Some of the educators were skeptical of the notion that schools could reinforce good behavior with what they considered "fuzzy" accolades and acknowledgments. In other words, they felt older students would reject such recognition. But the leadership literature shows clearly that older people never complain when they are showered with praise and compliments. Perhaps additional research needs to be done to ascertain if teachers really feel this way about older students, or simply feel this way about a certain type of student. The bottom line, according to Bohanon et al. (2006), is that students do want praise and recognition when they have done a good job, regardless of their age. Thus in order for SWPBIS to be effective, it is incumbent upon school leaders to do the proper preparation with their teachers. This means school leaders have to lead and be proactive along the way.

Conclusion

In this chapter, we highlight many common themes across age/grade levels with regard to PBIS. But we would like to emphasize that the most important concept we discovered is the notion of being proactive at every age/grade level. In order for PBIS to be utilized effectively, school leaders and educators must be upbeat about its potential benefits. The benefits are simple but substantial. When schools utilize PBIS models effectively, it can drastically reduce the number of students who are exposed to exclusionary discipline measures. As of now, the number of students being ushered out of the educative process is far too high. PBIS represents hope for all of us. But it requires educators at the early childhood, elementary, middle school, and high school grade levels to modify their notion of how to develop positive behavior or discipline students according to their developmental needs and the contextual factors influencing students' behaviors; it also requires administrators to assist teachers in this process. With teachers and school leaders working together, PBIS models have the potential to reduce disciplinary problems and to create effective learning environments for all students.

References

Bambara, L. M. (2005). Evolution of Positive Behavior Support. In L. M. Bambara & L. Kern (Eds.), *Individual supports for students with problem behaviors: Designing positive behavior plans* (pp. 1–24). New York: Guilford.

Beachum, F. D., & McCray, C. R. (2011). *Cultural collision and collusion: Reflections on hip hop culture, values, and schools.* New York: Peter Lang.

Bohanon, H., Fenning, P., Carney, K. L., Minnis-Kim, M. J., Anderson-Harriss, S., Moroz, K. B., ... Pigott, T. D. (2006). Schoolwide application of Positive Behavior Support in an urban high school: A case study. *Journal of Positive Behavior Interventions, 8*(3), 131–145.

Caldarella, P., Young, E. L., Richardson, M. J., Young, B. J., & Young, K. R. (2008). Validation of the Systematic Screening for Behavior Disorders in middle and junior high school. *Journal of Emotional and Behavioral Disorders, 16*(2), 105–117.

Crone, D. A., Horner, R. H., & Hawken, L. (2003). *Responding to problem behavior in the school: The behavior education program.* New York: Guilford.

Davies, D. E., & McLaughlin, T. F. (1989). Effects of a daily report card on disruptive behavior in primary students. *BC Journal of Special Education, 13*, 173–181.

Dougherty, E. H., & Dougherty, A. (1977). The daily report card: A simplified and flexible package for classroom behavior management. *Psychology in the Schools, 14*, 191–195.

Duran, J. B., Zhou, Q., Frew, L. A., Kwok, O., & Benz, M. R. (2011). Disciplinary exclusion and students with disabilities: The mediating role of social skills. *Journal of Disability Policies Studies, 24*(1), 15–26.

Fairbanks, S., Sugai, S., Guardino, D., & Lathrop, M. (in press). Response to intervention: An evaluation of a classroom system of behavior support for second grade students. *Exceptional Children.*

Filter, K. J., Tincani, M., & Fung, D. (2009). Surveying professionals' views of Positive Behavior Support and behavior analysis. *Journal of Positive Behavior Interventions, 11*(4), 222–234.

Filter, K., Benedict, E., McKenna, M., Horner, R. H., Todd, A., & Watson, J. (in press). Check in/check out: An efficient, secondary intervention for reducing problem behaviors in schools. *Journal of Positive Behavioral Intervention and Supports.*

Franzen, K., & Kamps, D. (2008). The utilization and effects of Positive Behavior Support on an urban school playground. *Journal of Positive Behavior Interventions, 10*(3), 150–161.

Glover, T. A., & Albers, C. A. (2007). Consideration for evaluating universal screening assessments. *Journal of School Psychology, 45*, 117–135.

Goh, A. E., & Bambara, L. M. (2012). Individualized Positive Behavior Support in school settings: A meta-analysis. *Remedial and Special Education, 33*, 271–286.

Hawken, L., & Horner, R. (2003). Evaluation of a targeted intervention within a schoolwide system of behavior support. *Journal of Behavioral Education, 12*, 225–240.

Hemmeter, M. L., Fox, L., Jack, S., & Broyles, L. (2007). A program-wide model of Positive Behavior Support in early childhood settings. *Journal of Early Intervention, 29*(4), 337–355.

Hunter, L., Elias, M. J., & Norris, J. (2001). School-based violence-prevention challenges and lessons learned from an action research project. *Journal of School Psychology, 39*, 161–175.

Kauffman, J. (1999). How we prevent the prevention of emotional and behavioral disorders. *Exceptional Children, 65*, 448–468.

Kaufman, R. (1995). *Mapping educational success: Strategic thinking and planning for school administrators.* Thousand Oaks, CA: Corwin Press.

Lane, K. L., Kalberg, J. R., Menzies, H., Bruhn, A., Eisner, S., & Crnobori, M. (2011). Using systematic screening data to asses risk and identify students for targeted supports: Illustrations across the K–12 continuum. *Remedial and Special Education, 32*(1), 9–54.

Lane, K. L., & Menzies, H. M. (2003). A school-wide intervention with primary and secondary levels of support for elementary students: Outcomes and consideration. *Education & Treatment of Children, 26*, 431–451.

Lane, K. L., Parks, R. J., Kalberg, J. R., & Carter, E. W. (2007). Systematic screening at the middle school level: Score reliability and validity of the student risk screening scale. *Journal of Emotional and Behavioral Disorders, 15*(4), 209–222.

Lane, K. L., Rogers, L. A., Parks, R. J., Weisenbach, J. L., Mau, A. C., Merwin, M. T., & Bergman, W. A. (2007). Function-based interventions for students who are nonresponsive to primary and secondary prevention efforts: Illustration at the elementary and middle school levels. *Journal of Emotional and Behavioral Disorders, 15*(3), 169–183.

Lane, K. L., Wehby, J. H., Robertson, J., & Rogers, L. A. (2007). How do different types of high school students respond to Schoolwide Positive Behavior Support programs? Characteristics and responsiveness of teacher-identified students. *Journal of Emotional and Behavioral Disorders, 15*(1), 3–20.

Lewis, T. J., & Sugai, G. (1999). Effective behavior support: A system approach to proactive school-wide management. *Effective School Practices, 17*, 47–53.

Lindle, J. C. (2008). School safety: Real or imagined fear? *Educational Policy, 22*(1), 28–44.

March, R. E., & Horner, R. H. (2002). Feasibility of contributions of functional behavioral assessment in schools. *Journal of Emotional and Behavioral Disorders, 10*, 158–171.

Masten, C. L., Juvonen, J., & Spatzier, A. (2009). Relative importance of parents and peers: Differences in academic and social behaviors at three grade levels spanning late childhood and early adolescence. *Journal of Early Adolescence, 29*(6), 773–799.

McCray, C. R., & Beachum, F. D. (2006). A critique of zero-tolerance policies: An issue of justice and caring. *Values and Ethics in Educational Administration, 5*(1), 1–8.

Nelson, J. R., Benner, G. J., Reid, R. C., Epstein, M. H., & Currin, D. (2002). The convergent validity of office discipline referrals with CBCL-TRF. *Journal of Emotional and Behavioral Disorders, 10*, 181–189.

Netzel, D. M., & Eber, L. (2003). Shifting from reactive to proactive discipline in an urban school district: A change in focus through PBIS implementation. *Journal of Positive Behavioral Intervention, 5*, 71–79.

Newcomer, L. L., Lewis, T. J., & Powers, L. J. (2002). *Policies and procedures to develop effective school-wide discipline practices at the elementary school.* Reston, VA: Council for Exceptional Children.

Obiakor, F. E., Beachum, F. D., & Harris, M. (2010). Special education in Milwaukee Public Schools: Processes and practices for African American learners. *Western Journal of Black Studies, 34*(4), 425–437.

Obiakor, F. E., Harris-Obiakor, P. H., Garza-Nelson, C., & Randall, P. (2005). Educating urban learners with and without special needs: Life after the Brown Case. In F. E. Obiakor & F. D. Beachum (Eds.), *Urban education for the 21st century: Research, issues, and perspectives* (pp. 34–58). Springfield, IL: Charles C Thomas.

Peterson, R. L. (2003). Teaching the social curriculum: School discipline as instruction. *Preventing School Failure, 47*(2), 66–73.

Skiba, R. J., & Peterson, R. L. (1999). Zap zero tolerance. *Education Digest, 64*(8), 24–30.

Stormont, M., Lewis, T. J., & Beckner, B. (2005). Developmentally continuous Positive Behavior Support systems: Applying key features in preschool settings. *Teaching Exceptional Children, 37*, 42–48.

Tavernise, S. (2010, December 1). A mission to transform Baltimore's beaten schools. *New York Times*, p. A19. Retrieved from http://www.nytimes.com/2010/12/02/education/02baltimore.html?pagewanted=all&_r=0

Todd, A. W., Campbell, A. L., Meyer, G. G., & Horner, R. H. (2008). The effects of a targeted intervention to reduce problem behaviors: Elementary school implementation of check in—check out. *Journal of Positive Behavior Intervention, 10*(1), 46–55.

Warren, J. S., Edmonson, H. M., Griggs, P., Lassen, S. R., McCart, A., Turnbull, A., & Sailor, W. (2003). Urban applications of School-Wide Positive Behavior Support: Critical issues and lessons learned. *Journal of Positive Behavior Interventions, 5*(2), 80–91.

Welch, K., & Payne, A. A. (2012). Exclusionary school punishment: The effect of racial threat on expulsion and suspension. *Youth Violence and Juvenile Justice, 10*(2), 155–171.

White, R., Marr, M. B., Ellis, E., Audette, B., & Algozzine, B. (2001). Effects of a model of school-wide discipline on office referrals. *Journal of At-Risk Issues, 7*, 4–12.

11. *When Good Intentions Are Not Enough: Essentials for Effective Leaders and Educators in Building and Leading Culturally Responsive Schools and Programs*

Rosa Milagros Santos and Lillian Durán

A foundational ingredient required to successfully implement Positive Behavioral Interventions and Supports (PBIS) in programs and schools is to create and promote culturally responsive environments for children, families, teachers, leaders, and community members. Culturally responsive schools and programs are essential if we are to ensure children's success both within and beyond the classroom walls. Culturally responsive schools need leaders who are committed to serving children and families from diverse cultural and linguistic backgrounds. However, in order to be culturally responsive, school and program leaders must also possess characteristics and skills that enable them to act effectively on their commitment to diversity (Santos, Cheatham & Durán, 2012).

Culturally responsive leaders are those who engage children, parents, and teachers in building and supporting a community that welcomes, appreciates, and values the different cultural and linguistic backgrounds represented in their schools, programs, and the larger community that they serve. Such leaders value and build on the unique strengths within each child, family, teacher, staff, and community member. They recognize the diverse voices and perspectives that these individuals bring to schools and programs and support the contribution of these diverse perspectives to the school.

In this chapter, we describe the importance of moving beyond good intentions when building and leading culturally responsive schools and programs.

We highlight the complex challenges schools and programs face in successfully implementing PBIS for all children and families. We also describe guiding principles upon which schools and programs can build culturally and linguistically responsive services within the framework of PBIS. Finally, we discuss five key roles and responsibilities that leaders must undertake in order for schools and programs to better serve the ever-increasing diversity in the children and families in our communities. These roles and responsibilities are based on a set of guiding principles related to cultural and linguistic diversity. As such, they can directly influence policies and professional development that in turn impact short- and long-term outcomes for children and families.

Terms and Definitions

To ensure a common understanding of some of the terms and concepts we use in this chapter, we offer the following definitions.

The most basic definition of "diversity" refers to variations or differences among people or things. In our current socio-political world, the term "diverse" has become a proxy for individuals or groups who are non-White. It is our belief that people are not diverse—populations are. Thus, in this chapter we use the term "diversity" to acknowledge differences and variations in behaviors, beliefs, values, priorities, customs, and practices. The most important concept in culturally responsive practice is to recognize that everyone is part of diversity and that diversity is "always life enhancing" (Barrera & Kramer, 2009, p. 43); that is, it adds to, rather than detracts from, available resources.

The term "culture" refers to the "ideations, symbols, behaviors, values, and beliefs that are shared by a human group" (Banks, 2008, p. 133). All individuals have a culture. "It is the perceptual and conceptual web of beliefs and understandings that undergirds all that people see and think, regardless of whether it can be given an ethnic label" (Barrera & Kramer, 2009). Moreover, Shonkoff and Phillips (2000) emphasized that culture is not static but instead is malleable, which allows it to be maintained or challenged, and means that over time it can evolve and change to adapt and survive.

"Cultural and linguistic diversity" refers to "behavioral, value, linguistic, and other differences ascribed to people's cultural backgrounds. Cultural diversity almost invariably includes some level of diversity in how language is understood and used whether a different language is spoken ... therefore [the terms] cultural diversity and cultural linguistic diversity [are often used] synonymously" (Barrera, Kramer, & Macpherson, 2012, p. xx).

In this chapter, we refer to "cultural competence and responsiveness" as defined by Lynch (2011), who stated, "the ability to think, feel, and act in ways that acknowledge, respect, and build on ethnic, [socio-] cultural, and linguistic diversity … is a process not an endpoint—a journey rather than a destination" (pp. 43–44).

Finally, we purposefully refer to "schools and programs" to denote the broad range of settings and services within which children and youth (birth through 21 years of age) with and without disabilities access education, interventions, and other services. We recognize that while the contexts for these schools and programs are just as diverse as the children and families they serve, the one key ingredient necessary for success is the leadership within these schools and programs.

A Complex Challenge

The cultural and linguistic background of the U.S. population is always dynamic and ever changing. Cultural and linguistic groups living in the country today include both new immigrants from all over the world, as well as U.S.-born populations with long histories in the U.S., such as Latinos, Native Americans, Asian Americans, and African Americans. Recognizing the similarities and differences within and across the cultural and linguistic groups living in the U.S. is important. One key commonality for educators to understand is that both U.S.-born and immigrant populations who are not from Anglo-European backgrounds represent a disproportionately higher percentage of individuals living in and dealing with challenging and often high-risk situations, such as racism, lack of or under-employment, and poverty (U.S. Census Bureau, 2010).

Many U.S.-born groups have experienced generations of inequity and oppression, ranging from genocide in the case of Native Americans, to slavery in the case of African Americans, to the extremely poor working conditions endured by Latinos and Asians (Central Pacific Railroad Photographic History Museum, 2013; Drescher, 2009; National Center for Farmworker Health, 2013; Szasz, 1999). To the nation's credit, much has changed in terms of our laws and attitudes to promote greater equity in our society. However, these hostile legacies continue to manifest in the ongoing marginalization of certain populations within the U.S. today. Educators must be vigilant in discerning school policies, approaches, and attitudes that may reinforce this marginalization (Delpit, 1995). Culturally responsive educators and leaders should ask themselves:

1. Does the curriculum content reflect the culture and languages represented in my community?
2. Do children have the opportunity to learn about their own history and their people's contribution to this country?

3. Do the teachers, administrators, and specialists reflect the diversity in the school?
4. What efforts have I made to welcome families and the community into the school building and to support their active engagement in the school?
5. What efforts have we made to implement Positive Behavioral Interventions and Supports that are culturally responsive and relevant to the communities we serve?

New immigrants face different but no less complex challenges. In Mary Pipher's book *The Middle of Everywhere*, she describes the experiences of several families in adjusting to life in the U.S. after arriving from various countries in Africa and throughout the Middle East (Pipher, 2003). New immigrants are often relocated to neighborhoods with low-income housing, and unfortunately, in the U.S., this generally translates into being exposed to dangerous communities replete with substance abuse, violence, street gangs, and poorly performing schools. This leaves new immigrants and their children vulnerable to a host of challenges and dangers, in addition to becoming accustomed to a new culture, language, and location (Matthews & Jang, 2007).

The salient points to consider for both newly arrived immigrants and U.S.-born populations are that educators and leaders need to know the communities in which they are situated and to be responsive to their unique needs. Schools do not operate in isolation, but within the context of the community being served. Given the compelling and overwhelming difficulties so many children and families face in the U.S. every day, "schooling" must be re-conceptualized to take into consideration children's overall well-being and security. Funding before- and after-school activities and family support programs are important ways that leaders can promote children's success outside of the typical school day. Partnering with the community is another important effort worth undertaking in the hopes that the school and its personnel will be perceived as allies rather than as representatives of the social power structures that reinforce the cycles of poverty within which many of these communities are entrenched (Delpit, 1995; Gay, 2000).

It is no secret that many schools in the U.S. have been failing (Chilcott & Guggenheim, 2010). However, many communities are devising innovative approaches to address the unique needs of the children and families in their neighborhoods. For example, Geoffrey Canada's work with the Harlem Children's Zone exemplifies hope for the future. Mothers are enrolled in the Harlem Children's Zone program during pregnancy, and children are followed into college (Tough, 2008). The goal of this model program is to create a secure and supportive pipeline for children by establishing a protective environment with high expectations within which they can grow and thrive despite the dangers and temptations they may face on a daily basis. The program has been highly successful, and although it is resource intensive, no one can argue the savings to society in terms of the prevention of criminality and poverty (www.hcz.org). No individual can single-handedly tackle the task of building this level of comprehensive support, but the first step in being a culturally responsive educator or leader is recognizing the steps that should be taken to offer more meaningful and effective support. Culturally responsive educators and leaders acknowledge the holistic needs of the children and families they serve and then operate within their capacity to meet those needs. Culturally and linguistically diverse populations within the U.S. face challenges beyond simply existing outside of White Anglo-European middle-class norms. The challenges are often structural and institutionalized. Thus, educators and leaders must acknowledge that the choices they make can either challenge the status quo and promote positive change or can serve to further exacerbate the difficult situations in which these children and families often find themselves.

There are additional challenges for children and families who speak languages other than English at home. The resources and services are simply not in place in most schools and programs across the U.S. to support ongoing and meaningful communication with families who speak languages other than English (Zehler et al., 2003). Therefore, a culturally responsive educator or leader must also be linguistically responsive. Fundamentally, schools are responsible for reaching out to families who speak languages other than English by providing interpretation (i.e., using oral modalities to translate English into the families' language and vice versa) and translation (i.e., using written modalities to translate English into the families' language and vice versa) services to support effective communication. This critical responsibility should not be compromised. Without effective interpreters and translators, families' and teachers' access to important information that supports children's growth and development is impeded. Educators, administrators, families, and children will have limited connections on which to build productive relationships. Creative approaches to interpretation and translation are sometimes needed given the many languages that can be spoken within a single classroom or school building, but the first step is embracing these interpretation and translation services as a necessity and not as an unnecessary burden on the system. Again, educators and leaders should get to know their communities and draw on already existing resources, such as cultural centers, hospital interpreters, phone line interpretation services, etc. For some larger language groups, schools may choose to hire bilingual staff to facilitate communication. For other low-incidence language groups, seeking community resources and exploring creative approaches may be the immediate action schools and programs can take to address the needs of children and families. In either case, making the effort is the critical first step toward creating successful partnerships with the linguistically diverse populations present in the school or program and in the larger community.

Families may also look to schools and programs to answer questions about maintaining their home language, as well as how doing so might affect their children's English language development. It is important for school and program leaders to know that supporting children's home language and helping them to maintain that language throughout their schooling has been shown to promote greater academic and reading outcomes in English (August & Shanahan, 2006; Goldenberg, 2008; Rolstad, Mahoney, & Glass, 2005). Thus, school and program leaders should support professional development activities that will enhance the knowledge of all school personnel about bilingual development, the role of the first language in second language acquisition, evidence-based instructional approaches with dual language learners, and appropriate screening and assessment practices. Without a coordinated, systematic, and ongoing training system focused on home language maintenance, families may receive mixed messages (e.g., unfounded comments such as, "You should just speak one language to your child because it will confuse her to hear multiple languages") that may lead them to abandon their home language in favor of English, even if the parents and other adults in the child's life have very limited English proficiency. The loss of home language by children can interrupt family communication patterns, which may in turn have long-term detrimental effects on the family's ability to relate and communicate with each other (Anderson, 2012; Kremer-Sadlik, 2005; Wong-Fillmore, 1991).

Cultural and linguistic responsiveness also means incorporating evidence-based practices into instruction, as well as interventions specific to the population. Where the intent is to support bilingualism and biliteracy throughout the early school years, developmental bilingual education has been shown to produce the best academic outcomes in English, with the added benefit of children maintaining their home language (Rolstad et al., 2005). However, when bilingual teachers are not available and the bulk of instruction occurs in English, evidence-based strategies should be used, such as visual supports, total physical response, sheltered English immersion, and small-group targeted instruction to enhance academic success (Hill & Flynn, 2006; Goldenberg, 2008). A pull-out or resource-room approach to instruction delivery and intervention for linguistically diverse students has been found to be the least effective approach (Goldenberg, 2008; Rolstad et al., 2005). Therefore, culturally and linguistic responsive educators and leaders should strive to ensure that children are receiving appropriate instructional supports to help them learn in their home and second language throughout the day, rather than just for short periods during each day (Paradis, Genesee, & Crago, 2010).

Appropriate screening and assessment procedures should also be in place so that dual language learners are not over-identified in the category of learning disabilities. Appropriate screening and assessment practices should include administering tests to the child in his or her home language when appropriate, understanding how differences in cultural background and life experiences could influence test performance, understanding the limitations in the reliability and validity of many standardized tests, and recognizing the limitations and biases in test results that may occur when tests are simply translated from English by interpreters or translators. While we describe some basic strategies, fully articulating recommended instructional and assessment strategies and approaches for dual language learners is beyond the scope of this chapter. Thus readers are encouraged to access additional resources; see Appendix A for a sampling of useful resources.

In sum, responsiveness to culture and language diversity includes valuing and tapping into children's and families' culture, language, and experiences to facilitate development and learning. Providing culturally and linguistically responsive services is a complex undertaking that demands serious consideration, specific content knowledge, and a sincere willingness to honor every individual's unique identity. It is important that our school and program leaders today have a clear understanding of the ambitious nature of responding to this overwhelming responsibility. Leaders must develop the capacity to meet the challenge of facilitating change in their schools and programs based on a commitment to honoring diversity and supporting equity in educational outcomes across all U.S. populations.

Building a Foundation for Culturally Responsive Schools and Programs

Culturally responsive schools and programs must be guided by a set of shared beliefs, values, and principles that focus on cultural and linguistic diversity. These principles set the tone within the learning environment when they are interwoven with school and program policies, practices, and services. Every member of the learning environment, including children, families, teachers, staff members, administrators, and community partners, need to understand these principles as they collaborate to build and support culturally responsive schools and programs. In this section, we discuss three guiding principles supported by evidence-based best practices. These guidelines are by no means exhaustive. For leaders, the guidelines described form the basis for understanding critical roles and responsibilities when leading culturally responsive schools and programs.

School and program leaders play a key role in leading their staff to reflect upon and consistently use these guidelines. The guidelines represent a starting point to help leaders begin to work with others to develop shared beliefs, values, and principles that will support, honor, and celebrate cultural and linguistic diversity in their schools and programs.

(1) **Culture and language are central to each individual's life.** The first principle is at the heart of systems change designed to help key stakeholders better understand cultural and linguistic diversity. Recognizing the dynamic nature of culture, as well as its complexity and multiplicity, is key for individuals coming to understand that each individual has a culture. Culturally responsive schools and programs recognize that each child, parent, family member, teacher, staff member, and community member has a culture that plays a central role in their individual beliefs, biases, assumptions, as well as in the decisions they make when teaching children and working with their families (Gilbert, Goode, & Dunne, 2007; Lynch & Hanson, 2011). This understanding is vital in helping each person see beyond the "difference" of others whose cultures are distinct from their own, and helps prevent the two from ultimately occupying positions across an invisible divide. By exploring one's own beliefs, family stories, attitudes, history, and early memories, one can recognize and begin to accept that everyone comes from dynamic and often complex cultures. Self-awareness is the first step toward developing the understanding that every individual has a culture that influences their behaviors, attitudes, and interactions with others (Barrera & Kramer, 2009; Kidd, Sánchez, & Thorp, 2004; Lynch & Hanson, 2011).

(2) **Language and culture are tightly interwoven.** The second principle relates to the understanding that language and culture have a transactional relationship and that each is manifested in the other. Language is one of the most powerful ways by which culture is passed on to the succeeding generation. Cultural beliefs, traditions, and practices are expressed and shaped through language. At a very early age, children begin to understand those around them and to express their own fears,

needs, and desires in the distinctive vocabulary of a home language that includes not only words, but also rhythms, gestures, patterns of speech, and silence. Language is the tool used to mediate the socialization process for members of cultural groups. Language and culture are the fundamental building blocks of identity. Culturally responsive leaders must be diligent in ensuring that their school and program policies, practices, and services do not sacrifice the cornerstone of each individual's identity by asking them to forsake their home language and culture.

(3) **Positive relationships serve as the foundation for the support of children, families, teachers, leaders, and organizations.** The third principle highlights the importance of human relationships and the impact of these relationships on growth and development (Shonkoff & Phillips, 2000). Relationships impact every dimension of development, and culture and language play a critical role in defining those relationships. One of the primary tasks for infants is the development of social skills to form strong, stable, secure relationships with others, which is a critical task as they strive to meet new challenges and forge relationships with people outside of their home environment. The need for relationships continues throughout life. Adults also need to feel secure as they move through their developmental pathways and face new challenges. Relationship building should be embedded at the core of school and program policies, practices, and services. Good relationship building often occurs in school settings through strong Positive Behavior Support programs that recognize relationships and pro-social behavior as fundamental to creating optimal learning environments.

Key to relationship building is recognizing the importance of families in children's development and learning. Regardless of when children enter the education system, they do so as members of a family. Families are the experts about their children's lives. It is from their families that children gain a sense of personal and communal history, learn the joy of having a shared meaning with others, and the security of knowing who they are and where they come from. Culturally responsive schools and programs are defined by the strength of their relationships with the families they serve, especially when each is able to willingly step outside of their comfort zones. For culturally and linguistically responsive policies, practices, and services to be possible, school and program administration and staff must value families. It is from them that school and program staff and administration will learn about the cultural, political, and economic forces influencing the lives of families different from their own; with this knowledge, they can then raise the awareness and compassion needed to mediate cultural differences and honor and respond in appropriate ways when planning, implementing, or evaluating policies, practices, and services.

The Role of Educators and Leaders

There is abundant literature that addresses the critical roles educators and leaders play in facilitating and promoting positive outcomes for children and families. In this section, we highlight five key leadership roles that are needed to support culturally responsive schools and programs. An atmosphere of acceptance and appreciation for the cultural and linguistic groups represented in schools and programs begins with well-informed administrators, teachers, and staff. Therefore, to build culturally responsive schools and programs, leaders must:

Role 1: Develop a shared vision, mission statement, and/or philosophy that respects and embraces the unique qualities and characteristics children, families, teachers, other staff members, and community partners bring to the table.

To build culturally responsive schools and programs requires changes at many levels, beginning with the stated vision, mission, and/or philosophy statement of the school or program. There are two key elements that leaders must consider when crafting a vision, mission, or philosophy statement. First, it must explicitly state how much the school or program values cultural and linguistic diversity. Leaders must take the first step of reviewing their school or program's current vision, mission, or philosophy statement to determine to what extent it explicitly declares its value of and respect for diversity. Second, the vision, mission, and/or philosophy statement must be shared by all and therefore, key stakeholders must have a hand in developing and enforcing it. In this instance, culturally responsive leaders adopt a participatory leadership approach in which they engage diverse voices, recognizing that a vision, mission, or philosophy statement cannot be developed in isolation.

Role 2: Develop and promote clearly stated policies that ensure that culturally and linguistically appropriate practices and services are provided to all children and families.

School and program policies provide a foundation for addressing specific pedagogical and content areas that are critical to the preparation and education of all children. These policies are the starting point for leaders in guiding and supporting families and teachers as they help children develop specific skills, such as literacy, numeracy, and social emotional development, in a culturally and linguistically responsive manner. Explicit policies should be developed and adopted to reflect the program's vision, mission, and philosophy statement with regard to cultural and linguistic responsiveness. The character of policies will vary from program to program, and school to school, based on the contextual issues facing the communities in which the program or school operates. Nonetheless, it is important for leaders to understand the impact their program and school policies will have on the entire population of students they serve, and the consequences of these policies for the families and the community. For example, adopting a policy that promotes the use of a standardized curriculum that is focused on teaching only one cultural group's history, language, and literature can send a message to children and families that other groups' backgrounds and experiences are valued less.

Role 3: Develop systems of accountability that hold school personnel and other key stakeholders responsible for the success of all of the children they serve and for enacting the stated policies.

Culturally responsive leaders must create and support a culture of accountability within their programs or schools. This means that all key stakeholders must understand and do their best to fulfill their responsibility to support each and every student in their program and school. Specialized training and expertise must be both valued, and at the same time transcended, in order to provide seamless and coordinated programming for students across the spectrum. As such, dual language learners are not the sole responsibility of the bilingual staff but rather are supported and taught by the entire teaching and support staff on a daily basis. The culturally responsive leader must therefore collaborate with key stakeholders to create and sustain a high-quality program that is valued by the teachers, staff, families, students, and community members. In such programs, culturally responsive leaders empower their teachers and staff to make key decisions and provide them with the necessary supports and instruction to ensure that they understand their accountability as professionals. Thus, a culturally responsive leader provides transformational (inspiring commitment and action in others) and moral (clarifying a sense of right and wrong) leadership for their teachers and staff in order to engage them in fulfilling their responsibility to all students (Leithwood & Duke, 1999).

Role 4: Use evidence-based and recommended practices that support the children and families they serve.

Leaders must create a culture of success in their school or program by seeking out and mandating the use of effective practices. Leaders can support the translation of research to practice by providing high-quality professional development opportunities and administrative support for the implementation of new evidence-based practices. Culturally and linguistically responsive policies, practices, and programs are linked to improved access, utilization, and quality of services and support for diverse populations (Goode, Dunne & Bronheim, 2006). Yet, the implementation of such responsive practices remains a great challenge for many systems, organizations, and their personnel for many reasons. Leaders have the responsibility of helping school or program personnel overcome these challenges to bring about positive changes in the quality and effectiveness of the services delivered. Culturally responsive leaders must have an ongoing and positive influence on the work of their teachers and staff in order for them to deliver culturally and linguistically responsive services and to continue to grow professionally and personally

Role 5: Engage in ongoing self-reflection and meaningful discussions with key stakeholders to plan, implement, and evaluate culturally responsive policies, practices, and services.

Critical reflection is at the core of successful professional development (Miller et al., 2003). Professional organizations, including the Division for Early Childhood of the Council for Exceptional Children, have recommended that personnel development programs prepare practitioners to be aware of the socio-cultural context of education and the role of education in a just, equitable, and democratic society. As such, professional development efforts need to create contexts that enable practitioners to embrace critical reflection so that they become better able to explore the cultural lens through which they view the world, their assumptions about the role of home language in relation to second language acquisition, and their attitudes toward bilingualism. Leaders must embrace the principles of relationship building and critical reflection in order to foster these traits in the staff they serve (Derman-Sparks & Phillips, 1997; Sleeter, 2001).

Embarking on a Journey Toward Cultural and Linguistic Competence

Becoming a culturally and linguistically responsive educator and leader is in reality a deeply personal experience. There is no one right path to take, or a single set of prescribed steps that will lead every person to the level of responsiveness necessary to be an effective educator or leader for the broad range of communities served throughout the U.S. However, initiating this personal journey is the critical first step in the process. A genuine curiosity and willingness to engage in self-reflection about one's personal beliefs, attitudes, and perceptions can lead to a better understanding of how your own worldview influences your interactions with others. Responsivity is about being flexible, adaptable, and engaged in interactions in the moment. Listen to the children and families you serve. Allow yourself to hear them. Become immersed in their stories, their histories, and their truth. In doing so you will be creating the possibility for shared stories to emerge as you cultivate your relationship and navigate new territory in the remarkable process of educating their children.

Appendix A

Resources for Instruction and Assessment Practices with DLLs

Baca, L. M. & Cervantes, H. T. (2004). *The bilingual special education interface* (4th ed.). Upper Saddle River, NJ: Merrill Prentice Hall.

Delgado-Gaitan, C. (2004). *Involving Latino families: Raising student achievement through home-school partnerships.* Thousand Oaks, CA: Corwin Press.

Graves, M. F., August, D., & Mancilla-Marinex, J. (2013). *Teaching vocabulary to English language learners.* New York: Teachers College Press.

Hill, J. D., & Flynn, K. M. (2006). *Classroom instruction that works with English language learners.* Alexandria, VA: Association for Supervision and Curriculum Development.

Paradis, J., Genesee, F., & Crago, M. (2010). *Dual language development and disorders: A handbook on bilingualism and second language learning* (2nd ed.). Baltimore, MD: Paul H. Brookes.

References

Anderson, S. R. (2012). *Languages: A very short introduction.* Oxford, UK: Oxford University Press.

August, D., & Shanahan, T. (Eds.) (2006). *Developing literacy in second language learners. Report of the National Literacy Panel on Language-Minority Children and Youth.* Mahwah, NJ: Erlbaum.

Banks, J. A. (2008). *An introduction to multicultural education* (4th ed.). Boston, MA: Pearson Education.

Barrera, I., & Kramer, L. (2009). *Using skilled dialogue to transform challenging interactions: Honoring identity, voice, and connections.* Baltimore, MD: Brookes.

Barrera, I., Kramer, L., & Macpherson, T. D. (2012). *Skilled dialogue: Strategies for responding to cultural diversity in early childhood* (2nd ed.). Baltimore, MD: Brookes.

Central Pacific Railroad Photographic History Museum. (2013). *A history of the Chinese in California*. Retrieved from http://cprr.org/Museum/Chinese_Syllabus.html

Chilcott, L. (producer), & Guggenheim, D. (director) (2010). *Waiting for Superman*. United States: Paramount.

Delpit, L. (1995). *Other people's children: Cultural conflict in the classroom*. New York: The New Press.

Derman-Sparks, L., & Phillips, C. B. (1997). *Teaching/learning anti-racism*. New York: Teachers College Press.

Drescher, S. (2009). *Abolition: A history of slavery and antislavery*. Cambridge, UK: Cambridge University Press.

Gay, G. (2000). *Culturally responsive teaching: Theory, research, & practice*. New York: Teachers College Press.

Gilbert, J., Goode, T., & Dunne, C. (2007). *Curricula enhancement module: Cultural awareness*. Washington, DC: National Center for Cultural Competence, Georgetown University Child Development Center, University Center for Excellence in Developmental Disabilities. Retrieved on February 15, 2013 from http://www.nccccurricula.info/documents/awareness.pdf

Goldenberg, C. (2008). Teaching English language learners. What the research does—and does not—say. *American Educator*, *32*(2), 8–23, 42–44.

Goode, T., Dunne, C., & Bronheim, S. (2006). *The evidence base for cultural and linguistic competence in health care*. New York: Commonwealth Fund.

Hill, J. D., & Flynn, K. M. (2006). *Classroom instruction that works with English language learners*. Alexandria, VA: Association for Supervision and Curriculum Development.

Kidd, J. K., Sánchez, S. Y., & Thorp, E. K. (2004). Listening to the stories families tell: Promoting culturally responsive language and literacy experiences. In C. M. Fairbanks, J. Worthy, B. Maloch, J. V. Hoffman, & D. L. Shallert, (Eds.), *Fifty-Third Yearbook of the National Reading Conference* (pp. 246–263). Oak Creek, WI: National Reading Conference.

Kremer-Sadlik, T. (2005). To be or not to be bilingual: Autistic children from multilingual families. In J. Cohen, K. T. McAlister, K. Rolstad, & J. MacSwan (Eds.), *Proceedings of the 4th International Symposium on Bilingualism* (pp. 1225–1234). Somerville, MA: Cascadilla Press. Retrieved August 29, 2013, from http://www.lingref.com/isb/4/096ISB4.PDF

Leithwood, K., & Duke, D. L. (1999). A century's quest to understand school leadership. In J. Murphy & K. S. Louis (Eds.), *Handbook of research on educational leadership* (2nd ed., pp. 45–72). San Francisco, CA: Jossey-Bass.

Lynch, E. W. (2011). Developing cross-cultural competence. In E. W. Lynch & M. J. Hanson (Eds.), *Developing cross-cultural competence: A guide for working with children and their families (4th ed.)* (pp. 41–77). Baltimore: Brookes.

Lynch, E. W., & Hanson, M. J. (2011). *Developing cross-cultural competence: A guide for working with children and their families (4th ed.)*. Baltimore: Brookes.

Matthews, H., & Jang, D. (2007). *The challenges of change: Learning from the child care and early education experiences of immigrant families.* Washington, DC: Center for Law and Social Policy.

Miller, P. S., Ostrosky, M., Laumann, B., Thorp, E., Sánchez, S., & Fader-Dunne, L. (2003). Quality field experiences underlying performance mastery. In V. D. Stayton, P. S. Miller, & L. A. Dinnebeil (Eds.), *DEC personnel preparation in early childhood special education: Implementing the DEC recommended practices.* Missoula, MT: Division of Early Childhood.

National Center for Farmworker Health. (2013). *About America's farmworkers.* Retrieved from http://www.ncfh.org/?pid=4&page=2

Paradis, J., Genesee, F., & Crago, M. (2010). *Dual language development and disorders: A handbook on bilingualism and second language learning* (2nd ed.). Baltimore, MD: Paul H. Brookes.

Pipher, M. (2002). *The middle of everywhere: Helping refugees enter the American community.* New York, NY: Harcourt, Inc.

Pipher, M. (2003). *The middle of everywhere: Helping refugees enter the American community.* Boston, MA: Houghton Mifflin Harcourt.

Rolstad, K., Mahoney, K., & Glass, G. (2005). The big picture: A meta-analysis of program effectiveness research on English language learners. *Educational Policy, 19,* 572–594. doi: 10.1177/0895904805278067

Romero-Little, M. E. (2006). Honoring our own: Rethinking Indigenous languages and literacy. *Anthropology & Education Quarterly, 37*(4), 399–402.

Santos, R. M., Cheatham, G. A., & Durán, L. K. (Eds.). (2012). *Young exceptional children monograph 14: Supporting young children who are dual language learners with or at risk for disabilities.* Missoula, MT: Council for Exceptional Children Division for Early Childhood.

Shonkoff, J., & Phillips, D. (Eds.). (2000). *From neurons to neighborhoods: The science of early childhood development.* Washington, DC: National Academy Press.

Sleeter, C. E. (2001). Preparing teachers for culturally diverse schools: Research and the overwhelming presence of whiteness. *Journal of Teacher Education, 52,* 94–106.

Szasz, M. C. (1999). *Education and the American Indian: The road to self-determination since 1928.* Albuquerque: University of New Mexico Press.

Tough, P. (2008). *Whatever it takes: Geoffrey Canada's quest to change Harlem and America.* Boston, MA: Houghton Mifflin Harcourt.

U.S. Census Bureau. (2010). *Language use in the United States: 2007.* Retrieved from http://www.census.gov/hhes/socdemo/language/data/acs/ACS-12.pdf

Wong-Fillmore, L. (1991). When learning a second language means losing the first. *Early Childhood Research Quarterly, 6,* 323–346.

Zehler, A. M., Fleischman, H. L., Hopstock, P. J., Stephenson, T. G., Pendzick, M. L., & Sapru, S. (2003). *Descriptive study of services to LEP students and LEP students with disabilities.* Final Report to the U.S. Department of Education, Office of English Language Acquisition. Arlington, VA: Development Associates.

12. *Accomplishments and Directions for Future Actions, Research, and Policy*

CARLOS R. MCCRAY, SU-JE CHO, CHUN ZHANG,
AND HEATHER WYNNE

Introduction

Positive Behavioral Interventions and Supports (PBIS) has received a lot of attention in the last few years due to the tremendous accomplishments that educators have achieved with this system over the past couple of decades. This attention is warranted, given the urgency of the need to assist students with their behavior in the classroom. Educators and school leaders who have bought into the concept of PBIS have been able to use it to cultivate a school climate and culture that is conducive for learning. Through the use of PBIS, teachers have been able to increase learning opportunities for students in a couple of ways. First, PBIS has given teachers the tools they need to help change the behavior of students so that the classroom climate and school culture reflect an atmosphere where cogent learning can take place (Bohanon et al., 2006). Second, through the utilization of PBIS, educators are often able to identify the students who are in need of additional learning assistance and make modifications to their instructional delivery (Lane, Wehby, Robertson, & Rogers, 2007). Throughout this book, we have touched on an array of topics regarding PBIS and how it has been used in schools to create authentic learning opportunities for all students.

The goal of this chapter is to take a critical look at PBIS from a leadership perspective—to consider how PBIS has been interpreted and implemented by educational leaders. This will help school leaders better understand the importance of PBIS and how to formulate structures to enhance its overall implementation. The framework that will be used in our analysis is the concept of *transformational leadership*. According to Leithwood, Jantzi, and Fernandez (1994), transformational leadership involves the leader (1) setting the course, (2) building people up, (3) cultivating a collaborative environment, and (4) placing the right personnel into the program. We believe the role of school leaders is crucial in the implementation of PBIS because it is the school leader who sets the tone of the school culture (Cunningham & Corderio, 2009; McCray, Alston, & Beachum, 2006). Also, despite the many successes achieved through PBIS, there is still much room for improvement in its implementation at the high school level (Flannery, Sugai, & Anderson, 2009; Lane et al., 2007; Yawn & Gibson, Chapter 9). We will look at why researchers have found that certain models of PBIS have not been as successful with certain student populations (Bohanon et al., 2006). But first, we would like to begin by highlighting some PBIS success stories, especially at the elementary level, and then talk about its future direction, along with the program or school leader's role in transforming the school culture to ensure the implementation of PBIS at all age/grade levels.

As we have indicated, the successes of PBIS have been numerous. PBIS has in many ways been a catalyst for educators and school leaders to examine best practices in order to determine how to deal effectively with students who bring behavioral issues to the educative process. We readily applaud the efforts of these educators and school leaders in assisting their students to navigate their educational matriculation. Such assistance via PBIS includes educators helping students learn appropriate ways in which to conduct themselves within the classroom and the overall school setting; the corollary is increased academic achievement for all students, as well as decreased problems with discipline (Lane et al., 2007).

One of the main models that educators have used consistently throughout elementary and middle grade levels is the School-Wide Positive Behavioral Interventions and Supports (SWPBIS) model. This model has proven to be extremely effective in modifying students' behavior. Scholars (Coffey & Horner, 2012; Eber, Hyde, & Suter, 2011) have recognized that the success of the SWPBIS model is due to the fact that it has been incorporated into the entire school culture. One of the benefits of SWPBIS is that it gives faculty and staff the opportunity to engage all students at the Tier 1 phase. By making no assumptions about any particular students, the SWPBIS model is a systematic approach to ensuring that all students have access to a high level of education. We believe that Tier 1 SWPBIS has the potential to reduce Beachum and McCray's (2011) notion of cultural collusion. In Chapter 10, McCray, Zhang, Cho, and Martin mentioned that cultural *collusion* occurs between teachers and students as a result of cultural *collision*. Because of the clashes in culture between students and teachers, educators often look upon students from a culture different than their own with contempt. As a result of this disdain, students without the requisite cultural and social capital often capitulate to a negative, self-fulfilling prophecy and display even more disruptive behavior (McCray, Grant, & Beachum, 2010). And unfortunately, in many instances, teachers are only too happy to help usher such students out of the education system.

The success of SWPBIS has been undergirded by its emphasis on prevention (Colvin, Kame'enui, & Sugai, 1993). As Beachum and Gullo (see Chapter 8) indicated, SWPBIS is similar to PBIS in general. SWPBIS makes the assumption that all students in the school are in need of some form of behavioral support. Once again, we believe this to be one of the most important aspects of a SWPBIS plan. When school leaders and educators simply assume that the entire student population is deserving of behavior modification, it has the potential to reduce educators' bias toward students with little social and cultural capital (McCray et al., 2010). Beachum and Gullo (see Chapter 8) point out that this is one of the major successes of SWPBIS. In addition to the first tier focusing on all students in the school building, two additional tiers help support students who have not shown improvement as result of their exposure to Tier 1 (Lewis & Sugai, 1999; Sugai, Sprague, Horner, & Walker, 2000). Tier 2 of SWPBIS is designed to provide "interventions such as small-group instruction, data-based decision making about specific student behavior, and explicit feedback on behavioral progress towards goals" (Yawn & Gibson, Chapter 9). Finally, Tier 3 is designed for students who have not benefited from the first two tiers. Thus, Tier 3 is intended for those students who are at extreme risk of displaying aggressive behavior and total noncompliance (Lane et al., 2007).

We have chosen the SWPBIS model to showcase the successes of PBIS for several reasons. First, as mentioned above, it makes no assumptions as to which students merit the Tier 1 intervention. In this way, we believe it dramatically decreases what Obiakor, Harris-Obiakor, Garza-Nelson, and Randall (2005) have referred to as the misidentification, misassessment, and miscategorization of students. Second, SWPBIS is a behavior intervention model that entails educators and school leaders approaching behavioral issues from a holistic perspective. SWPBIS has an array of support mechanisms that educators and school leaders can pull from in order to ameliorate negative behavior in students. Some of the interventions embedded in SWPBIS at the first and second tiers consist of the enhancement of pedagogy to reflect diverse learners, constructive behavior reinforcement, data collection on students' behavior, data-based decision making on students' behavior, and critical feedback to students and parents (Yawn & Gibson, Chapter 9). And finally, the third tier of intervention for students with persistent behavioral issues consists of more focused one-on-one intervention (Yawn & Gibson, Chapter 9). We feel that that this multi-level behavioral intervention is a welcome departure from the traditional forms of discipline educators have haphazardly applied over the last few years. Traditional forms of discipline usually involve little to no data collection or any one-on-one teacher-student support, especially in urban schools (Beachum & McCray, 2011; Duran, Zhou, Frew, Kwok, & Benz, 2011; Ferguson, 2001; Lindle, 2008; McCray & Beachum, 2006; Welch & Payne, 2012).

Future Directions of PBIS and SWPBIS

Eradication of Exclusionary Punishment

As much success as SWPBIS has gained, it has also failed in many instances, especially in urban high schools. This failure has been due at least in part to urban high school educators' perceptions of who actually benefits from SWPBIS. In many instances, teachers in urban high schools with a high concentration of students of color feel that PBIS is intended for younger students (Bohanon et al., 2006). There is also evidence that teachers tend to use harsher disciplinary measures when a school population includes a higher concentration of students of color (Welch & Payne, 2012). Welch and Payne (2012) found that use of such harsh measures is strongly related to the racial threat theory. This theory posits that increased presence of minority groups leads to the perception of increased threat on the part of the White population and results in "more punitive criminal punishment and harsher student discipline" (Welch & Payne, 2012, p. 155). Thus, the concept of racial threat is undergirded by the power differential, and social threat theories indicate "punitive social control will expand in response to a larger proportion of minorities—particularly Blacks—relative to Whites because of the presumed economic and political competition they would present ... (Blalock, 1967; Blumer, 1958), as well as the presumed criminal threat they pose (Liska, 1992)" (Welch & Payne, 2012, pp. 157–158). Welch and Payne (2012) found that schools with a higher percentage of African American students tend to use exclusionary policies (i.e., zero-tolerance policies, suspensions, and expulsions) more often than schools with a lower percentage of students of color. They and other researchers have concluded that urban schools are growing increasingly prison-like (Fabelo et al., 2011) and using policies such as zero tolerance (i.e., suspension and expulsions) to exclude undesirable students.

The notion that educators and school leaders are steering some of our most precious students—and, moreover, those in most desperate need of formal academic training—out of the educative process, is educational malpractice at its highest level. Again, many researchers (Black, 2004; Cartledge, Tillman, & Johnson, 2001; Casella, 2003; Keleher, 2000; Mosca & Hollister, 2004; Raffaele Mendez, Knoff, & Ferron, 2002; Skiba & Peterson, 1999; Welch & Payne, 2012) have consistently found that schools tend to disproportionately suspend and expel students of color, especially African American students. According to McCray and Beachum (2006), currently in the U.S., "African American students make up 16.9% of the student population, but account for 33.4% of all school suspensions (Day-Vines & Day-Hairston, 2005)" (p. 2). Of course, the more students are suspended and expelled from school, the greater their chances of dropping out of the educative process all together (Skiba & Peterson, 1999). It has also been well established that once students—especially African American students—drop out of school, their chances of going to prison increase (Day-Vines & Day-Hairston, 2005; Wilson, 2009).

These statistics indicate a major breakdown in the implementation of effective disciplinary measures for African American students at the classroom level. Although African American students are suspended and expelled more than any other group of students, research has made it abundantly clear that African American students do not tend to misbehave at a higher rate than other students (McCarthy & Hodge, 1987; Shaw & Braden, 1990; Skiba, Michael, Nardo, & Peterson, 2002; Skiba & Knesting, 2001; Wallace, Goodkind, Wallace, & Bachman, 2008). In fact, many researchers have found that African American students are much more likely to be sent to the principal's office or suspended for subjective infractions, as opposed to objective infractions (Skiba et al., 2002). Subjective infractions include instances such as student not moving from point A to B in a timely fashion, talking to a teacher in what is perceived to be a negative or disrespectful manner, wearing inappropriate articles of clothing (i.e., sagging pants), and horsing around with peers. Objective infractions, in contrast, include much more concrete violations such as bringing a weapon to school, fighting with another classmate, or bullying peers. Ergo, subjective infractions are possible violations of rules in which the educator has to make a snap judgment as to whether or not to discipline a student.

The future direction of PBIS should therefore include the possibility of strengthening its presence in urban high schools, especially those in which the notion of racial threat is potentially pervasive. PBIS alone cannot solve the multitude of challenging issues that many urban high schools face. These issues include the well-documented distresses that many students bring with them from home to school (Beachum & McCray, 2011), as well as the "anxieties" of educators and school leaders. These anxieties concern how to educate and relate to urban students in a way that is free of disdain or contempt. Presently, urban educators and school leaders appear to be lacking in this skill set; the number of school suspensions adds credence to this argument. We believe that in offering urban educators and school leaders a better understanding of transformational leadership, PBIS can become an effective tool to help ameliorate some of the aforementioned issues with students of color, especially African American students.

Transformational Leadership for the Enhancement of SWPBIS

Earlier in the chapter we mentioned that research has shown that teachers in urban high schools struggle with the concept of SWPBIS. McCray, Zhang, Cho, and Martin (see Chapter 10) also found in their research that PBIS at the high school level was not utilized effectively. According to McCray et al. (Chapter 10), Bohanon et al. (2006) discovered five specific challenges that high schools face in implementing SWPBIS: "(1) the school-wide acknowledgment system, (2) teaching behaviors in a high school setting, (3) logistics of implementation, (4) enacting consistent policies to address behavioral issues, and (5) modifying office disciplinary referrals (ODR) forms to track data." We believe that if leaders gain a better understanding of transformational leadership, they will be more apt to structure the school's culture to be more responsive to the aforementioned challenges. As we indicated, transformational leadership entails (1) setting the course, (2) building people up, (3) cultivating a collaborative environment, and (4) putting the right personnel in place (Leithwood et al., 1994). These strategies of transformational leadership can help sustain a SWPBIS within urban high schools by addressing the challenges identified by Bohanon et al. (2006).

Strategy 1: Setting the Course

Educational leadership researchers (Anderson, 1990; Capper, 1998; Shields, 2004; Theoharis, 2007) have found that it is the school principal who ultimately sets the tone for the school's culture and climate. Shields (2004) declared that "educational leaders are expected to be transformative, to attend to social justice and academic achievement" (p. 111) (as cited in Scanlan, 2011). Expounding on Capper's work regarding school leaders being transformative and setting a vision, Scanlon (2011) pronounced that school leaders should "catalyze school communities to examine power relationships and change policies in order to redistribute power more equitably"

(p. 294). Likewise, the research of Theoharis (2007) led him to declare that school leaders have an obligation to structure their schools to benefit "marginalized students and families, to address issues of race and class, and to focus their vision on developing a just school" (p. 224). Finally, McCray and Beachum (2010) found that school leaders have a responsibility to ameliorate oppressive policies within their schools. This entails school leaders being cognizant of such policies and mobilizing others to act in concert with them. Each of these scholars focuses on the leader as a visionary, while pointing out the leader's role in making the school more socially just. Beachum and McCray (2011) argued that in order for schools to become more socially just in terms of African American students and exclusionary discipline policies, school leaders must ensure that these students are not being suspended or expelled for minor or trivial reasons.

One of the components of SWPBIS entails educators acknowledging and reinforcing the positive behavior of students, as well as modeling desired behaviors. Bohanon et al. (2006) found that high school teachers, especially in urban areas, struggle with this concept. If educators do not completely buy into the idea of acknowledging and teaching positive behavior, there is simply no point in implementing a SWPBIS plan in an urban high school. It is imperative for school leaders in urban high schools to cultivate a culture in which teachers feel comfortable with acknowledging and teaching positive behavior. And it must begin with the leader articulating his or her vision for SWPBIS.

The initial step in cultivating a vision entails providing a critique of the organization's current culture (Kouzes & Posner, 1995; Starratt, 1991). The administrator must ask hard questions regarding the teachers and their enthusiasm toward a SWPBIS. This critique will require the school leader to confront the moral issues involved when s/he finds teachers who are treating some students in the school better than others (McCray & Beachum, 2006; Starratt, 1991). Once the school leader has critiqued the organization's culture, s/he must provide the vision (Kouzes & Posner, 1995). Furthermore, the leader should be able to easily share his or her vision with stakeholders, and once articulated, the leader must become a champion of his or her vision (Cox, 1994). The leader can accomplish this by making it clear that the vision is just as important as any other concept in the school.

Strategy 2: Building People Up

The concept of building people up is premised on the notion of good professional development. Undoubtedly, there are many educators who come into urban high schools completely unprepared for the challenges they will encounter. These challenges consist of an array of issues ranging from lack of administrative support to managing student behavior. In essence, the destiny of urban students is often in the hands of educators who may not share their culture (McCray et al., 2010). In Chapter 8 of this book, Beachum and Gullo quote Villegas and Lucas (2002, p. 3): "While children of color constituted about one-third of the student population in 1995, they are expected to become the numerical majority by 2035. This change will render the expression 'minority students' statistically inaccurate." Beachum and Gullo continue:

> At the same time, most school leaders and teachers are White, middle class, and monolingual, which may result in cultural misunderstandings, cultural mismatch (Delpit, 2006), and/or cultural collision (Beachum & McCray, 2004, 2011). These problems will inevitably force school leaders and the core of teachers in America to reassess their pedagogical approaches and leadership strategies, and result in a deeper look at students, their behaviors, and their academic performance.

Beachum and Gullo make a very strong case for school leaders focusing on more rigorous professional development in order to circumvent some of the problems facing students of color in urban schools. The very essence of these problems is epitomized in Beachum and McCray's concept of cultural collision and collusion. According to Beachum and McCray (2011), the problem can sometimes be that the culture of the educator clashes with that of their students, resulting in a phenomenon called cultural collision. Collusion, on the other hand, occurs when students feed off educators' deficit thinking and begin to engage in a self-fulfilling prophecy of destructive behavior (McCray et al., Chapter 10). Beachum and McCray argued that while educators may have little control over the collision that occurs due to students' culture, they absolutely have control over their own dispositions, which students will readily perceive.

School leaders must thus become the intermediaries, offering educators cogent professional development to mitigate the miscommunication that leads to office referrals, suspension, and expulsions. Building people up with regard to SWPBIS requires school leaders to make investments in professional development opportunities. And one of the best forms of investment school leaders can make in terms of professional development is putting more emphasis on educators' soft skills.

Oftentimes, professional development in schools consists of educators having hard skill sets reinforced. Professional development undergirded by hard or technical skills usually consists of training around the enhancement of pedagogy. In contrast, professional development centered on PBIS usually includes a focus on the proper implementation of best practices.

But the intersectionality of professional development and PBIS should also include softer skills sets, such as making teachers more aware of the need to interact with and understand the community in which the school is located. Ballard-Krishnan and colleagues (2003) found that when school administrators attempted to incorporate PBIS into their schools, one major component that was often missing was teacher training on how to engage with parents and other community stakeholders. Ballard-Krishnan et al. (2003) advocated including parents more in educational decisions. "Parent participation is optimized when positive behavior [intervention] support (PBIS) involvement moves significantly beyond simple parent cooperation to true parent and professional collaboration" (p. 122).

The Merriam-Webster Online Dictionary defines cooperation as "assistance, especially by ready compliance with request"; collaboration, in contrast, is "the action of working with someone to produce or create something." Clearly, there are subtle differences between the notion of cooperation and collaboration. The former seeks compliance while the latter emphasizes the notion of truly working together to produce something positive. Alas, the extent of parents' involvement in the educative process is often reduced to passive compliance rather than active creation. Thus, in order for educators to be successful with PBIS, they need to become more aware of their students and the community in which their students live. Parents can be of vital assistance in helping teachers achieve this understanding (Bambara, Nonnemacher, & Kern, 2009). The research of Bambara et al. (2009) found that "parents can help the team gain insight on the student's behavior as well as provide other critical information needed to develop effective support" (p. 172). Therefore, it is crucial that school leaders begin to focus more on the soft skills that will enhance teachers' ability to connect and work with parents in the community. Professional development opportunities in these skills will, in essence, build up educators as well as parents.

Strategy 3: Cultivating a Collaborative Environment

As we argue above, the concept of collaboration is founded on the notion of working together to create something positive. With regard to SWPBIS, what is created is a system that fosters a mindset among all key stakeholders (Turnbull, Wilcox, Stowe, & Turnbull, 2001) to enhance learning within the school. Turnbull et al. (2001) found that the effective implementation of PBIS requires not only a high level of personnel training but also a systems change. We broached the idea of personnel training in Strategy 2, building people up, and it will be highlighted again in Strategy 4, placing the right personnel in the program. Meanwhile, according to Turnbull et al. (2001),

"Necessary systems change involves development of collaborative efforts across settings (i.e., different classrooms) to enable implementation of PBIS for any particular child" (p. 16). Although every strategy listed here as being necessary for transformational leadership is vitally important, the concept of cultivating a collaborative environment is truly the basis of transformational leadership with regard to ensuring PBIS is implemented properly. A genuinely collaborative environment will become the catalyst for a systems change. Without cogent collaboration, it will be difficult for educational leaders to change the system from within.

Idol and West (1991) researched schools and collaboration and discovered eight common characteristics shared by schools that collaborated effectively. These common characteristics are: (1) faculty shares a common language about instructional techniques, (2) faculty frequently observes one another, (3) faculty has frequent discussions about best practices, (4) faculty works together to master new methods and strategies, (5) faculty plans and designs new materials together, (6) faculty shares resources together, (7) faculty creates opportunities to learn from one another, and (8) at faculty meetings, time is dedicated to discussing new, innovative strategies and techniques, and informal discussions center on best practices.

The characteristics identified by Idol and West (1991) can only come to fruition if the leadership team promotes an environment in which each is embraced by faculty and staff. As McCray et al. have pointed out (see Chapter 10), faculty and staff are often unsure of or reluctant to try PBIS approaches with high school students due to misapprehensions about how to reinforce positive behavior in older students. They note:

> The challenge of *teaching behaviors in high school* is also undergirded by educators' beliefs and expectations regarding high school students … [Many] educators do not believe it is possible to teach corrective behaviors to high school students. This probably explains why we see so many suspensions and expulsions at the high school level. (p. 198, emphasis added)

When faculty and staff collaboration brings about positive results in high school students' behavior, this can reinforce the benefits of SWPBIS in the eyes of faculty and staff members who remain unenthusiastic about its merits. Undoubtedly, such collaboration not only has the potential to strengthen support for SWPBIS, but it can also begin to change the structure and system within the school that often undermines system implementation, resulting in anemic versions of the SWPBIS model (Turnbull et al., 2001).

Idol and West's (1991) eight criteria for effective collaboration in schools truly underpins the notion of transformational leadership and is the antithesis to the bane of transitional leadership. Only sustained transformational leadership can create opportunities for change within the system. The corollary of transformational leadership is transactional leadership, where leaders in essence become managers of the status quo in their organizations. Although transactional leadership may be necessary in certain instances, it is not a leadership style conducive to helping high school teachers become more comfortable with SWPBIS, particularly when many of them are struggling with the notion of positive intervention for older students. Idol and West (1991) maintained that one of the best ways for school leaders to become transformational leaders and increase collaboration in their schools was by modeling the importance of teamwork. As they put it, "The principal [has] to provide leadership in creating or enhancing collaboration by modeling collaboration with the [faculty] in appropriate situations and by reinforcing collaboration as an important professional role" (p. 74). Such modeling by the school leader, especially as it relates to SWPBIS, can increase faculty and staff's understanding of its relevance and perhaps institutionalize it within the school culture.

Strategy 4: Staffing

The final component to enhancing SWPBIS via transformational leadership is the strategy of placing in the school people who not only believe in SWPBIS but also are culturally sensitive to diverse student populations. Some scholars have found that schools need to do a better job of recruiting faculty and staff who are familiar with their student populations, especially in urban areas. Thus, staffing the program involves school leaders finding the best and most qualified individuals who can engage in cogent teaching, while relating to diverse students. McCray et al. (see Chapter 10) asked whether educators who were skeptical of reinforcing positive behavior in urban high schools might have an inherent bias against SWPBIS at this level, or an inherent bias against urban students. This question merits some attention. If teachers are apprehensive about reinforcing positive behavior with older students, regardless of the school location, perhaps the remedy is more professional development. However, if teachers are uneasy about SWPBIS due to a bias against urban students, maybe it is also a staffing issue.

Haberman (2005) has been adamant that urban schools need to do a better job of recruiting teachers who are committed to the student population. Haberman (2005) argues that when urban school leaders recruit teachers, they should look to hire teachers who have a certain familiarity with the community. In his research, Haberman (2005) found that teachers who grew up in urban areas were more familiar with community stakeholders, and tended to stay in positions longer than teachers who had no knowledge of the community in which they worked. Haberman (2005) also noted that older teachers and teachers who had switched professions tended to stay longer than teachers coming directly out of pre-service teacher programs. In essence,

> After many years of working with urban school districts, Haberman (1999) has concluded that the standard qualifications required by teacher preparation programs (e.g., B average, satisfactory interview with faculty, and/or a well-written essay on teaching) are only predictors of the likelihood of a candidate's completion of a program of teacher education, not a predictor of who is likely to be a successful teacher of the inner city youth. (p. 41)

Schools all across the United States have begun to suffer staffing problems, but over the last few years, these problems have been exacerbated in urban schools. Kolbe and Strunk (2012) noted:

> Despite its importance, many districts and school leaders experience difficulties staffing their classrooms with qualified teachers. Staffing challenges arise because of an inadequate supply of qualified teachers, difficulties recruiting teachers for specific positions, trouble retaining teachers and challenges with distributing teacher talent between and within school districts (Rice, Roellke, Sparks, & Kolbe, 2009).... [T]hese problems are particularly acute in schools that serve large proportions of minority, low-income, and low-performing students (Jacob, 2007).... (p. 780).

Thus, researchers acknowledge that while staffing is a problem all over the United States, the difficulty is more severe in urban schools and schools situated in low socioeconomic communities (Kolbe & Strunk, 2012). Nevertheless, in order for school leaders to increase their chances of implementing and institutionalizing SWPBIS, they must make an extra effort to staff the school with appropriate individuals (Haberman, 1999).

The notion of educators in urban schools being uneasy about the benefits of SWPBIS with older students (Bohanon et al., 2006) is a cause for concern. School administrators should try to ascertain whether teachers have such reservations prior to recruiting them. Undoubtedly, once educators are selected and hired, school leaders have every obligation to ensure that they are receiving high-quality professional development to enhance their skills in areas such as SWPBIS. However, when given the opportunity to fill a position, school administrators should ensure that the potential hire is indeed the right person for the job. Researchers have often found that it is better for a school to forego a potential hire than to select someone who is not the appropriate person for the position. Thus, if school leaders are serious about implementing SWPBIS, they also have to become serious about the teachers they hire to implement such programs (Stotko, Ingram, & Beaty-O'Ferrall, 2007).

SWPBIS is founded on the premise that negative behavior can be modified or corrected. SWPBIS has the potential to reduce the negative outcomes that are often associated with student discipline (i.e., excessive school suspensions) by focusing on behavior modification. Faculty and staff must, however, be committed to the principles of tiers one, two and three for SWPBIS to succeed, especially in urban schools. Stotko, Ingram, and Beaty-O'Ferrall (2007) found that urban teachers' persistence is the key. And this trait is something that school leaders should look for when making hiring decisions.

> Effective urban teachers believe it is not easy to improve student learning and performance. [But] they are persistent: They refuse to give up on their students. They are flexible: They are willing to modify various aspects of the practice (e.g., planning, classroom management, instructional strategies) to improve student learning. They set high standards for their students. (p. 41)

In order for SWPBIS to become institutionalized within the school culture, educational leaders must do a better job of recruiting and selecting teachers who understand the importance of not giving up on their students.

Conclusion

Throughout this chapter we have highlighted the accomplishments of PBIS, as well as the need for future direction and research. We found that one of the major accomplishments of PBIS was how it has helped educators begin to rethink and re-conceptualize the notion of student discipline. As we mentioned earlier, far too often students receive office referrals to the principal's office when the matter could be handled differently. Rethinking and re-conceptualizing student discipline has made educators more cognizant of the need to reinforce positive behavior in students instead of simply ushering them to the principal's office. At the end of the day, SWPBIS allows educators to maintain control of their classes in a more cogent way, while offering students the opportunity to receive corrective feedback on their behavior within a reliable modification system. Undoubtedly, PBIS has the potential to have an enormous impact on how school leaders and educators approach the discipline of students.

Despite the fact that many teachers and school administrators have bought into the concept of PBIS and are having some success with it, the disposition of many urban teachers toward it is troubling. Bohanon et al. (2006) concluded that many educators and school leaders in urban schools are not totally convinced of the benefits of SWPBIS. Essentially, these educators and school leaders have not completely bought into the notion that older urban students' behavior can be modified via the SWPBIS model. The conclusions of the Bohanon et al. (2006) study are somewhat troubling in that they reveal one of the reasons why we see such a high number of suspensions and expulsions in urban schools. This is why we argue in this chapter that for urban school educators to reduce the high level of disciplinary exclusion measures within their schools, there has to be a drastic change in school culture.

In order for the SWPBIS model to work in urban high schools, school leaders will need to cultivate a culture that promotes and reinforces the principles of SWPBIS. As we indicated earlier, a transformational leadership style can help facilitate the structural change in school culture necessary to institutionalize PBIS within the school. We relied on Leithwood, Jantzi, and Fernandez's (1994) notion of transformational leadership, which involves the leader (1) setting the course by providing a vision, (2) building people up through solid and effective professional development, (3) cultivating a collaborative environment by promoting the sharing of best practices among educators, and (4) staffing the program with the right personnel through a rethinking of who is best qualified to teach in urban schools.

Many urban students today face the threat of being jettisoned from the educative process. We believe that school leaders with the ability to transform school culture could improve this grave situation tremendously. Currently, many urban teachers do not believe that the behavior of older urban students can be modified via PBIS. If this line of thought is pervasive, the problems we witness in terms of high suspensions and expulsions, leading ultimately to high dropout rates, are understandable (McCray & Beachum, 2006). If urban school leaders are going to be successful in implementing SWPBIS, they need to carefully assess whether or not the culture of their school is in dire need of total transformation. The SWPBIS model is only as good as the people implementing its principles. Thus, it is imperative that school leaders provide the best training and find the right personnel to work with our most precious resources. Our future depends on it.

References

Anderson, G. L. (1990). Toward a critical constructivist approach to school administration: Invisibility, legitimation, and the study of non-events. *Educational Administration Quarterly*, *26*(1), 38–59.

Ballard-Krishnan, S. A., McClure, L., Schmatz, B., Travnikar, B., Friedrich, G., & Nolan, M. (2003). The Michigan Positive Behavior Support initiative: Advancing the spirit of collaboration by including parents in the delivery of personnel development opportunities. *Journal of Positive Behavior Interventions*, *5*(2), 122–126.

Bambara, L. M., Nonnemacher, S., & Kern, L. (2009). Sustaining school-based individualized Positive Behavior Support: Perceived barriers and enablers. *Journal of Positive Behavior Intervention*, *11*(3), 161–176.

Beachum, F. D., & McCray, C. R. (2004). Cultural collision in urban schools. *Current Issues in Education, 7*(5). Retrieved from http://cie.asu.edu/volume7/number5/

Beachum, F. D., & McCray, C. R. (2011). *Cultural collision and collusion: Reflections on hip hop culture, values, and school.* New York: Peter Lang.

Black, S. (2004). Safe schools don't need zero tolerance. *Education Digest, 70*(2), 27–31.

Blalock, H. (1967). *Towards a theory of minority group relations.* New York: Capricorn Books.

Blumer, H. (1958). Race prejudice as a sense of group relations. *Pacific Sociological Review, 1*, 3–7.

Bohanon, H., Fenning, P., Carney, K. L., Minnis-Kim, M. J., Anderson-Harriss, S., Moroz, K. B., ... Pigott, T. D. (2006). Schoolwide application of Positive Behavior Support in an urban high school: A case study. *Journal of Positive Behavior Interventions, 8*(3), 131–145.

Capper, C. A. (1998). Critically oriented and postmodern perspectives: Sorting out the differences and applications for practice. *Educational Administration Quarterly, 34*(3), 354–379.

Carnegie Council Task Force on Education of Young Adolescents. (1989). *Turning points: Preparing American youth for the 21st century.* The report of the Task Force on Education of Young Adolescents. Washington, DC: Author.

Cartledge, G., Tillman, L., & Johnson, C. T. (2001). Professional ethics within the context of student discipline and diversity. *Teacher Education and Special Education, 24*(1), 25–37.

Casella, R. (2003). Zero tolerance policy in schools: Rationale, consequences, and alternative. *Teachers College Record, 105*(5), 872–892.

Coffey, J. H., & Horner, R. H. (2012). The sustainability of Schoolwide Positive Behavior Interventions and Supports. *Exceptional Children, 78*, 407–422.

Colvin, G., Kame'enui, E., & Sugai, G. (1993). Reconceptualizing behavior management and school-wide discipline in general education. *Education and Treatment of Children, 16*, 361–381.

Cox, T. H. (1994). *Cultural diversity in organizations: Theory research and practice.* San Francisco: Berrett-Koehler.

Cunningham, W. G., & Corderio, P. A. (2009). *Educational leadership: A bridge to improved practice* (4th ed.). Boston, MA: Pearson.

Day-Vines, N. L., & Day-Hairston, B. O. (2005). Culturally congruent strategies for addressing the behavioral needs of urban, African American male adolescents. *Professional School Counseling, 8*(1), 236–243.

Delpit, L. (2006). *Other people's children: Cultural conflict in the classroom.* New York: The New Press.

Duran, J. B., Zhou, Q., Frew, L. A., Kwok, O., & Benz, M. R. (2011). Disciplinary exclusion and students with disabilities: The mediating role of social skills. *Journal of Disability Policy Studies, 24*(1), 15–26.

Eber, L., Hyde, K., & Suter, J. C. (2011). Integrating wraparound into a schoolwide system of Positive Behavior Supports. *Journal of Child & Family Studies, 20*, 782–790.

Fabelo, T., Thompson, M. D., Plotkin, M., Carmichael, D., Marchbanks, M. P., III, & Booth, E. A. (2011). *Breaking schools' rules: A statewide study of how school discipline relates to students' success and juvenile justice involvement.* New York: Council of State Governments Justice Center.

Ferguson, A. A. (2001). *Bad boys: Public school in the making of Black masculinity.* Ann Arbor, MI: University of Michigan Press.

Flannery, K. B., Sugai, G., & Anderson, C. M. (2009). School-Wide Positive Behavior Support in high school: Early lessons learned. *Journal of Positive Behavior Interventions, 11*, 177–185.

Haberman, M. (1999, September/October). Selecting future teachers of youngster in poverty. *Action in Teacher Education*, 3–7.

Haberman, M. (2005). Personnel preparation and urban schools. In F. E. Obiakor & F. D. Beachum (Eds.), *Urban education for the 21st century: Research, issues, and perspectives* (pp. 34–58). Springfield, IL: Charles C Thomas.

Idol, L., & West, J. F. (1991). Educational Collaboration: A catalyst for effective schooling. *Intervention in School and Clinic, 27*(2), 70–78.

Jacob, B. A. (2007). The challenges of staffing urban schools with effective teachers. *Future of Children, 17*(1), 129–153.

Keleher, T. (2000, February 18). *Racial disparities related to school zero tolerance policies: Testimony to the U.S. Commission on Civil Rights.* Educational Resource Information Center (ERIC), ED454324, 1–12. Retrieved from http://files.eric.ed.gov/fulltext/ED454324.pdf

Kolbe, T., & Strunk, T. K. (2012). Economic incentives as a strategy for responding to teacher staffing problems: A typology of policies and practices. *Educational Administration Quarterly, 48*(5), 779–813.

Kouzes, J. M., & Posner, B. Z. (1995). *The leadership challenge.* San Francisco: Jossey-Bass.

Lane, K. L., Wehby, J. H., Robertson, J., & Rogers, L. A. (2007). How do different types of high school students respond to Schoolwide Positive Behavior Support programs? Characteristics and responsiveness of teacher-identified students. *Journal of Emotional and Behavioral Disorders, 15*(1), 3–20.

Leithwood, K. A., Jantzi, J., & Fernandez, A. (1994). Transformational leadership and teachers' commitment to change. In J. Murphy & K. S. Louis (Eds.), *Reshaping the principalship: Insights from transformational reform efforts* (pp. 72–98). Thousand Oaks, CA: Corwin Press.

Lewis, T., & Sugai, G. (1999). Effective behavior support: A systems approach to proactive schoolwide management. *Focus on Exceptional Children, 31*(6), 1–24.

Lindle, J. C. (2008). School safety: Real or imagined fear? *Educational Policy, 22*(1), 28–44.

Liska, A. E. (1992). *Social threat and social control.* Albany: SUNY Press.

McCarthy, J. D., & Hodge, D. R. (1987). The social construction of school punishment: Racial disadvantage out of universalistic process. *Social Forces, 65*, 1101–1120.

McCray, C. R., Alston, J. A., & Beachum, F. D. (2006). Principals' perceptions of multicultural education and school climate. *Multicultural Teaching and Learning, 1*(1), 12–22.

McCray, C. R., & Beachum, F. D. (2006). A critique of zero tolerance policies: An issue of justice and caring. *Values and Ethics in Educational Administration*, *5*(1), 1–8.

McCray, C. R., & Beachum, F. D. (2010). An analysis of how gender and race of school principals influence their perception of multicultural education. *International Journal of Education Policy and Leadership*, *5*(4), 1–11.

McCray, C. R., Grant, C. M., & Beachum, F. D. (2010). Pedagogy of self-development: The role the Black Church can have on African American students. *Journal of Negro Education*, *79*(3), 233–247.

Mosca, F., & Hollister, A. (2004). External control and zero tolerance: Is fear of our youth driving these policies? *Educational Horizons*, *83*(1), 2–5.

Obiakor, F. E., Harris-Obiakor, P., Garza-Nelson, C., & Randall, P. (2005). Educating urban learners with and without special needs: Life after the Brown case. In F. E. Obiakor & F. D. Beachum (Eds.), *Urban education for the 21st century: Research, issues, and perspectives* (pp. 3–19). Springfield, IL: Charles C Thomas.

Raffaele Mendez, L. M., Knoff, H. M., & Ferron, J. M. (2002). School demographics variables and out-of-school suspension rates: A quantitative and qualitative analysis of a large, ethnically diverse school district. *Psychology in the Schools*, *39*(3), 259–277.

Rice, J., Roellke, C., Sparks, D., & Kolbe, T. (2009). Piecing together the teacher policy landscape: Multi-level case study findings from three states. *Teachers College Record*, *11*(2), 511–546.

Scanlan, M. (2011). How principals cultivate a culture of critical spirituality. *International Journal for Leadership in Education*, *14*(3), 293–315.

Shaw, S. R., & Braden, J. B. (1990). Race and gender bias in the administration of corporal punishment. *School Psychology Review*, *19*, 378–383.

Shields, C. M. (2004). Dialogic leadership for social justice: Overcoming pathologies of silence. *Educational Administration Quarterly*, *40*, 111–134.

Skiba, R. J., & Knesting, K. (2001). Zero tolerance, zero evidence: An analysis of school disciplinary practice. *New Directions for Youth Development*, *92*, 17–43.

Skiba, R. J., Michael, R. S., Nardo, A. C., & Peterson, R. L. (2002). The color of discipline: Sources of racial and gender disproportionality in school punishment. *Urban Review*, *34*(4), 317–342.

Skiba, R. J., & Peterson, R. L. (1999). Zap zero tolerance. *Education Digest*, 64(8), 24–30.

Starratt, R. (1991). Building an ethical school: A theory for practice in educational leadership. *Education Administration Quarterly*, *27*, 185–202.

Stotko, E. M., Ingram, R., Beaty-O'Ferrall, M. E. (2007). Promising strategies for attracting and retaining successful urban teachers. *Urban Education*, *42*(1), 30–51.

Sugai, G., Sprague, J. R., Horner, R. H., & Walker, H. M. (2000). Preventing school violence: The use of office discipline referrals to asses and monitor school-wide discipline interventions. *Journal of Emotional and Behavioral Disorders*, 3, 94–101.

Theoharis, G. (2007). Social justice educational leaders and resistance: Towards a theory of social justice leadership. *Educational Administration Quarterly*, *43*(2), 221–258.

Turnbull, H. R., Wilcox, B. L., Stowe, M., & Turnbull, A. P. (2001). IDEA requirements for use of Positive Behavior Support: Guidelines for responsible agencies. *Journal of Positive Behavior Intervention*, *3*(1), 11–18.

Villegas, A. M., & Lucas, T. (2002). *Educating culturally responsive teachers.* Albany: SUNY Press.

Wallace, J. M., Jr., Goodkind, S., Wallace, C. M., & Bachman J. G. (2008). Racial, ethnic, and gender differences in school discipline among U.S. high school students: 1991–2005. *Negro Educational Review*, *59*, 47–62.

Welch, K., & Payne, A. A. (2012). Exclusionary school punishment: The effect of racial threat on expulsion and suspension. *Youth Violence and Juvenile Justice*, *10*(2), 155–171.

Wilson, W. J. (2009). *More than just race: Being Black and poor in the inner city.* New York: W.W. Norton.

Epilogue

Supporting Success (K to 12) for Diverse Students: What Works, and Why, Now for Teens!

Bruce S. Cooper

This book is critical now and in the future for anyone working in or concerned about our American schools, as the number of students from other nations, speaking other languages, and living different cultures, has dramatically risen. Called "culturally and linguistically diverse," or CLD, these children are our future, and schools must welcome, accommodate, teach, and promote these youngsters if we as a country are to prosper.

In fact, over the last 150 or more years, public schools, and many private ones, have absorbed and helped children from dozens of cultural and language groups. For example, my grandparents were from both Hungary on my dear mother's side, and from a "schtetle" later destroyed by the Nazis in Poland on my father's. One grandpa whom I spent precious time with had been a house painter, his son (my dad) was a shop owner, and I am a professor, showing how Yiddish-speaking people from Europe were accommodated, grew, and learned from American education—and progressed up the social-economic ladders of life.

Thus, this book on cultural-linguistic diversity—and how to work in classrooms with these kids—is essential for teachers, administrators, parents of CLD students, and policymakers, if we are to continue to see progress from our school graduates. This book, then, helps us to understand: (1) the meaning of and research on linguistic and cultural diversity; (2) what we know from "the literature," based on prior research and findings; and (3) critically what we know now about how to promote and improve school programs, curricula, classes, and practices for CLD students.

Importantly, too, this book is both practical and helpful for educators and their schools (systems) to offer Positive Behavioral Interventions and Support (PBIS), thus taking us through key steps of understanding the problem and research on cultural-linguistic diversity; what's working and lacking in this critical field; and what schools should do to help: that is, what models work and how?

Contributors of this book introduce theories, practices, and policies to help educators and their families understand failures and successes with these students within the context of their particular schools and communities. What works with one group and age cohort may change as students grow up, socially, within local and regional contexts.

Students of color in the U.S. have seen four stages of development, including Stage 1, the right to an equal—and shared—education under the 1954 *Brown v. Board of Education* that made conscious segregation policies and practices illegal. Stage 2 attempted to apply some of the same ideas and principles to children living in poverty-stricken areas, as states like California begin to have *Serrano v. Priest* (1971) cases that attempted to equalize educational spending, regardless of local property wealth.

Next, in Stage 3, similar equity concerns were applied in the 1970s and beyond (see Hanushek, 1996) to help children with "special needs," disabilities, and limitations (and "handicaps"). Today, the federal government sponsors programs under the Individuals with Disabilities Education Act (IDEA), to identify and help children with any limitations or abilities. We did research on the spending of these students, using a weighted student formula (WSF), to see how large cities spent "how much more" on these children, who might require both physical assistance (e.g., transportation to and within schools) and pedagogical assistance, including staff devoted to helping them.

And, most recently, Stage 4 sees us measuring and accounting for student progress, sometimes called Gain Scores or Value-Added models. Interest in Gain Score models is in part being stimulated by teacher and school leader accountability, meaning that teachers are evaluated by how much each student gains, not how many pass a common test.

Thus, if a teacher has a group of sixth graders reading at the start of the year at the third-grade level or lower, and has pulled them up to fifth grade in one year, a two-or-more yearly gain, then the teacher is both successful and competent (even if all students are not yet at grade level in these skills).

To expect every child to read at the same level or above at the start of the year just doesn't happen. And working with diverse groups, both "culturally" and "linguistically," may mean that some of the students are behind in language arts at school opening. Teachers can then be evaluated, and even helped, in improving students' growth, and "gain scores" on local, state, and national tests.

Thus, this book is about both kids and their education, and educators' values and practices. Do schools collaborate to help students from diverse backgrounds and families? For example, Diane Rodriguez explains in the first chapter of this book what a successful classroom teacher does. Rodriguez indicates that successful classroom teachers instill in students the ideas of having respect for self, respect for others, and respect for property.

Thus, what we learn from this book has universal appeal to any good teacher and effective classroom—and school. If we fail to respect each other, our property, and ourselves, then what will our kids learn from our schools and us?

The book shows that teachers of younger children from diverse backgrounds are learning to help these students adjust. However, the problem occurs with older, secondary school pupils in urban schools, where teachers are often more connected to their subjects, than to the special needs of these teenagers. Beachum and McCray's important research (2011) is a useful anchor for understanding how schools can read and accommodate to the culture, styles, and languages of different students, and help school teachers and administrators grasp how to help and support children from different ethnic-language-cultural backgrounds.

And somehow educators must adjust to the age-changes as students grow up, and require different treatment. It appears that we are better with the younger children, where we can control and tolerate their cultural differences; but what happens when these kids are teens? How do we adjust to them and their attitudes and behaviors? This book is key. Individualized PBIS is key to helping schools prepare students for tests as they grow older.

Positive Behavioral Interventions and Supports involves helping children by selecting good behaviors, and rewarding them, rather than picking on kids who do not conform. Individual Positive Behavioral Interventions and Supports (IPBIS) for learning is even better. And making secondary schools better and more helpful for these children is critical, as these students by ages 15 or 16 are either well-adjusted or often out of step, as high schools are neither consistent nor prepared to help. Thus, focusing on diverse cultural and language communities is critical if these teens are to learn, pass grades, and graduate and go on to higher and further education.

This book is right there, right on. We know much of what this book tells us, but we need to re-learn, practice, and coordinate "best practices for respect" if any school is going **to** work, particularly for children from other language and cultural groups. Yes, now!

References

Beachum, F. D., & McCray, C. R. (2011). *Cultural collision and collusion: Reflections on hip-hop culture, values, and schools.* New York: Peter Lang.

Hanushek, E. A. (1996). Rationalizing school spending: Efficiency, equity, and externalities, and their connection to rising expenditure. In Victor Fuchs (Ed.), Individual and Social Responsibility: Child Care, Education, Medical Care, and Long-Term Care in America (pp. 45–57). Chicago: University of Chicago Press.

About the Authors

Tachelle Banks, PhD, is an associate professor of Special Education, Department of Teacher Education, Cleveland State University. Dr. Banks conducts research primarily in emotional behavior disorders and cognitive behavior interventions in multicultural/urban contexts. She focuses on the development of emotional competence in children and youth, particularly those identified as having emotional behavior disorders. Her other studies have addressed implementing preventative mental health curriculum and instruction in urban educational settings and examining the initial commitment of culturally and linguistically diverse (CLD) teachers in special education. Currently, her research focuses on the role that culture and ethnicity play in emotional competency development and instruction. Banks is executive managing editor of *Multicultural Learning and Teaching*, a multidisciplinary, peer-reviewed international journal devoted to the education of people with diverse multicultural life experiences and backgrounds. Dr. Banks is the author of more than 25 publications and has presented at numerous national and international conferences advancing her commitment to bridging the gap between special education research and practice.

Floyd D. Beachum, PhD, is the Bennett Professor of Urban School Leadership at Lehigh University. He is also an associate professor and program director for the Educational Leadership program in the College of Education. He received his doctorate in Leadership Studies from Bowling Green State University with an emphasis in Educational Administration. He also holds a master's in education and a bachelor of science in social studies education from Alabama State University. He has a total of 18 years in education (K–12 and higher education) as well as experience as a substitute teacher, student teacher, classroom teacher, and lead teacher for social studies. Before coming to Lehigh, he served as associate professor and program coordinator for Educational Administration at the University of Wisconsin–Milwaukee. His research interests include: leadership in urban education, moral and ethical leadership, and social justice issues in K–12 schools. He has authored several peer-reviewed articles on these topics in many journals. In addition, he is co-editor (with Festus Obiakor) of the book *Urban Education for the 21st Century: Research, Issues, and Perspectives* (Charles C Thomas, 2005); a co-author of *Radicalizing Educational Leadership: Dimensions of Social Justice and Cultural Collision* (Sense, 2008), and (with Carlos McCray) *Cultural Collision and Collusion: Reflections on Hip-Hop Culture, Values, and Schools* (Peter Lang, 2011); and co-author of the forthcoming book *School Leadership in a Diverse Society: Helping Schools to Prepare All Students for Success.*

Kwang-Sun Cho Blair, PhD, is an associate professor in the Department of Child and Family Studies and faculty of the Applied Behavior Analysis Program at the University of South Florida. Dr. Blair's primary research interests have centered around developing and evaluating assessment methods and interventions for young children with social-emotional and behavioral challenges. She is currently project director of Project Tiered System Behavior Analyst (TSBA), funded by the Office of Special Education Programs, U.S. Department of Education, and designed to prepare school-based tiered system behavior analysts. She has published numerous journal articles and been an active member of editorial boards and guest reviewer for journals related to early intervention and special education, including *Topics in Early Childhood Special Education, Remedial and Special Education, Early Intervention, Journal of Autism and Developmental Disorders, Journal of Positive Behavior Interventions, Journal of Behavioral and Emotional Disorders, Korean Journal of Early Childhood Special Education*, and *Korean Journal of Special Education.*

Angie Chai, PhD, is currently a certified school psychologist and the director of the Abilis autism program and behavioral support program at Abilis in Connecticut. Within those programs, she coordinates an autism-specific early intervention program, conducts assessments, provides behavioral consultations, and provides therapeutic services for children and adolescents. She has been an adjunct professor at Fordham University since January 2011.

Su-Je Cho, PhD, is an associate professor of special education in the Division of Curriculum and Teaching at Fordham University. Dr. Cho's research interests include adaptation of families to their children with disabilities, and assessment and interventions for children with challenging behavior. Dr. Cho has published articles in journals including *Topics in Early Childhood*

Special Education and *Focus on Autism and Other Developmental Disabilities.* Dr. Cho is currently directing Project REACH, funded by the Office of Special Education Programs, U.S. Department of Education, and designed to prepare school-based tiered system behavior analysts.

Bruce S. Cooper, PhD, is professor of Education Administration and Leadership in the Graduate School of Education at Fordham University, NYC. He's a former president of the Politics of Education Association.

Yi Ding, PhD, is an assistant professor in School Psychology at Fordham University. Her research interests include reading disabilities, mathematics disabilities, and special education and school psychology issues based on a multicultural perspective.

Lillian Durán, PhD, is an assistant professor in the Department of Special Education and Rehabilitation at Utah State University. She helped to begin the first Spanish-English Head Start bilingual preschool program in the state of Minnesota and conducted a three-year experimental, longitudinal study comparing the language and literacy development of the children who attended the bilingual classroom to children in an English-only setting. She is currently collaborating with Centro de la Familia, the lead agency for Migrant Head Start in Utah. Dr. Durán has delivered numerous presentations on the topic of recommended practices in assessment and instruction with young dual-language learners (DLLs) at regional, state, and national conferences. Prior to Dr. Durán's work in higher education, she worked for 10 years as an Early Childhood Special Education (ECSE) teacher both in Prince George's County, Maryland, and rural Minnesota. She became interested in researching evidence-based practices for young DLLs when she and her family moved from the Washington, DC area to rural south-central Minnesota where she worked as an ECSE teacher in many communities with high Latino, Somali, and Sudanese populations.

Lenwood Gibson Jr., PhD, is an assistant professor of Special Education at Queens College, the City University of New York. He received his PhD in Special Education from the Ohio State University. Dr. Gibson's area of expertise is in the identification and treatment of behavioral deficits for high-risk student populations, particularly for culturally and linguistically diverse students. His current research interests include: (a) the use and effectiveness of computer-assisted instruction as a supplemental tool for students at risk for academic failure, particularly in urban schools; (b) closing the academic achievement gap between minority students and their non-minority peers; (c) the effective use of positive behavioral approaches for classroom management.

Gina L. Gullo received her bachelor's degree in biopsychology from the College of New Jersey and continued to study behavioral neuroscience at Rutgers University. After transitioning to pharmaceutical research, Gina returned to study special education at Lehigh University where she is currently pursuing her master's degree. Gina works collecting data for various intervention programs, teaching science programs, and assisting in the educational leadership program at Lehigh University.

Cynthia Hudley, PhD, is a professor of Child and Adolescent Development in the Gevirtz Graduate School of Education at the University of California, Santa Barbara. Dr. Hudley has also served as an associate dean of the UCSB Graduate Division; vice president of Division E of American Educational Research Association (AERA); and a past member of the Board of Educational Affairs and current president-elect of the Committee on Socioeconomic Status, both for the American Psychological Association. Dr. Hudley's scholarship addresses children's social cognitions, with a specific focus on social and cultural influence on achievement motivation and aggressive behavior. Hudley has focused on how ethnic minority students' academic motivation and school engagement are affected by social cognitions.

Ji-Ryun Kim, PhD, is an assistant professor at the State University of New York at Cortland. She teaches courses related to inclusive special education at undergraduate and graduate levels. Her research interests include the influence of school-level variables on the academic progress of students with various disabilities and the influences of specific instructional practices on students' achievement in various subject areas for students with and without disabilities. Currently, she is using Early Childhood Longitudinal Study—Kindergarten Cohort (ECLS–K) Restricted-Use Data, and National Assessment of Educational Progress (NAEP) Data to examine the students' achievements and their behavior in relation to teacher-related variables and disability-related variables.

Samuel Martin is a doctoral candidate at the University of Missouri in the department of Educational Leadership and Policy Analysis. His research interests include the development of school culture and college access with a focus on how race, class, and gender impact student performance and school leadership. Samuel has a BSED in Middle School Language Arts and a MSED in Counseling Psychology, both from the University of Missouri. He has taught courses in Government, Literacy, and African-American Literature. For the past six years Samuel has been employed as a professional school counselor with Columbia Public Schools in Columbia, Missouri.

Dr. Carlos R. McCray is an Associate Professor and Chair of the Educational Leadership, Administration, and Policy Division at Fordham University in the Graduate School of Education at the Lincoln Center campus in New York City. Professor McCray was the first program chair for the Leadership for Social Justice Special Interest Group of the American Educational Research Association in 2006. He was also a participant in the University Council of Educational Administration's Urban Curriculum Leadership Development commission, which developed guidelines for colleges of educational leadership to assist in training urban educational leaders. Professor McCray has co-authored two books titled, Cultural Collision and Collusion: Reflections on Hip-Hop Culture, Values, and Schools and School Leadership in a Diverse society: Helping Schools to Prepare all Students for Success. Overall, he has over fifty publications on topics dealing with school building leadership, multicultural education, and Black male academic achievement. Professor McCray has worked with school administrators and educators in the metropolitan areas of Atlanta, New York City, and London, England.

Festus E. Obiakor, PhD, is department head and professor, Early Childhood and Special Education, Dewar College of Education and Human Services, Valdosta State University, Valdosta, Georgia. A teacher, scholar, and consultant, he has served as distinguished visiting professor at a variety of universities. He is the author of more than 150 publications, including books, articles, and commentaries; and he has presented papers at many national and international conferences. He serves on the editorial boards of reputable nationally and internationally refereed journals, including *Multicultural Learning and Teaching* (MLT) in which he serves as executive editor. Obiakor is a leader who has been involved in many landmark scholarly works in the fields of general and special education, with particular focus on African American and other culturally and linguistically diverse (CLD) learners and he continues to prescribe multidimensional methods of assessment, teaching, and intervention for these individuals. Based on this premise, Obiakor created the Comprehensive Support Model (CSM), an intervention model that values the collaborative, consultative, and cooperative energies of students, families, teachers/service providers, communities, and government agencies.

Diane Rodriguez, PhD, is an associate professor at Fordham University, Graduate School of Education. She specializes in the areas in bilingual special education, bilingual education, and second-language teaching and learning. Dr. Rodriguez has been an invited speaker at national and international conferences on special education and bilingual education. Dr. Rodriguez' publications include articles in many journals such as *Urban Education Journal*,

English Language, *The Bolder Walking Journal*, *Exceptional Children*, *Early Childhood*, and *Journal of Research in Childhood Education*.

Rosa Milagros Santos, PhD, is a professor of Special Education at the University of Illinois. Her research work has focused on understanding the way culture and language impact early intervention and early childhood special education services for young children with disabilities and their families. Dr. Santos has published and presented widely on topics related to the complex nature of relationships among children, families, and professionals who do not share similar cultural and linguistic backgrounds. Dr. Santos believes that the translation of research to practice can make a lasting impact on the day-to-day practices of professionals who touch the lives of young children with disabilities and families. Dr. Santos is past president of the Division for Early Childhood (DEC) of the Council for Exceptional Children (CEC). She is currently the editor of the *Young Exceptional Children* journal. She is a recipient of the prestigious CEC Leadership Award and DEC's Merle Karnes Award for Service to the Division.

Heather Wynne is a PhD candidate in Fordham University's School Psychology program. She received her MSEd in Educational Evaluation and Intervention at Fordham University. Trained in cognitive-behavioral, client-centered, and psychodynamic approaches, she has worked in specialized schools, foster care, inpatient, and general education settings. Ms. Wynne has experience in program implementation, academic remediation, social-emotional interventions, identification of student strengths/weaknesses, progress monitoring, Positive Behavioral Support systems, and trauma-focused care. Her research interests include stress, resiliency, self-regulated learning, and achievement motivation. As a scientist-practitioner, she believes that theory and research should promote and create better services to children and improve school systems.

Christopher D. Yawn, PhD, is an assistant professor and director of the Special Education Program at the City College of New York (CCNY). He earned his PhD in Special Education from the Ohio State University. His research interests revolve around the utilization of evidence-based methods to produce positive outcomes for the advancement of culturally and linguistically diverse (CLD) students considered at risk. Specifically, his research interests are (a) effective CLD parents of students with disabilities and school collaboration models, (b) academic and behavioral interventions for incarcerated youth with disabilities, and (c) culturally relevant pedagogy.

Chun Zhang, PhD, is a professor at the Division of Curriculum and Teaching, Graduate School of Education, Fordham University. She was a Fulbright scholar in 2013. Her research focuses on early prevention and intervention of developmental delays and disabilities for young children birth to age eight and family-professional partnerships and collaboration. Dr. Zhang has published widely in childrearing and parenting differences of culturally and linguistically diverse (CLD) families, and in preparing educators to be culturally competent in supporting young children and families from CLD backgrounds in urban settings. She directs several major grants in training early childhood special education teachers in cross-cultural competence and in enhancing teacher effectiveness.

Dake Zhang, PhD, is an assistant professor in Special Education at Rutgers University. Her research interests include assessment and interventions for students with math learning disabilities, meta-analysis, and children's strategic development.

Index

C

D

E

F

G

H

I

J

K

L

M

N

O

P

Q

R

S

T

Y

Z

Educational
PSYCHOLOGY

Critical Pedagogical Perspectives

Greg S. Goodman, *General Editor*

Educational Psychology: Critical Pedagogical Perspectives is a series of relevant and dynamic works by scholars and practitioners of critical pedagogy, critical constructivism, and educational psychology. Reflecting a multitude of social, political, and intellectual developments prompted by the mentor Paulo Freire, books in the series enliven the educator's process with theory and practice that promote personal agency, social justice, and academic achievement. Often countering the dominant discourse with provocative and yet practical alternatives, *Educational Psychology: Critical Pedagogical Perspectives* speaks to educators on the forefront of social change and those who champion social justice.

For further information about the series and submitting manuscripts, please contact:

Dr. Greg S. Goodman
Department of Education
Clarion University
Clarion, Pennsylvania
ggoodman@clarion.edu